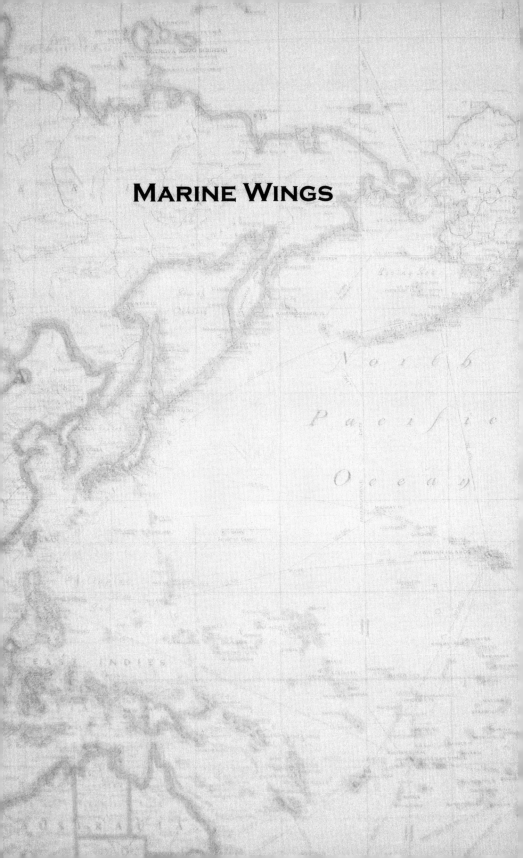

MARINE WINGS

MARINE WINGS

by
Minnesota Marine Air Reserve authors:

Harry Anderson	Carlyle Lageson
Austin "Jim" Bailey	Goodwin Luck
Sherman Booen	James Magnus
Lyle Bradley	Bill Messerli
Tom Brinkman	Ohrn O'Dette
Andy Danielson	Jim O'Neil
Myron Engel	Herb Pfremmer
Ralph Engelking	Tony Plattner
Louie Farrell	Clyde Slyman
Harry Goodyear	Darrell Smith
Richard Hansen	Edward Sovic
Robert Kilgore	John Wastvedt

MARINE
WINGS

Stories of war and peace as written by the pilots

by
Minnesota Marine Air Reserve, LLC

 **DeForest Press**
Rogers, Minnesota

Permission gratefully acknowledged for "Mud Marine Ohrn O'Dette" article by Mac MacKechnie.

Published by:
DeForest Press
P.O. Box 383
Rogers, MN 55374 USA
www.DeForestPress.com
Toll-free: 866-509-0604
Shane Groth, Publisher
Richard DeForest Erickson, Founder

Cover design by Linda Walters, Optima Graphics, Appleton, WI
Maps and illustrations in text body by Robert A. Kilgore
Cover photographs of F4U Corsairs by Dave Pease
Photo on page 240 © Bob Perzel

ISBN 978-1-930374-25-6
Printed in the United States of America
10 09 08 07   5 4 3 2 1

                    Library of Congress Cataloging-in-Publication Data

Marine wings : stories of war and peace as written by the pilots / by Minnesota Air Reserve.
    p. cm.
Includes index.
ISBN 978-1-930374-25-6
1. Air pilots, Military--United States--Biography. I. Minnesota Marine Air Reserve.
UG626.M37 2007
359.9'6--dc22
[B]
                    2007019203

This book is dedicated
to all the members of the
Minnesota Marine Air Reserve,
past and present.*

*For a listing of the members of the
Minnesota Marine Air Reserve, see Appendix A.

CONTENTS

PREFACE

This book got a rocky start in 1995 as a group of Minnesota Air Reserve Marine pilots gathered for a monthly social meeting at the Fort Snelling Officers' Club in Minneapolis. Aviation anecdotes always flowed freely at these gatherings. An idea was floated that the group should put in writing some of those "talked about" experiences for family, friends, and Marine Corps history before we pass into the state of "non-communicators." Several concurred that many of our aviation experiences were unique and had never before, nor would in the future, be repeated.

Over the next few years there were a few articles written. It was obvious that most of the group were more articulate in talking rather than in writing. However, some of the articles were not only interesting but very professionally written and comments about writing a book surfaced. Two successful authors visited our group to share their writing experiences. This brought a spurt of new stories from our group and by 2001 we had 25 interesting stories in the file.

The age of the group ranged from 50 to 94 years, the military rank ranged from captain to colonel and covered the period from 1938 to 1998. Everyone had aviation experience as a pilot or ground officer. Most were reservists on active duty during World War II, Korea, or Vietnam, with continued non-active duty as members of the Minnesota Marine Air Reserve during peacetime. Aviation experiences in their civilian occupation are also included in the book. These pilots and ground officers were involved in intercepts of enemy aircraft, close air support (CAS) of ground troops, bombing, transportation, ordnance, communication, engineering, testing and air/sea rescue. Almost every phase of aviation is covered in their stories.

The Air Expo Show in 2002 at Flying Cloud Airport near Minneapolis gave the group more incentive to write a book. Many people stopped at our Corsair booth and asked if we had a book or some literature about our aviation experiences. Adjacent to our booth, the Enola Gay books were being sold and signed by Paul Tibbetts, the pilot of the B-29 that dropped the atomic bomb on Hiroshima. We helped them unload at least 500 books for their booth, which were all sold in 24 hours.

Conversations with people at the Experimental Aircraft Association (EAA) in Oshkosh, Wisconsin, libraries, bookstores, and museums all encouraged us to get our stories into print. We presented our ideas to Deforest Press in Minneapolis, which was excited about publishing such a worthwhile project. More stories were written and by Christmas of 2006 sixty stories were in the file along with many photographs. The book has truly been a team effort.

That being said, the group would like to acknowledge the work of member Lyle Bradley—in spite of his strongly opposing any mention of his name and effort—who managed to get the articles written by inviting, encouraging, persuading, and cajoling; by setting one deadline after another, by reading all the material, and by giving order to the enterprise. And he did it all with patience, a generous judgment, and confidence in the group. We are all in his debt.

Regrettably, this book did not start earlier because many possible participants have gone to "Aviation Heaven" or have been lost in the shrouds of geographic space. A list of most of the members of the Minnesota Marine Aviation Reserve follows in Appendix A.

We hope this book has added to U.S.M.C. aviation and Minnesota history, has preserved cherished stories for family and friends, and has provided you, the readers, some interesting first-hand accounts lived and written by those Marine aviators and ground personnel who had "front row seats for the action." It has given our reserve group greater interaction and rapport. We hope aviation enthusiasts will get much pleasure and information from their reading of this book.

THE MINNESOTA MARINE
AIR RESERVE

The Minnesota Marine Air Reserve was founded in 1931 at the Naval Air Station in Minneapolis, Minnesota. Named VM-7MR, it was commanded by Second Lieutenant Sweetser.

In 1934 Major Melvin J. Maas became the commanding officer (CO) and the unit was renamed VO-MR. The squadron trained in fabric-covered bi-planes, amphibians, Curtiss "Helldivers" and F2Fs. Drills were one weekend per month. No uniforms, no pay, but marines nonetheless.

In the fall of 1940, a year before Pearl Harbor was bombed by the Japanese, the unit was activated and absorbed into the regular Marine Corps, which included eight officers and thirty-two enlisted men. Some of these men were at Pearl Harbor on December 7, 1941. They served with valor and distinction throughout the Pacific in World War II.

Following World War II, the Twin City Marine Air Reserves was again established. Three squadrons were designated: Fighter Squadrons VMF-213, VMF-234 and Marine Air Control Squadron 16 (MACS 16). Pilots were flying the famed F4U Corsair. There were plenty of aircraft and lots of flying for the World War II veterans. The three squadrons had a complement of more than 500 officers, NCOs and enlisted men.

The Korean War started in June 1950. Twin City Marine Air Reservists were called to active duty August 1, 1950, and were given five days to prepare to leave for the Far East, both by plane and by ship. The entire squadrons were called and were to be integrated into the First Marine Air Wing at El Toro, California, and Kobe, Japan.

The Twin City Marine Air Reserve served with distinction in the Korean Conflict. The pilots were flying in combat to support the beleaguered ground troops within 30 days after call up in August. Sadly, six pilots were killed in action within 90 days after leaving their home and families. It is with respect and admiration that their names are listed here: Bill Nitz, Bob Crocker, Homer Cornell, Walter Jung, Joe Stonelake and Tom Odenbaugh.

Twin City Marine Air Reserve pilots served an entire tour with distinction. Operating from both land and carriers, these pilots were involved in every theatre of operation, including Inchon, the Chosin area, and the evacuation of the ground marines when the Chinese came into the war. Decorations were numerous for the marine pilots.

Twin City Marine Air Reservists returned to stateside in 1951 after a year in Korea and were released from active duty in 1952. They returned to Minnesota and resumed Reserve Training with the same squadrons, VMF-213, VMF-234 and MACS-16.

In 1955 the Twin City marines said goodbye to their beloved Corsairs and were checked out in their first jets, the F9F Panther.

In 1958 the pilots checked out in the AD-5 Skyraiders, back in recip engines again. These were designated attack units, VMA-213 and VMA-234. A new squadron was added to the Twin City Marine Air Reserve, Helicopter Squadron HMR-766. They were flying HUP-2, one of the first inventory helicopters. In 1961 the squadron was named HMM-766, and the new aircraft was the sonar-equipped SH-34J.

In 1962 pilots of the two attack squadrons were joined to form VMR-234, and the aircraft was the R4Q—a C-119 twin-engine transport airplane. MACS-16 was renamed Marine Air Traffic Control Unit 71 (MATCU-71).

In 1965, Marine Air Maintenance Squadron 47 was established along with a headquarters squadron.

All the squadrons and personnel were disbanded in 1969 when the Naval Air Station was closed. Some joined units in Chicago to continue their participation. A volunteer squadron, VTU-14, was formed, the members serving without pay in the ready reserve.

The Twin City Marine Air Reserve Squadron established an outstanding record of efficiency, readiness and aviation safety. The marine fighter, attack, and transport squadrons were awarded nine safety citations, the Pete Ross Safety Award, and three safety awards from Naval Operations. The helicopter squadron earned three safety citations and the Marine Air Reserve helicopter trophy.

Because of the Marine Air Reserve's efficiency, readiness, and spirited participation, the Twin Cities Marine Air Reserve training detachment was awarded the M. Drill attendance award.

In 1973 the annual conference of the Marine Corps Reserve Officers Association was held in St. Paul by the Richard Fleming chapter. Letters on file indicate that it was one of the best annual conferences ever held.

By Sherman Booen

INTRODUCTION

There was a time in the 1930s when the whole world, the whole developed world, tensed up over the likely outbreak of a large war, only two decades after World War I, which was supposedly the "war to end all wars."

There was a time when the whole world, both developed and undeveloped countries, regions, oceans, and islands were caught up in the bloody hostilities of World War II, either as aggressors, defenders, or unfortunately, as innocent victims.

The earliest of this time was in 1931 to 1937, when Japan bloodily attacked the much larger but less advanced country of China. This time in the life of our world continued with Germany's suspenseful, mostly bloodless maneuvering to usurp control of Austria and Czechoslovakia in 1938. Then the time of war erupted more fully, and officially became World War II on September 1, 1939, with Adolph Hitler's invasion of Poland—the Blitzkrieg, or Lightning War—and quick conquest of most Scandinavian countries, and then of France in May, 1940. Britain was pushed out of France at this point—exiting through the embattled port of Dunkirk—and its initial time of bloodletting continued through the desperate Battle of Britain, the conclusion of which saw Britain's Royal Air Force outlasting Germany's Luftwaffe, thus avoiding a fatal end-time for Great Britain. Next, starting in June 1941, it was time for Russia's monumental bloodletting at the hands of Germany's Operation Barbarossa—the invasion of Mother Russia.

And finally it became America's time of trial. On Sunday morning, December 7, 1941—the "Day of Infamy" in America's memory—when without warning, a large force of Japanese naval warplanes swept out of the skies above the Pearl Harbor navy base and above other American army and marine bases on the island of Oahu in the Hawaiian Islands. These Japanese forces sank many of the U.S. Navy's battleships, a number of other naval vessels, destroyed many army and navy aircraft on the ground, and killed nearly 2,400 American servicemen, as well as a number of Hawaiian citizens.

So after over four years of growing brutal worldwide conflict, it now became time for the Minnesota marine pilots in this book—time for them to leave homes and families, jobs and college, and time to begin the largest and most intense experiences of their lives. This time typically began with initial military training and preflight, a time like no other up to that point in the lives of most of these young men. It moved to flight school, then ultimately to some of them going down to the sea in ships, in order to be transported under Spartan and sometimes miserable conditions, to link up with their aircraft or with other duties near or in combat zones in the Pacific Theater of Operations (PTO). Some were carried, unceremoniously and uncomfortably, in a variety of aircraft to their duty areas in the Pacific.

And now it was time for these young men to begin active operations and combat in the war zones of the Pacific, and to fully assume awesome responsibilities, carry out frightening duties, and to mature as young men very quickly, and in some cases, old men very quickly. For some of these young marine aviators this was the time of legendary, desperate, and bloody places in the South, Central, and Western Pacific:

• The Solomon Islands (Guadalcanal, New Georgia/Munda, Bougainville, others), the tip of Japan's spear, where the momentum of Japan's thrust south and towards Australia and New Zealand was blunted.

- The Bismarck Islands (New Britain, New Ireland/Rabaul, and others) where the long push back against Japan's expansion continued.
- The Central Pacific, with actions in the Gilbert Islands (Tarawa, Makin, and others) and the Marshall Islands (Eniwetok, Kwajalein, Wotje, Maloelap, and others), in an effort to grind down Japanese strongholds.
- And the Western Pacific region, where Japan was finally pushed back to the point of her home island shores due to hard fighting in places such as Saipan, Peleliu, the Philippines, Formosa (Taiwan), Hong Kong, and off the coast of China, including Hainan Island, Iwo Jima, Okinawa, and finally Japan.

Throughout these struggles, the USMC aviators in this book performed both combat and noncombat service, all of which was part of America's long wartime experience in the Pacific Theater. This included aerial combat against experienced Japanese pilots (both day and night, as well as against kamikaze/suicide pilots), bomber escort, ground attack, strafing, land-based flight operations, and seaborne aircraft carrier operations. Landing signal officer (LSO) duties were also carried out on carrier combat stations. This is the dangerous, intense, and precise guiding of aircraft landing on carriers after completion of their missions, as well as launching and catapulting aircraft from aircraft carrier decks. Noncombat wartime work included stateside flight training, bombing training, and headquarters duty in war zones, among other activities.

And then it was time for the Nuclear Age—the single White Sands Proving Ground Test in July 1945 and the deathly and effective atomic bomb drops on Hiroshima and Nagasaki on August 6 and

August 9, 1945, respectively. The Japanese surrendered September 2, 1945, onboard the battleship USS *Missouri* in Tokyo Bay, six years and one day from the start of World War II.

World War II had caused approximately 50 million deaths worldwide. This was equivalent to 37% of America's complete 1940 population of 131.5 million people! The United States suffered approximately 400,000 deaths, and many more wounded or maimed among its armed forces during its four years of participation in World War II.

At this point it was time for many of these pilots to come home, some to a combination of the Marine Reserves and civilian life, some fully to civilian life.

After all of this there was yet another time, a time in June 1950 when North Korea, without warning, attacked South Korea across the 38th Parallel of latitude, a geographic line that served as a common border between these two countries. Korea had been divided as a nation because of a split protectorate/political agreement between several victors of World War II, and this foretold a long stressful Cold War between Western Bloc democracies and Eastern Bloc communist countries. The Korean War has been viewed as a "Police Action" by those with a hopeful vision of a world managed more rationally and cooperatively under the umbrella of a participatory United Nations arrangement. But in fact and in the end, Korea was, plain and simply, a war in the same and ugly old-fashioned sense of what war has always been.

And so again it was now time for this contingent of Minnesota marine aviators, spread across several squadrons, to embark on a second wartime tour of duty, this time fully across the Pacific into Korea. As before, it was again the time for a mixture of disruption, excitement, boredom, chaos, privations, and mortal danger—all the experiences of war—as these men flew from Korean and Japanese land bases and from the sea on aircraft carriers.

These USMCR aviators from Minnesota were among the very first squadrons to be recalled and sent to Korea. This was due both to awareness of Minnesotans' ability to operate in cold weather, and because at one time perhaps 40 to 50 F4U Corsair fighter bombers were based at the Naval and Marine Corps Reserve Stations at the Minneapolis-St Paul International Airport (Wold-Chamberlain Airport at that time) during the postwar period. Because of the availability of these World War II warplanes, these Marine Reserve pilots had been able to maintain their flight experience as well or better than most bases elsewhere in the country. The Korean air war, while eliciting lasting images of American F-86 Sabre jet verses communist MiG-15 jet aerial battles, was in fact, more of a very dangerous down and dirty ground attack aerial war, where close support of ground troops and low level interdiction of communist ground forces and supplies was the order of the day. These airmen saw ground attack duty from aircraft carriers and from land bases, in summer, and in the frozen Korean winters.

Looking back at the Korean War, this was the time that some have described as a yo-yo experience up and down the 650-mile Korean Peninsula:

- The rapid retreat into, and the desperate defense of the Pusan Perimeter.
- Back and forth movement across the 38th Parallel of latitude.
- General Douglas MacArthur's successful end-around amphibious landing at Inchon harbor, a classic move from the pages of Admiral William Halsey and General MacArthur in the South Pacific during World War II.
- The ensuing rapid advance of United Nations forces fully up the

North Korean peninsula to the Yalu River (China's border with North Korea).

- The entry of communist China into the war with an overwhelming number of troops moving south into North Korea and forcing a major retreat by United Nations forces.
- The frozen, desperate fighting retreat by the First Division of United States marines from the Chosin Reservoir to relief on the Korean coast.
- And eventually the lengthy, frustrating peace negotiations at Panmunjon, while full combat continued.

The Korean War raged in all of its ferocity for three years (1950 to 1953). It resulted in re-establishing approximately the original border region between North and South Korea. American casualties included 34,000 killed, and a much larger number wounded or maimed. And then national memories faded, regardless of the higher motives and urgencies that drove the United Nations and the United States to commit troops to the defense of South Korea, and Korea became, unfairly, the "Forgotten War."

And finally, it was time, for the second time, for these marine airmen from Minnesota to come home. For those who came back—and all did not—from the great Pacific War of 1941 to 1945 and from the bitter Korean War of 1950 to 1953, it was time to begin building (or rebuilding) their peacetime lives, careers, and families. Some stayed in military service, and some fully joined civilian life. Not surprisingly, some developed exceptionally varied and successful careers in commercial aviation or as test pilots.

Many kept with them their memories of intense wartime experiences and events, these of a magnitude larger than life for most people who were not there, and larger than anything many of these pilots were to experience in their postwar lives. And many, after all of this time, carry still, the pain of missing friends, acquaintances, and comrades who did not return, or who were maimed and disabled, and of exciting or violent scenes branded into their memories.

Now, after all of these historic events of the 1940s and 1950s, after all of this time has past, we are at a time where many of these fine men are passing into history before our very eyes. Their sacrifices, experiences, triumphs, losses, and their dedicated contributions from these timeframes were made a long time ago, yet this is not the time when our society should be unaware of, or forget, these marine pilots and their experiences.

This book contains the stories of these pilots, experiences they lived, struggled through, and survived. Unlike other collections of veterans' experiences, the pilots in this book have written their own stories, the most personal of all accounts.

It is now your time—to read their stories, to appreciate, to honor, to learn, and to remember.

By Tom Brinkman

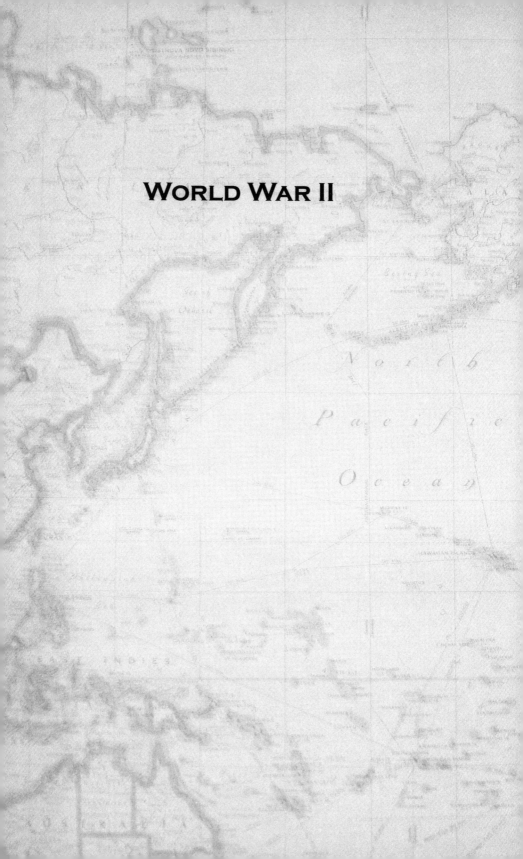

WORLD WAR II

South Pacific Duck Rescue
By Goodwin Luck

I arrived at Henderson Field, Guadalcanal, at dawn the first part of February 1943 via a SCAT C-47 with a marine crew. "Pistol Pete," a Japanese firing a canon, started to shell the field so the SCAT crew quickly unloaded. They then loaded the wounded and took off without being hit.

I reported to General Francis Mulcahy who was ComAirSols (having just relieved General Geiger), and I was assigned as an operations officer on his staff. Our main mission was to control all air activity (American marines, navy and air corps, Australian and New Zealand). We scrambled fighters as required, organized bombing raids and fighter sweeps, set condition red and green as required, and acted on messages from coast watchers and from higher commands. A message from "Pearl" enabled our fighter command using P-38s to shoot down Admiral Yamamoto at Kahili, Bougainville. We also provided rescue missions, anti-sub patrol for the fleet, and night spotting for our cruisers and destroyers shelling enemy positions at Munda and Kolombangara using "black cat" PBYs. Although I was fortunate not to get hit by snipers, artillery fire, bombs, or antiaircraft, I did contract malaria and had to take Atabrine. Malaria, plus eating a regular diet of K-rations, caused my weight to drop to 121 pounds.

The next big mission was to take Munda airfield on New Georgia Island some 170 nautical miles northwest of Guadalcanal.

General Mulcahy was designated ComAir New Georgia and on June 30, 1943, with his ComAirSols staff, landed on the island of Rendova about 10 miles across the channel from Munda. A large number of infantry troops landed at several beaches on New Georgia. They would surround Munda and force the enemy out. The command that planned this operation estimated it would be completed in about ten days and that ComAir New Georgia would then control all allied air operations.

Major V. A. Peterson, also an air operations officer, and I convinced the general that until Munda was taken and made operational, our fighters from Guadalcanal (170 miles away) would need to be rescued if downed in the Munda/Rendova area. I volunteered to fly a J2F Duck in the Munda/Rendova area because I had more J2F experience (obtained at NRAB Minneapolis) than other flight officers on the staff. We also obtained a high-speed boat to aid in rescues. The Duck was flown to Rendova on July 3 with about 30 F4U3s as cover. A marine sergeant and I took over the Duck and the navy pilot who flew it from Guadalcanal departed in a PBY. Unfortunately the J2F did not have an electric starter so we had to use the hand-cranked inertia starter. The rear cockpit machine gun was also missing; in fact, the aircraft had no weapons.

One of the biggest problems was to hide the Duck from the daily air attacks by the Japanese. A camouflage net, overhanging jungle trees, and frequent relocation of the J2F solved the problem. When needed, 100-octane fuel was obtained from PT boats in the area. On one occasion gasoline was pumped from a PT boat commanded by John Kennedy. This occurred shortly before his PT boat was demolished at night by a Japanese destroyer.

Instead of 10 days it took about 44 days to capture Munda Airfield. General Mulcahy wanted to fly the first American aircraft to land on Munda. However, on August 14, when the field was declared secure, he requested that I fly him to Munda from Rendova Harbor in the Duck after I first checked the condition of the field. It was in poor condition, being narrow, short, and peppered with bomb craters;

The J2F Duck

however, I was able to land on it. When I reported the condition of the field to the General he said, "Luck, you fly me in." And that's what I did.

The Japanese also had an airfield at Vila on the island of Kolombangara some 16 miles northwest of Munda. Vila was kept neutralized by marine and navy aircraft from Guadalcanal and the Russell Islands. On the morning of August 16, Major Turner landed his TBF on Munda, which was open for emergency landings only. He reported to me and Major Peterson that on the pullout of his bombing run on Vila he noticed someone waving from the shore of Arundel Island. He thought the person might be a downed marine or navy airman. Several were missing from previous bombing runs on Vila.

We decided that the person waving should be rescued as soon as possible. Major Peterson and Sergeant Happer volunteered to fly with me in the Duck on this extremely risky mission. We had an inflatable rubber raft in the Duck but the CO_2 cartridges had been used when I rowed the general to the plane at Rendova. A bicycle-type tire pump was located which would do the job. The plan was to fly low over the water around the west side of Arundel Island, turn east across Arundel and fly very close to the tops of the trees of the jungle. The Japanese floatplanes that operated frequently from the channel between Arundel and Kolombangara sounded like the Duck when the propeller was set in low pitch. To make the enemy think the airplane they heard was one of their floatplanes, I put the Duck's propeller in low pitch.

Major Turner's instructions were accurate because when we cleared the jungle there was a man on a coral reef near shore waving. I made a short landing, made a turn towards shore, got as close to shore as the coral permitted, cut the engine and dropped anchor. The man on shore then disappeared into the jungle. We thought this was a trap; however, Major Peterson said he didn't think so because the man had red hair and a red beard, so the major continued to pump up the raft.

The man returned to the shore carrying some assorted Japanese items. Major Peterson hurriedly paddled him out to the Duck. Sergeant Happer and I cranked the starter by hand, being extra careful not to drop the crank in the ocean. When I started taxiing, the anchor caught in the coral. I had a six-inch hunting knife, which most pilots carried in case the seat life raft inflated accidentally and pushed the control forward, thereby nosing the aircraft down. Sergeant Happer cut the anchor rope with my knife, permitting me to takeoff and return to Munda. Fortunately I parked in a Japanese built revetment because the Japanese started to shell the field and surrounding area with artillery. One or more shells hit near the Duck, putting many holes in it from shrapnel and pieces of coral. The artillery projectiles were coming from the southwest tip of Arundel Island as a complete surprise to us. We had marine SBDs from Guadalcanal bomb the Japanese guns and the shooting stopped. Apparently they became angry to see a small U.S. aircraft land and takeoff in their front yard and they foolishly revealed the position of their big guns.

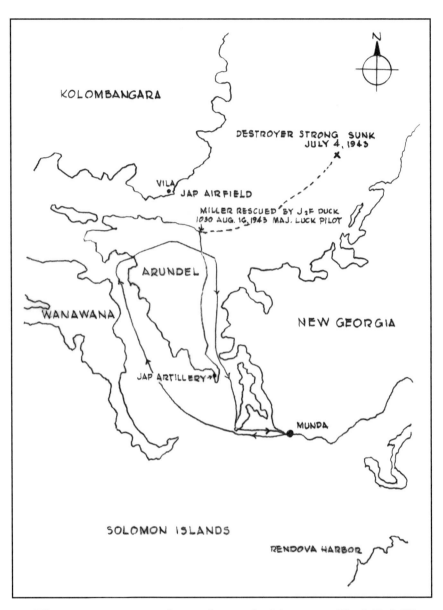

The person we rescued turned out to be Lieutenant Hugh B. Miller. He was on the destroyer USS *Strong* when it was sunk by Japanese torpedoes on July 4, 1943. He drifted ashore on Arundel Island and survived until rescued. His story is covered in the November 8, 1943, issue of *Life* magazine and is also included in *The Best 100 True Stories of World War II*. Several other publications cover Miller's story but are not accurate. In January 1957, Miller, Luck, Peterson, Happer and others appeared on the television program "This Is Your Life, Lieutenant Hugh B. Miller." Ronald Reagan was the host.

On September 27, 1943, with allied landings scheduled for the island of Bougainville, I flew coast watcher Evans and three of his native scouts to the northeast shore of the island of Choiseul. Evans was to observe Japanese air and ship operations around the Shortland Islands and Bougainville. The natives on Choiseul were known to have been headhunters and possible cannibals; however, they apparently were on our side since they had a smoky fire on the beach as a signal that a landing was okay.

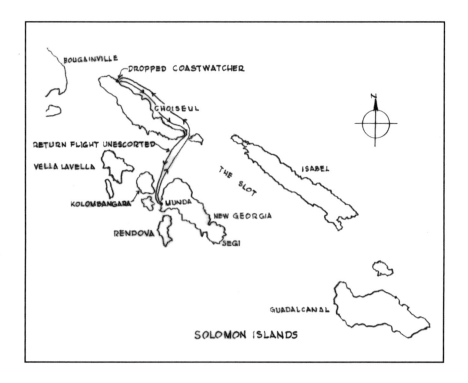

I anchored off shore and some natives in large canoes paddled out to the Duck to pick up Evans, his helpers, and supplies. The native leader wanted to shake hands with me. I did not hesitate when I noted several shrunken heads around his neck. Sergeant Happer and I hand-cranked the starter to get out of there but the engine failed to start. Our escort of some 18 F4Us got low on fuel and had to wave goodbye. Sinking the Duck was an option, but one more try and the R1820 Wright engine came to life. We took off flying low to stay out of radar. I observed many large crocodiles sunning themselves on the mangrove/coral shore of Choiseul. We were glad to get back to Munda.

The following letter was sent a few months after the rescue.

September 2, 1943

Dear Mrs. Luck:

I am a Lieutenant in the Naval Reserve and I was an officer on a destroyer which was sunk in Jap waters on the night of July 4, 1943, the U.S.S. Strong. I had the misfortune to drift ashore behind the Jap lines on Arundel Island between the north end of New Georgia Island and Kolombangara Island and I managed to live there until the 16th of August.

On that morning I attracted the attention of a low flying torpedo plane piloted by a marine first lieutenant—he flew over to Munda Airfield, which we had occupied only a few days before, and reported it to marine fighter headquarters.

Major Vernon A. Peterson, Master Sgt. John J. Happer, and your Major Goodwin R. Luck, all in headquarters, volunteered to get me. I was several miles behind the Jap lines and there were Jap planes in the air at the time—despite this and despite the fact that they did not know whether I was an apprentice seaman or an officer, or what, this small expedition set out without fighter plane coverage to get me—all they knew was that I was an American in a dangerous spot and in trouble. They flew a small, slow, amphibious plane we call a "Duck"; in order to land on the water in front of me, they were forced to circle within gun range of the very powerful position the Japanese have at Villa Plantation on Kolombangara Island—which they did—and then lit in front of me and calmly inflated a boat, came ashore and got me. Because they could see that I was weak, they would not allow me to cover the last 30 yards of water, which would have been dangerous for me, but made me wait until they could come and get me—at all times considering only my safety while they risked their own skins—and they flew me out to Munda.

The appreciation which I feel toward them for saving my life cannot be put into words, but more important than that is the purely impersonal courage and daring which they displayed and which, surely, is the reason why a fighting marine is superior to any other fighting man alive. Though one can never tell, I sincerely hope that they will be decorated for this act of bravery.

Your Major Luck piloted the plane. When I last saw him on August 18, I promised to wire a message to you when I reached the States—it appears that I will be a month or so getting back and that is the reason I am writing. He was in the best of health and spirits when I left Munda.

You may be perfectly sure that the Luck family may feel free to call on me at any time for anything. I can always be reached through my home address of 1925 8th St., Tuscaloosa, Alabama.

Sincerely,
Hugh Barr Miller, Jr.

Tally Ho!

By John Wastvedt

World War II was, for most young men of the time, a defining experience—probably the major event of our lives. The attack on Pearl Harbor evoked an intense feeling of patriotism in most of the country with many thousands of young men rushing to enlist the day after the attack, myself included. I was eighteen years old and in my second year of college at the time, dreaming of becoming a naval aviator, flying off carriers and engaging in swirling dog fights that thrilled me as a boy reading pulp magazines such as *Wings* and *Flying Aces*. However, the recruiter informed me that I had to complete my two years of college to be eligible for the navy flight training program. I should wait and come back in May, he said, when I would be finished with my second year. This I did, and after over two years of intensive training I was shipped overseas in the early fall of 1944. At that time the war with Japan was moving northward by the U.S. Navy's fast carrier task forces, striking closer to the Japanese homeland.

On January 16, 1945, Task Force 58, comprised of a dozen or so large carriers and many battleships, cruisers and destroyers, was a couple of hundred miles off the coast of China and Hainan Island ready to strike with fighter sweeps and bombing raids. Some of the squadrons were assigned targets on the coast, others to targets on Hainan Island. Marine Squadron VMF-124, to which I was assigned as a pilot officer flying the most advanced naval fighter at the time, the F4U Corsair, was based on the large carrier USS *Essex*. We were scheduled for the first strike on Hainan Island early in the morning.

When I joined them, VMF-124 was reforming in late 1943 at the Mojave Marine Corps Air Station on the Mojave Desert of California after a combat tour on Guadalcanal in the South Pacific. After almost a year of intensive training together all the pilots were bonded, much as a college fraternity and actually, not much older. There were many accidents, some fatal, and any loss was particularly hard. Most of us pilots were in our very early twenties, first and second lieutenants. Out of about forty pilots, six were captains and three were majors, including our skipper. Most of these were veterans of combat on Guadalcanal. These veterans led divisions, the smallest tactical unit, consisting of four aircraft to which pilots were permanently assigned. My division was led by Captain Bill Bedford, an "old man" of 26, the other three being Gill Boyd, George Strimbeck, and myself as tail-end Charlie.

The division assignments and intelligence briefing were conducted the evening before the strike. Intelligence officers laid out the information they had on targets, such as numbers, kinds and locations of antiaircraft batteries, and estimates of the numbers and types of enemy aircraft. Escape and evasion techniques were discussed and local currency handed out (which, incidentally, would be charged to our account and would have to be repaid). The approximate location of a rescue submarine, which would be lying submerged offshore with only a tailing antenna visible, was given. A "shackle" code for contacting the submarine regarding any downed airman, which changed every day, was issued, and of course we were reminded no reply should be expected as this was extremely hostile territory and the enemy could track any radio signal. Expected weather was discussed and it didn't look good.

The carrier position for the morning launch, its planned course and speed, was also laid out so that by dead reckoning we could find our way back after the strike. Each aircraft had a navigation plotting board located below the instrument panel that slid out horizontally when you worked out your navigation problem using estimated winds or whatever winds the weather people told you to expect. This was not very precise and you could miss your final destination by many miles when flying over open ocean with no landmarks back to the carrier. You would think that the task force spread out over a large area would be hard to miss, but it was easy to fly between groups, especially in low visibility conditions. If you missed, the next land-fall was San Fancisco! There was, however, a homing beacon called YEZB with a range of about twenty miles. The beacon put out Morse code signals on a pie chart format with the carrier being the chart center. So, for instance, when you heard a B signal (-...), you could look at your chart and tell the direction to fly to the carrier. This was changed every day so the enemy couldn't use it, and we received the sector code letters at the briefing.

For the marines, the first launch was scheduled for dawn and was to be two divisions totaling eight Corsairs led by Major Marshal. Our mission was to sweep the area for enemy fighters, but we also carried a 500-pound bomb so if fighter opposition didn't materialize we could drop it on a "target of opportunity." Each aircraft had six 50-caliber machine guns, three in each wing, bore-sighted for about a thousand feet. The pilot had a gun sight with rings around the "pipper" to en-able him to estimate the lead distance, just as in pheasant or duck hunting. In addition to the bomb, we carried an external, jettisonable fuel tank to enable us to reach the target (about 200 miles away), complete the mission and return. Of course our six wing-mounted 50-caliber machine guns were fully loaded with about 600 rounds per gun. Switches on the armament panel allowed the pilot to choose how many guns to fire. At a firing rate of 400 rounds per minute per gun, our ammunition would last a minute and a half with all guns firing. Although we had trained in the use of rockets, these were used only for surface targets. Apparently the planners had intended us to be primarily fighter interceptors since we had no rocket rails and couldn't carry rockets.

Before dawn we breakfasted on steak and eggs and suited up in the ready room for a final briefing by Major Marshall, the mission leader. Then we climbed into our aircraft, spotted on the deck behind a navy squadron of Hellcats assigned a mission on the China coast. We waited for the signal to start engines just before the carrier turned into the wind. Those few minutes of waiting, shivering in the cold, looking out on the savage ocean just as dawn was breaking and thinking of what lay ahead, always gave me a strong sense of mortality.

Finally the carrier turned into the wind, the "start engines" signal was given over the bullhorn, and from there on we were too busy to be afraid. We launched, switched fuel to the external belly tank, and rendezvoused into formation, throttling back and leaning the fuel mixture to conserve fuel. About an hour or so later the Hainan coast loomed ahead. We were low, just below a 5,000-foot overcast, when the major spotted some ships in a small unfortified harbor. He led us in an attack, strafing and bombing. Fortunately their antiaircraft fire missed and we left them burning. The tracer 20 and 40 mm shells they were using seemed to float by slowly, so slow I felt I could almost dodge them. Unfortunately, my bomb release failed and I was unable to drop the bomb, so I had to carry it for the rest of the mission.

We regrouped and started toward the major harbor on the southwest shore of the island, climbing through the overcast to about 12,000 or 14,000 feet on top. About 20 minutes later, radar-directed enemy antiaircraft fire began to bear on us. Puffs of black smoke started appearing all around us and we could feel the light tap on our aircraft as the concussion wave struck, indicating our arrival at the harbor. Major Marshal led the attack, down in a steep dive into the clouds. I stuck tight to the wing of George, and when we broke out below the overcast we were at full power and high speed, but alone! None of the rest of the flight was anywhere to be seen. In front of us was the harbor full of ships. We flew through at a couple of hundred feet firing at any thing in our sights. The sky was filled with a hail of tracers streaking every which way but mostly behind us. Miraculously, we weren't hit in any vital spot and as we exited the harbor we throttled back to conserve fuel and started a slow climb toward the overcast. Radio silence had long since been broken and we heard the major (where he was we didn't know) ordering a rendezvous for the scattered flight at a prominent landmark on the coast away from the harbor.

George and I headed in that direction climbing through about 1,500 feet when in front of us, just below the overcast, was a flight of aircraft passing at 90 degrees to our course and about five miles away. At first I thought it was the rest of our group but instantly realized there were nine when there should have been no more than six—and besides, they were not Corsairs! At the same time we realized they were enemy fighters they saw us and turned in our direction, holding a huge advantage in altitude. I immediately jettisoned my belly tank, made sure all guns were charged and went to full power. We positioned ourselves for a defensive weave, a tactic taught all navy and marine fighter pilots in which the aircraft are side-by-side about 400 or 500 yards apart. A scissor action is then initiated in which the two defending aircraft head towards each other, and when crossing abruptly, reverse course heading back to repeat the maneuver. This allows the guns on each aircraft to be trained on the tail of the other to ward off attackers. However, during the course reversal you are exposed and undefended by your companion aircraft.

As the enemy descended on us in a line astern, I slid out to the side and we tried to time our turn into each other to meet the first few attackers to get them in our sights. As we crossed I was firing at the plane on George's tail and reversed course only to see he had partially reversed his course. He still had his belly tank and it was on fire and he was bailing out. I saw his chute open and then I was in the midst of a swirling maelstrom, feeling a lot like the fox when cornered by the hounds. Turning, dodging, firing at any thing in front of me, I was desperately trying to get to the overcast! Tracers filled the sky around me. Survival was the goal! After what seemed like an eternity, but was probably only two or three minutes, I entered the clouds.

Whew!! As far as I could tell no vital parts had been hit. Whether I downed anyone I haven't a clue. All the gun camera film developed later just showed aircraft flashing by mixed with tracers from my guns as I fired.

I now descended to just below the overcast, heading in the direction of the rendezvous point, looking for enemy aircraft. This time I might have the altitude advantage. I called in the blind on the rescue submarine frequency using the shackle code, giving the approximate position of George's bailout, which I estimated to be maybe a mile or so off the coast. As I was nearing the rendezvous point I saw two aircraft in the distance just below the overcast coming in from another direction. I heard Major Marshall shout, "Benny, stop shooting at me!" Bennewitz, who was Marshall's wingman and was separated from him, replied "Major, I'm not shooting at you." Then, as I was getting closer, I heard, "Goddam it, Benny, stop shooting at me!" At that instant the second aircraft pulled up into the clouds. I realized that it was an enemy fighter doing the shooting and Marshall was the target. My approach had frightened the attacker off.

We all managed to rendezvous, but low fuel state meant heading back for the carrier immediately. Marshall's aircraft had been hit and was leaking hydraulic fluid but seemed otherwise okay. Other than minor damage to the rest of flight's aircraft, no one was wounded.

The weather had deteriorated to a visibility of three or four miles and we were flying at about 4,000 or 5,000 feet just under an overcast. The two division leaders, Major Marshall and Captain Bedford, were computing time, distance, and heading to the carrier, which was moving northward on a predetermined course at 30 knots, which also had to be accounted for in their calculations. Things looked pretty dicey. The Corsair had unreliable fuel gauges, but you knew what the initial fuel load was and could calculate fuel burn, and thus time remaining. Also, you always fed off the belly tank till it was dry or you dropped it—then you knew you had about 200 gallons remaining. The main internal tank (230 gallons) had a reserve position on the valve that held back 50 gallons. When the engine started bucking as fuel was shutting down you could switch to reserve and know you had exactly 50 gallons left. This wasn't much, since leaned out and throttled way back you would burn about 80 gallons an hour. So 50 gallons meant about 40 minutes of flight time before the engine quit.

As we were approaching our calculated time of fleet intercept we were very concerned about our low fuel. No one had picked up the YEZB radio signal yet and everyone was listening intently. Then I thought I could just hear a very faint signal, a C (-.-.). Referring to the pie chart indicated that the fleet was off our beam—we were as close as we were going to get on our present heading! Continuing on the same course would bypass the fleet and all of us would perish. At about the same time several of us had to switch to reserve, giving us only about 40 minutes to go. I told the major I thought I was picking up a signal and he immediately turned the lead over to me. I made a 90-degree turn as indicated on the chart and began to breathe again as the signal strength increased and everyone began receiving it.

The rest of the flight mission was routine except for the bomb I hadn't been able to release. Fortunately we landed aboard the *Essex* without incident after slightly over five hours, the longest flight in the

Left to right: John Wastvedt, George Strimbeck, Bill Bedford, Gill Boyd

Corsair I had ever had. Emotionally drained and tired but extremely thankful to be back, relatively safe and secure, we were all debriefed by the intelligence officers. No word of George had come through but of course I didn't expect it for a day or two.

That night in my room, with a bunk next to the ship's hull at the water line, listening to the crashing of the waves as the carrier steamed along, reflecting on the day's events, hoping the rescue submarine had heard my transmission and George would be saved, I thought of other scenarios. Maybe he was injured in the bailout and died in the water. Maybe he was captured and executed. Maybe he was shot in his parachute. Maybe he was a prisoner of war.

A few days later, as no word of his rescue by the submarine was received, we thought possibly he had been taken prisoner. One of our other pilots had been shot down over Japan and we never heard of his fate until the end of the war when he was released from a prisoner-of-war camp. No word was ever again heard of George's fate and how he died. He was listed as "missing in action" and, after a year, as "killed in action."

Battle For Okinawa
By Richard Hansen

In January of 1945 while on Kwajalein, I was transferred to Marine Fighter Squadron 224. They were scheduled to go to Okinawa, and thanks to Colonel Classen, I was to go too. I was delighted because now I had a chance for some air-to-air combat, which is every fighter pilot's desire.

In January and February we continued bombing and strafing the four Japanese islands. Also, we did a lot of practice with bombing and gunnery, and were introduced to rockets. We were well trained after those two months. All this training was in preparation for the invasions of Okinawa and Japan.

The invasion of Okinawa was scheduled for April 1, 1945. The squadron was to be there the day of the invasion and we would be operating off of one of Okinawa's two airstrips, Yontan, on April 4. Because I had no seniority in VMF-224 I had to go on an LST (landing ship tank) with some of the squadrons' equipment and half of the pilots. The senior pilots went aboard a carrier and would fly the planes in after the airfield was secured.

I was happy to be going, but it was a long trip on the LST and we were on board for over a month. The LSTs are shallow depth vessels designed to get close to the shore, but they roll with every wave, resulting in seasickness. We made it to Palau, met with other ships in the convoy, then proceeded to Okinawa. Another convoy came up from the Philippines; in total there were 1,200 ships.

The invasion came off as planned and on April 2, I was on Okinawa in the rain. That night I found a piece of cardboard to try and sleep under, but there was so much noise from all the vehicles and shooting that it was useless. On the next day we got our tents up and the planes came in. I see by my logbook that I did fly on April 4.

The first few days we flew air patrols as directed by the radar combat center, looking for kamikazes. This was an interesting time, both in the air and on the ground.

The fleet's carriers were operating between Japan and Okinawa and their pilots were getting most of the action. The radio network was busy directing intercepts, and there was constant chatter over our radios. The kamikazes were out in force and most were shot down before they could inflict their damage, but some were able to crash into the ships, with some as far south as Okinawa. A few of our pilots got in action west of Okinawa where the Japanese were coming over from Formosa.

Our squadron tent site on Yontan Field was located between the two runways. We were getting bombed every night, as the shrapnel hole in my logbook confirms. Consequently, we had to go to our foxholes, which were always filled with water because it rained every night. In Asia they fertilize their fields with human waste, so we were standing in four feet of water diluted with human excrement. We stayed at the field for three nights and then moved to some large tombs in a cemetery on the side of a hill overlooking the airfield.

One moonlit night we were sleeping in the tomb when the antiaircraft guns started firing. We went to the front of the tomb overlooking the runway to see what was happening. A Japanese bomber had flown over our heads and landed on the runway 300 yards in front of us.

A suicide (Giretsu) squad jumped out from the plane and for the next few hours all hell broke loose. They came well prepared, mainly with grenades and rifles. They killed the tower duty officer, blew up the fuel dump that had hundreds of barrels of gasoline in it, and started blowing up transport planes and some of the other planes parked on the field. The army, who was in charge of the base defense, finally got organized. By morning, the Japanese that hadn't been killed committed suicide.

The next few days we were involved in combat air patrol and a few more kamikazes from Formosa were shot down. Most of these planes were trainers. As such they were not armed, but they probably carried explosives. If there was cloud cover we would go up on top of the clouds, at times 20,000 feet, and circle up there as we watched for enemy aircraft, but it wasn't very productive.

At the airstrip, almost everyday there was some kind of excitement with a kamikaze getting through the air cover. Antiaircraft fire was a common happening. One day shortly after we landed, the firing started. Above the command ship, coming straight down in a dive, was a kamikaze. The plane hit the bridge of the ship and killed a lot of the crew, including the fleet commander. From the airfield we could look out over the vast multitude of ships and watch these things taking place.

Another day antiaircraft fire knocked down a Japanese Betty-type bomber about fifteen thousand feet up, and it seemed to take forever to come down in a big wide spin. It was a great show the first few weeks.

Late one afternoon, when it was still daylight, two of our night-fighter planes were taking off from our field when the army antiaircraft guns, just 300 yards away, started shooting at them. The night-fighters' commander saw this and went over to raise a riot like you have never seen or want to see. These planes had our stars and stripes on them, which can be seen a thousand yards away.

A day or two later a navy type floatplane was catapulted off a cruiser and was shot down by another navy ship 300 yards away. There was a lot of confusion those first days because everyone on a ship was concerned about being the target of a kamikaze. All the ships were on full time alert, so the antiaircraft guns were always manned and there were too many mistakes. A navy vessel shot down one of our marine pilots while in the landing pattern for our own field. When we came back to the base from a flight, we always hoped that we wouldn't be mistaken for a Japanese plane.

On April 14 we had our first ground support action with the First Marine Division and we used all our weapons, including bombs, rockets, and machine guns. This would be a regular action from then on. To combat sneak kamikaze attacks at Yontan Field we provided what was called ready alert. On the airfield at the head of the runway, we had four Corsairs parked, two of them with pilots ready to start the engines and go. The other two planes were not manned, but the pilots were standing by in event of an attack. We would alternate the two crews hourly. This was not too boring as we had other planes taking off on ground support missions all day.

One day, all of a sudden two Japanese planes came down from behind hills east of the airport. Undetected by radar, they attacked us. I was out of my plane at that time and saw them coming. I alerted everybody and jumped behind a dump truck along with the other waiting pilot. The Japanese were strafing us and fortunately nobody was hit. The airplanes were hit but were still flyable. The Japanese planes were shot down by the antiaircraft defense groups on the field.

Within a few days after the invasion the navy established a ring of picket patrols around Okinawa to thwart the kamikazes that were coming thick and fast. The patrols consisted of two destroyers and five or six LCI antiaircraft ships. Since the harbor on the west side of Okinawa had over a thousand of our ships anchored there, it was one of the prime targets of the kamikazes. About the third day after the landing a kamikaze attacked the command battleship by coming straight down. It hit the bridge on the ship and killed numerous people, including the admiral in charge of the invasion.

Our primary purpose was to provide air cover for the picket patrols, which we did by having two Corsairs circling over the ships at all times during the day. We would be on station for about four hours and then would be relieved to refuel, at which time we came back on station for another four hours or more. This circling was boring, but there was a lot of activity on the radio to listen to.

One day a call came from the command destroyer saying there was an unidentified airplane coming towards the fleet from the west. My wingman was at 12,000 feet and I was at about 10,000 feet. All of a sudden I looked up and saw a Japanese Tony fly over me, with my wingman behind him. The antiaircraft fire started up and the wingman pulled off from pursuing it.

I decided I had to go after the Tony myself, even though my wingman should have continued his pursuit. There was no way I was going to carry the burden of 200 or more sailors dying, knowing in my heart I might have saved them. I went after him in spite of the antiaircraft fire coming directly at me.

When I saw the Tony fly over me, I quickly turned around and started my pursuit. The Tony fighter was a fast airplane. I pushed the throttle into war emergency power and went after him. In a short period of time I was gaining some and still accellerating, but he was still a long way out of range of my guns as I played catch up.

Eventually he started into his dive for the ship, but it was a fairly flat dive as he was still 800 yards out from the fleet. I was now gaining on him rather quickly. The antiaircraft fire was intense by this time, but it just left my mind and didn't bother me as I was completely preoccupied in the pursuit. I was sure the Tony would be going for the fleet command destroyer.

I armed my guns and waited to get as close as possible. When the Tony was about 600 feet above the water and 1,000 feet from the ship I was closing on him very fast. I figured when I got within 600

THE SECRETARY OF THE NAVY

WASHINGTON

The President of the United States takes pleasure in pre-senting the NAVY CROSS to

FIRST LIEUTENANT RICHARD O. HANSEN,
UNITED STATES MARINE CORPS RESERVE,

for service as set forth in the following

CITATION:

"For extraordinary heroism as Pilot of a Fighter Plane in Marine Fighting Squadron TWO HUNDRED TWENTY-FOUR in action against enemy Japanese forces at Okinawa, Ryukyu Islands, on 6 May 1945. While flying on radar picket patrol, First Lieutenant Hansen observed an enemy plane attempting a suicide run on a friendly destroyer and, courageously diving through an intense barrage of antiaircraft fire from seven ships, succeeded in shooting down the Japanese plane fifty feet from the destroyer, thereby undoubtedly saving the ship from damage or possible destruction. His daring airmanship, courage and gallant devotion to duty were in keeping with the highest traditions of the United States Naval Service."

For the President,

John L. Sullivan

Secretary of the Navy.

The presidential letter, along with the Navy Cross (inset).
The Navy Cross is the second highest medal awarded
in the armed services.

feet I would fire off a quick burst to align my aim. At this point we were passing over some of the LCIs in the fleet.

I fired off a burst and saw the tracers going down a little to the left of him. I adjusted my angle, and by this time the destroyer was dead ahead about 200 yards. I started firing continuously and suddenly I saw pieces coming off both the Tony's left wing and the cockpit. I knew I got him. The Tony turned slowly to the left, just about at the ship. It flew across the bow of the destroyer, about thirty feet above it, and crashed into the China Sea, just fifty feet past the ship.

As the Tony disappeared into the ocean, I followed over the bow of the destroyer. I immediately dove down as close to the water as I could and turned 90 degrees away from the ships, as I knew the antiaircraft guns were still firing. I moved on out at full throttle for about a mile and heard the command ship broadcasting, "Stop your firing! He's a friendly!"

The fleet commander radioed me that it was a great show from the fleet and thanked me about 10 times for shooting the Tony down. I told him not to expect an encore. Then he asked me why I didn't pull off with all the antiaircraft fire going on. I said, "I didn't think the battle was over since he was still attacking the fleet."

Tricky Crash Landing

By Darrell Smith

April 28,1945, is a date that sticks in my mind. Our squadron, VMF-312, was one of three squadrons flying Corsairs out of Kadena, a one-runway fighter strip on Okinawa that had been captured from the Japanese. The main invasion of Okinawa by the United States had taken place early in April off the seaward end of the strip. The Japanese still occupied both ends of the island. Much of the United States invasion fleet was still there, including a couple battleships and some cruisers, all loaded with antiaircraft guns. We had been catapulted off carriers as soon as the Seabees had patched up the strip and had been flying from it for about two weeks.

It was a warm and cloudy day. I had already flown one combat air patrol. When we came back we were put on "Ready Alert," which meant staying near our planes while they were refueled and rearmed. Late in the afternoon our four-plane division was scrambled. I was flying in the number two position on the wing of the division leader. We contacted the radar controller and were immediately vectored onto a bandit (an identified enemy aircraft).

A low overcast at about 1,500 feet had moved in and we were soon into it, three of us trying to stay close enough to the leader to see his running lights. Our target was heading northeast toward Japan. We soon broke out above the overcast into broken clouds, but something wasn't right. We were getting readings from the Controller like "Bandit 11 o'clock, one-half mile," then "Bandit 12 o'clock, three-fourths of a mile," "Bandit 1 o'clock, one mile," and so forth. Instead of closing in on our target, we were losing him. We thought

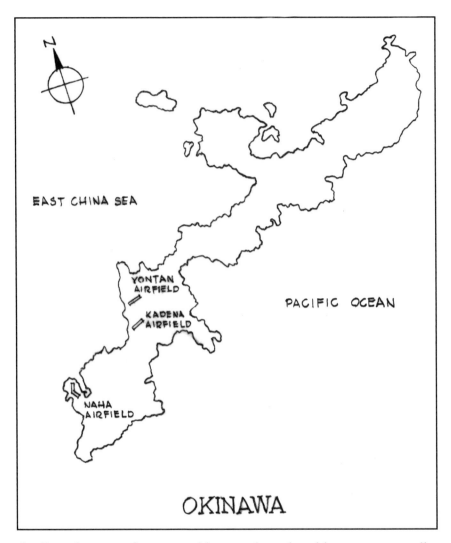

OKINAWA

the Corsair was as fast as anything out there, but this target was walking right away from us! It became obvious that we weren't going to catch him although we had been going full throttle for some time. The controller called us off and gave us a vector back to Kadena.

By then we were over the Pacific somewhere between Okinawa and Japan. We throttled back and went to 1,750 RPM which gave us maximum fuel range but at the price of a slower speed, and started a gradual let down. It was late in the afternoon but Kadena could easily be reached before dark. Soon we were back in the overcast. We broke out at about 1,500 feet right over Ie Shima, a small island about 35 miles northwest of Okinawa. We knew this island was occupied by our forces and was heavily fortified with an active airstrip. Nothing to cause concern. What we didn't know was that they had just been bombed by two Japanese Betty aircraft that had slipped in under the overcast.

Within seconds of our appearance over Ie Shima, what seemed like every gun on the island opened up. The sky lit up and we were sitting ducks, still hanging on our props just a little over stalling speed. I was waiting for our leader to take some kind of evasive action but he just kept going straight ahead. Suddenly there was a loud bang! My control stick started shaking back and forth, part of the console on the right side of the cockpit was in my lap, and my radio went dead. From the noise and the damage in the cockpit I knew I'd taken a direct hit from some kind of explosive.

My first thought was that the engine had been hit and I was in big trouble. I looked for the oil pressure gauge on the instrument panel, but part of the panel was curled in front of the gauge and my view was blocked. I glanced back and there was enough light to see that the right elevator was mostly gone. What was left was fluttering rapidly up and down. That accounted for the control stick shaking back and forth, but I was still worried about the engine. I tried desperately to peel back the damaged panel so I could see the oil pressure gauge. All I accomplished was to slice up my fingers, which began to bleed through my glove.

I looked for the other planes to signal for help but there was no one in sight. I was all alone, and without my radio I was out of touch. By then I was out of the field of fire and still headed in the general direction of Okinawa. What were my options?

Going back to Ie Shima didn't seem like a good idea. Even though there was an active airfield there, getting shot up by them once was enough.

Should I bail out? I was over the water at maybe 1,200 feet and it was getting dark. Even if I got out safely, and the chute opened before I hit the water, and if I got out of it and into my life raft, I'd still be somewhere on the water all night. Air rescue couldn't start looking for me until daylight. I knew from experience that a downed pilot in the ocean, even in a yellow life raft, was extremely hard to find.

Should I attempt a water landing before it got dark, or the engine quit, or the rest of the elevator came off? Same problems! Being on the water all night seemed like the worst option. That left heading back to Kadena, provided the engine kept running and the elevator didn't break completely loose. Although the stick was shaking I still had some control, but I had no way of knowing for how long.

About this time a trickling sensation down the back of my left leg got my attention. I reached down with my left glove and came up with blood. My first thought was if the leg was broken I wouldn't be able to control a landing. I tried pushing the rudder pedal and the leg still worked. I decided to try for Kadena.

It was only 35 miles across the water but it seemed twice as far. It was starting to get dark and I was beginning to wonder if I'd be able to find the strip. Finally, I began to see a slight glow in the sky. That had to be the fleet's lights coming on. Kadena would be just beyond that.

To land at Kadena I would have to fly over the fleet. I would be out of the approved approach pattern and I had no radio to let them know I was a friendly. I started thinking about the previous week when I had been standing with some other pilots on the Kadena runway. An F4F flew down the coastline and both the fleet and the shore-based antiaircraft opened up on it and followed it with their fire until it was out of sight. We knew from the sound of the engine that he was a friendly and guessed that the pilot had become separated from his group or had somehow become lost. Obviously he hadn't identified himself or used the proper approach, so the fleet had no way to know if he was friend or foe. Was the same thing going to happen to me? It seemed like the control stick fluttering was getting worse and I was increasingly concerned that the elevator might pull off or the engine quit. I headed for the runway for a straight-in approach right over the fleet. Although I should have been a prime target, not a shot was fired.

I also had no way to contact the Kadena tower to identify myself or explain my problem. I had no idea if anyone was in the tower so I figured I was on my own. All I wanted to do was get that airplane down on the strip, whatever way I could. To my amazement, suddenly I got a green light to land. I dropped the wheels and heard them chunk down and lock. I lowered the flaps and pulled back on the stick, but without the elevator intact the nose dropped and suddenly I was diving right for the runway. I jammed on full power and managed to get the flaps back up! I pulled out somewhere just over the runway but I was already at the far end. I would have to go around for another try. This meant making another approach over the fleet. But again, their guns were silent.

This time I came in faster and left the flaps up. As I slowed for the landing I began to lose control, and the plane started to slip to the left. I landed hard and the guns on my plane went off. The plane skipped sideways off the runway, through a shallow ditch and up onto a coral taxi way where it stopped. I didn't go though the regular shut down procedures—I just reached up and turned off the switch.

I was devastated about that burst of gunfire down the runway. I hadn't even thought about my guns still being armed. During flight training we had been told in no uncertain terms that prior to landing we were to be sure the guns were on safety. Failure to follow this procedure, we had been told, would result in being grounded permanently and possibly even a court martial.

By now it was dark. In just a few minutes the lights of a jeep appeared. Someone jumped up on the wing, shined a flashlight in my face and started to chew me out for shutting down on the taxi strip. It was our engineering officer. But before he got very far he saw the blood on my gloves and the damage in the cockpit. He broke off his lecture and started calling for help. In no time I was literally lifted out of the cockpit, carried to the jeep, and on my way to the medical tent.

My blood pressure was sky high, the fingers on my right hand were sliced up, and the flak wound on my leg, while it bled quite a bit, wasn't too serious. They determined I was in pretty good shape. While they were checking me out our commanding officer arrived and asked, "How you doing, Son?" (I think he was 24 or 25 at the time—about a year older than me). I said, "Sir, I'm all right, but those were my guns that went off on the runway." The thought of never being able to fly again was uppermost in my mind. With no hesitation he said, "You let me worry about that." I never heard another word about it.

It was routine during the flight debriefing to be given a small bottle of "medicinal" brandy to settle us down. That night I was given three bottles. I don't remember how I slept that night but it was probably pretty good. My logbook shows I was back in the air again the next day.

Sixty years later, I still remember that day. I've often wondered if someone in the fleet recognized the silhouette of the Corsair's gull wings and that's why they didn't shoot. And who can explain that landing? I still don't know why the plane didn't nose over or flip on its back when it went through that ditch.

The airplane didn't fare as well as I did. It wound up in the bone pile with other damaged aircraft to supply badly needed spare parts to other aircraft. I'll never forget that she brought me all the way back to Kadena. And some people wonder why we loved the Corsair!

Can an experience like that give a person religion? You bet! I believe I had a lot of special help that night.

Birding, Bombing, and Binoculars
By Lyle Bradley

My fascination with flight started about 1930 (at 6 years of age) by watching birds, dragonflies, kites, and a rare airplane. Never did I think about military aviation until my first year in college at the University of Dubuque. I had already enlisted in the Marine Corps and was awaiting the call when a military group of aviators visited the college and told about the changes for accepting aviation cadets. I decided to go with the Marine Corps and Naval Aviation.

Birding can create problems. As an aviation cadet, I was accused of cheating on aircraft recognition tests because of my perfect scores. A navy commander asked me bruskly, "Cadet, do you realize cheating is a court martial offense?" I'm not sure how I responded to the surprised accusation but he continued, "We are projecting 50 new slides of aircraft on the screen and you'd better get them correct." Three other officers were present as the projector rolled at 1/100 of a second for each slide. I did get them all correct. One officer with my file in front of him declared that several letters in my file indicated my expertise in bird identification and this might carry over to aircraft identification. They excused me and I never heard anything else on the subject.

During combat missions in the Pacific Theatre, I carried my birding binoculars with me to observe targets from altitude. On missions during 1944 and 1945, our primary work was to stop Japanese kamikaze aircraft from hitting our ships. We watched airfields closcly from altitude. On one mission I spotted the edge of a wing about a mile from the Okinoyerabu airfield. As we circled the island at

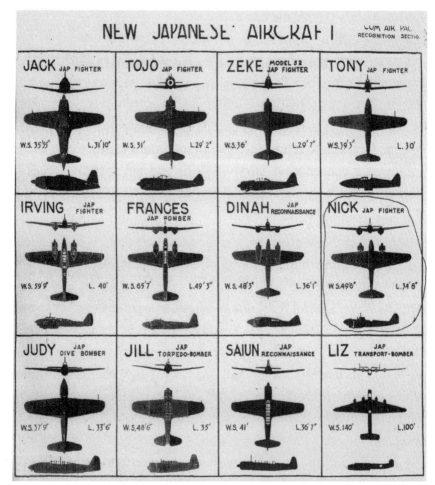

One of the many pages that each pilot must learn at 1/100th of a second
in recognition classes or Ready Room reviews.

20,000 feet I scrutinized the area carefully and could make out several
camouflaged aircraft. When I alerted Major Frame, who was leading
the mission, he turned the lead over to me. I described the spot for
the flight and started the dive. My eight rockets were armed and my
50-caliber guns were off safe. Among our planes we had bombs and
rockets, and when my first rockets hit the area aircraft parts flew in
every direction. Between us, we estimated that 40 aircraft had been

destroyed. They gave me credit for nine of them. Birding binoculars got a high priority from fellow aviators that day.

Several episodes during the Korean War also gave binoculars and birding skills high marks for neutralizing the enemy. At the Chosin Reservoir when the marines were pinned to the small area of Yudamni, our Corsair fighters, good eyes, and binoculars helped the First Marine Division to return safely with minimum losses.

Birding can improve survival skills and aid friendly forces in time of war. On our two aircraft carriers, the USS *Bennington* and *Sicily*, several other men who were birders enjoyed watching the three species of albatross, a flock of golden plovers that used our flight deck for resting, and an array of gull species. We pilots were always concerned about ending up in a life raft and hoping to be picked up. Watching gulls at sea is an indication, in the evening, where land is located. One species, however, the swallow-tailed gull, feeds at night, so it flies away from land in the evening.

While acting as a flight instructor at the Naval Air Station in Pensacola, Florida, I was asked to accompany another birder to explore the Suwannee River in 1952 to see if any ivory-billed woodpeckers still existed in the United States. We gave the National Audubon Society a no-see report, as did other teams. One year later they asked me to be a warden-biologist for them on the coast of Texas, where I prevented human interference with the colonies of nesting birds. While there, Robert Sisson, of the National Geographic Society, tented with me while photographing for the article in the November 1954 issue of the magazine titled, "Saving Man's Wildlife Heritage."

My passion for birds started early. My fascination of flight led me to a career in aviation and also a career in biology. I have been on fieldtrips with several famous birders such as Roger Tory Peterson, and have fantasized on birding with other great birders of the past like Leonardo DaVinci, Thomas Jefferson, John Muir, Franklin D.

Roosevelt, H. D. Thoreau, and John Audubon. They, along with others such as Meriweather Lewis, have all written detailed accounts about their birding experiences.

Birds affected my choice of where to build our home in Minnesota along the Rum River. On the oxbow selected we have observed 216 species of birds (almost tops in the state) as well as all the normal mammals, reptiles, and other life forms.

In 2004 a group of us were kayaking the Columbia River in Washington. Our history group tied our kayaks together in the middle of the river and read excerpts from the Lewis and Clark trip about the birds they observed at that spot 200 years ago. It gave me impetus to put on programs entitled "Birds of Lewis and Clark" for birding and historical groups.

We owe birds a debt of gratitude. They keep some destructive insects under control, aid miners by detecting gases, give color and song to our environment, and push many to travel beyond the horizon or in their backyards. Birds are one of the best indicators of environmental problems—we can thank Rachel Carson for her efforts and her book, *Silent Spring*. Think of all the people who use birds for photography, hunting, teaching, food, writing, art, and pleasurable hobbies.

If you are one who considers birding weird, try it before judging. One couple with whom we play cards told us, "Always thought you were off your rocker on birds, but now in our new house we have a Peterson Bird Guide on our kitchen table—so I guess we are off our rocker also." Birding adds an interesting dimension to anyone who indulges.

Don't worry about being weird—you will have much company. It will improve your senses, give you pleasure, and might save your life—as it did mine. Birding and aviation makes a superb survival combination—good for individuals and our country.

A Night to Remember
By Edward Anders Sovik

There was a brief news item from the *Associated Press* one day in 1981 that reported a volcanic eruption on the island of Pagan. It was a minor event as such eruptions go, on a minor island a couple of hundred miles north of Saipan in the Marianas, that minor archipelago of the western Pacific. It caught my attention because I once visited Pagan and never expected to see or hear anything about that island again.

The occasion of my brief but troublesome visit occurred on July 18, 1944. My Marine Corps night fighter squadron, VMF(N)-532, was based on Saipan at the time. Saipan, which has frequently been mentioned in various wartime accounts and has been occupied by Americans for various purposes since, was attacked by marines in June 1944, and by the middle of July, following some bloody engagements with the Japanese, was secured. VMF(N)-532 had been sent to provide aerial cover at night in defense against the likelihood of Japanese bombing threats.

One night about midnight Major Vaughan, our skipper, was notified that he should lead a flight to attack the Japanese installation on Pagan. Admirals King and Nimitz were due to visit Saipan the following day. Though no Japanese planes had been seen on Pagan for some days, a navy reconnaissance plane had reported that a Japanese seaplane had been sighted there, and the possibility occurred that the enemy had learned of the admirals' visit and were preparing an attack on Saipan.

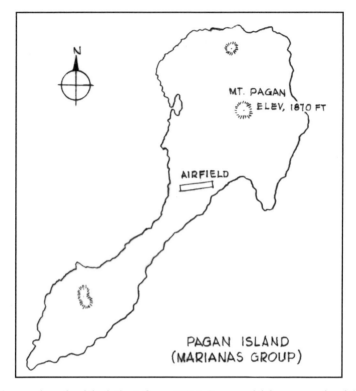

The major decided that four F4U-2s would be armed with two 250-pound bombs to make a bombing and strafing run on the Pagan installation with the intent that if the reported planes were really there they would be destroyed.

Pagan is perhaps three miles long, and is shaped roughly like an hourglass or dumbbell. The northern half is the little volcanic cone; the southern half is palisaded, rising sharply out of the ocean. Between the two is the isthmus, perhaps half a mile across. Running east and west was the little airstrip, ending in the west with a seaplane ramp at the harbor. The military buildings were on the north side of the strip at the foot of the volcano; along the south side of the strip and close to it rose a steep palisade, the continuation of the perimeter of that half of the island. From charts and reconnaissance, we knew that much about Pagan.

Takeoff was timed to arrive at the very earliest light. Major Vaughan led, I was on his right wing. Captain Bedell led the other section to the left, with Captain Bollmann on his left wing. We were to attack by sections (pairs), diving in from the west and hoping for a surprise. There was a small weather front between Saipan and Pagan so we climbed to 16,000 feet to get over it, and we found the island by our airborne radar before we could see it in the darkness. It did of course appear, a dead black shape in the ocean that reflected the sky, so we cut back power and came in diving. I was flying on the major, but opened up the space between us so I could look at the target.

We did surprise the garrison; there was no welcoming fire. But at the last instant as he came across the shoreline ahead of me I lost the black shadow of the skipper's F4U against the black shadow of the island. With thumb on the bomb release and fingers on the trigger, I pulled up and held fire for fear that I might shoot down the major's plane. What to do? Surely not drop the bombs and strafe at random, surely not fly back home with the load I came with.

So I crossed the isthmus and flew out over the water until I was sure the second section had flown clear. Then I turned back west, gave the engine full power and went down to try to do some damage.

This trip was no surprise. Gunfire began, tracers sparkling like the spray from dozens of lawn hoses from both sides, following me in my erratic path. I was trying to find targets below and in front for my own tracers. I saw some buildings and dropped my bombs, getting a fairly close look at the seaplane ramp and harbor, absent of aircraft.

I was hit, almost inevitably I suppose. I saw my fabric wing tips aflame and found control of the plane uncertain. As I pulled up, taking advantage of the full-power speed, I had one hand on the hatch release, wondering in an instant whether I might first explode, whether

I might find myself in the water, whether I was high enough to invert the plane and parachute, or whether I could get to shore and survive on the island. In the same moment I saw that the fires had blown out and that I was at 1,500 feet heading south, able to keep the plane under control.

My throttle was at full power, my controls were crossed, full left rudder, full right stick, but I was doing 165 knots, holding altitude, engine gauges steady. But when I tried to raise the other planes on VHF radio I got no response.

In the dawning light, I could see the burned-away openings in the wing tips. One of the hinged access doors on the starboard wing was open with a belt of machine gun ammunition bulging up, causing drag. No wonder I couldn't get more speed. I wondered what other damage there was and whether gas would hold out at full power. So I tried cutting back, but couldn't keep altitude and control. I settled down to a straight course at 1,500 feet, full power, crossed controls, 165 knots, and I set about fiddling with the radio. There was no response on low frequency antennas—something else probably gone, and no response on channel two VHF. Perhaps I was too distant to talk with base, but not too far to reach airplanes in flight. No luck.

About halfway home I saw one of our destroyers in the water ahead, and on VHF channel six I could make out speech. As I flew over I called and asked the ship to get in touch with Saipan (Copper Base) to say they should prepare for a crash landing. I didn't get a response; but in fact the destroyer did hear me, saw me overhead, and alerted Saipan. What goodness!

I tried once again as I approached the field at Saipan to see how slow I could fly and still keep control. Not much luck. I speculated about parachuting into the harbor, but reflected that to get out of the plane at that speed without getting in the way of the tail fin was high risk; and furthermore, the radar in that plane was one of the best ones we had, and it would be a shame to lose it in the drink. So I decided to avoid sparks and fire by landing on the grass alongside the runway at Saipan. I flew the plane in, wheels up.

How much damage the plane had taken at Pagan I never learned. Corsair F4Us were tough. We had gas tanks that could absorb bullets and engines where you might be able to lose some of the 18 cylinders and still fly. The frame and its parts were rugged. We sat on a quarter-inch thick steel plate that extended up to make the seatback. There was the rub. Under that grass into which I flew was no ordinary earth, but in the black earth great hard knobs of coral. They stopped the plane, but they didn't stop the engine, which broke away and kept going for a hundred yards or more. And they didn't stop me. My harness, fastened to the armor plate, held, but the bolts that fastened the armor plate to the airplane frame gave way, and I plunged forward against the instrument panel.

I remember climbing out of the airplane. I walked a few feet and collapsed. The "meat wagon" and fire engine, having been alerted, had been poised for action. I was transported to surgery, where Doc Vroman, our squadron physician, sewed me up before sending me to Hawaii for a hospital stay of about a month.

The plane after the crash.

The next hour is less objectively defined and harder to describe. It is to some degree mysterious, perhaps mystical.

I was in some residual state of consciousness when in a matter of seconds I was put on a stretcher and brought to the hospital tent, but I was not conscious of that activity for some time; my consciousness was as if I was seeing and feeling with the sensibilities of eternity. The terrible sin and cruelty of war surged like a wave in my awareness, and I felt as if I were in God's company observing the world—a sphere in blue space—with God's utter disappointment, and the most profound compassion.

How long this lasted I have no way of knowing—not very long perhaps. I became aware of people and voices, and the first voice I recognized was that of Vin Edwins. Vin was a meterologist in an army air force unit at Saipan. He had been on duty when the destroyer sent the message of my disabled arrival, had learned that I was the pilot of the plane, and came out with the ambulance to collect me from the wreck. We had discovered each other only a few days earlier at the field mess, but had known each other from infancy and had been close friends in high school in China.

Our surgeon was an expert, and put my face together so there is little apparent damage. When he began the stitching together, however, I recovered enough to complain of the pain, and wondered impatiently why there was no anesthetic. He explained that in head injuries anesthetics were unwise, so I shut up through what seemed innumerable sutures in head and face and inside nose and mouth. Then bandaged over, swelling, sightless, I was transported to the DC-4 hospital plane en route to Oahu. While being carried aboard I heard a feminine voice say, "Oh, the poor fellow." I thought she might know something I didn't, that I was going blind.

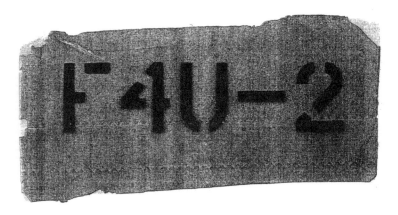

Garry Gramman cut from the wreckage a piece of fabric from the tail of the F4U. He kept it
and the photo for 57 years until the occasion came for him to give it to Sovik. Semper fi.

The fact, of course, is that although my eyes were bloodshot—one of them had no white for a year—I have had good vision. And I have sometimes thought that I had the best of the war; I learned a great deal, had good friends, was never bored, saw danger enough to know whether I had courage, and saw death and life face to face.

A Friend Dies; A Daughter Gets a Name
By Austin J. "Jim" Bailey Jr.

In September 1943 Marine Fighter Squadron 314 was formed at Oak Grove, a satellite marine air station for Marine Corps Air Base Cherry Point, North Carolina. In a few weeks the squadron moved to Mitchell Field, another satellite field for Cherry Point. The training program consisted of a 180-hour Corsair syllabus taught by experienced marine pilots Mike Yunck and Frank Presley, aces just back from the Pacific. The program was scheduled to be completed in three to four months.

In October, Second Lieutenant Dale W. Baird joined the squadron. He had just completed the Navy Corsair Fighter Program at Jacksonville, Florida. I was scheduled with him for an individual battle practice flight. It was a draw and neither one of us could shoot the other down. This was the start of a good friendship. During aerial gunnery Dale would consistently get 30 percent of his bullets in the target, so his nickname became Trigger. Most pilots had scores of 10 percent, so Dale was definitely a good shot. Joe Foss, who later became Governor of South Dakota, was also a good shot and felt it was because he had hunted ducks and pheasants with his brothers since he was seven years old.

Trigger was from St. James, Minnesota. He told me about the dust storms, the Depression, and how he spent a lot of time in the Civilian Conservation Corps (CCC) working to clean up the forests and so on.

In March of 1944 while still in intensive training, our commanding officer announced that two of us had been promoted to first lieutenant and were made division leaders. I was one of the two promoted. Being a division leader meant that I was responsible for navigation, communication, and tactics of four Corsairs. The commanding officer said we could pick three pilots to become part of our division. I got together with Trigger and we picked two other pilots to fly with us. Trigger wanted to be my wingman. We picked "Stretch" Keller (Boise, Idaho) to lead the second section and "Westy" Westover to fly on his wing. We made a great team and it was very exciting flying together. (Keller was killed in 1945 near Iwo Jima.) Upon completion of our training we boarded a troop train for California, then boarded an aircraft carrier bound for Pearl Harbor. We overnighted at Pearl. The next day we were airlifted to Midway Island over 1,000 miles west of Pearl Harbor and close to the center of the North Pacific.

On Midway we flew gunnery, tactics, and dawn and dusk patrols. One early morning on dawn patrol I spotted a submarine on the surface. It made a crash dive upon seeing me. I reported my sighting to the navy fighter director and after a long five minutes he cleared us to attack with our depth charges. Midway was a United States Navy submarine base so we had to be careful and not attack one of our own. Before we landed a United States Navy destroyer took up a search for the sighted sub and reported a contact. The rest of the day the destroyer dropped depth charges and reported possibly sinking the sub.

On August 1, 1944, during a practice mission, two divisions of Corsairs made a training attack on Kure Island 55 miles west of Midway. One division carried 500-pound bombs and my division was instructed to strafe Kure just ahead of the bombing. I gave the attack signal and rolled into a 40-degree dive at about 350 knots. After the firing run we were level at 500 feet. Before starting a climbing turn, I looked over my left shoulder to see where Trigger was. At that exact moment I saw a small piece of his elevator break off. Quickly the whole horizontal tail surface broke off, causing the fuselage to swing in such a way as to put a very high angle of attack on the wings. Both the wings broke off outboard of the fold mechanism, leaving only the fuselage and vertical fin tumbling toward the water. On impact there was smoke, a little fire and an oil slick. It all happened in a second and the canopy never opened. My best friend had been killed. I called on the emergency radio channel and a navy torpedo boat came in about 15 minutes and inspected the area, finding nothing.

After returning to Midway and listening to my description of the structural failure our commanding officer ordered an inspection of Corsair elevators. They discovered a number of elevators where the ribs had separated from the trailing edge, leaving only fabric to hold things in place. All Corsairs were grounded and inspected. A number of elevators had to be replaced.

There is not a day that passes that I don't think of Trigger. His picture in the cockpit of a Corsair is over my desk this very day. When I married in 1946 my wife and I decided to name our first child Dale, after Trigger. Our daughter, Dale Bailey Norris, who has a Ph.D. in English literature, is very proud of her name.

The Somnolent Sentry

By Edward Anders Sovik

Captain Howard Bollmann was the only one in VMF(N)-532, I believe, who had been in the war zone before the squadron sailed into what were considered to be enemy waters aboard the CVE *White Plains* en route to Tarawa. Bollman came late to 532. He had been in the Solomons, and when his outfit was shipped back stateside he was so impatient to get back into action that he persuaded someone to cut him loose and reattach him to 532; our squadron's departure from Cherry Point was imminent. He was senior to everyone but Major Vaughan, who said he would accept Bollmann on condition that our table of organization wouldn't be upset. This was fine with Bollmann—he wanted to fly, nuts to rank and privilege.

The rest of us were moving from one new experience to another as we sailed southwest. Our F4Us were tied down on the flight deck from which they would be catapulted. The hangar deck was occupied by the squadron's equipment, piled helter-skelter—ammunition, bedding, tools, C-rations, paint, canned goods, everything—in a great mountain that almost covered the deck and rose almost to the 20-foot overhead. On top sat a private first class on guard duty, armed and supposedly alert, watching not for the enemy, but for any wandering swab jockey who might come by and adopt for his own some attractive or useful item from the miscellaneous heap.

One night on the way I had the duty, which meant mostly sitting around in a little room off the hangar deck that was the squadron HQ, and occasionally strolling around to look and listen for trouble. The sentinel on duty was one of the line crew, one of the youngest among us, a gung ho marine from Brooklyn. On one of my outings I looked up to see him sitting with his rifle across his knees and head down, apparently drowsing. I called to him and got no answer, so I started a noisy climb up the mountain. It seemed to me to be my duty to check on the somnolent sentinel. I had learned somewhere that if one could take his rifle away from a sentry that would be prime evidence of sleep, so I lifted the piece from his knees and then woke him up. It seemed to be my duty, so I reminded him that sleeping on watch in enemy waters was grounds for a general court martial. He was due to be relieved soon; I thought it would be proper to let him stew a little bit—and I thought I could use a little time to think, too—so I said, "Come see me at 0900 in the morning."

We were both, of course, members of the Corps—the toughest outfit in the world, where attention to duty is impeccable, and the discipline unrelenting. But we were both just barely into enemy waters on our first trip. So when we met again at nine in the morning I said, "I won't say anything about last night and I don't want you to either." But I know neither one of us forgot it, because he would come running to carry my chute or be otherwise helpful when we met on the flight line.

Bombing of Bloody Nose Ridge at Peleliu
By Harry J. Goodyear

The island of Peleliu, part of the Palau Islands located approximately 500 miles east of the Philippine Islands, was secured after a fierce battle between the First Marine Division and the Japanese beginning on September 15, 1944. On November 15, 1944, the First Marine Division was relieved by the Army 81st Wildcat Division to continue the fighting. The airfield on Peleliu, located on the most southern island of the Palau chain, became the airbase for the fighter-bomber squadron VMF-122 and other Marine Corps fighter-bomber and night fighter squadrons.

A few days after the First Marine Division had secured the airfield at Peleliu, fighter squadron VMF-122 was ordered to make a napalm bombing mission on the Japanese gun and cannon positions in caves on Bloody Nose Ridge, located on the highest elevation on the island of Peleliu.

The caves had cannons that the Japanese troops would roll out on tracks in position to fire at the attacking marines. The F4U Corsairs, loaded with external tanks of napalm, took off on a northeasterly direction with wheels down, gained an altitude of a few hundred feet, turned in a northwesterly direction, flew approximately a half mile to Bloody Nose Ridge, dropped the napalm over the caves, turned to the left, and landed on the airstrip on Peleliu to receive another load for the next mission.

The bombing helped the First Marine Division secure the Ridge, and later became known as one of the shortest bombing flights of the war.

Dive-bombing Devil Dogs
By Edward Anders Sovik

Our night fighter squadron, VMF(N)-532, was sent with half its planes and a GCI up to Kwajalein after a month at Tarawa. Before we came, the Fourth Marines had taken the atoll from a strong garrison of whom few, if any, remained alive, and within a few days had departed in favor of a base garrison. Seabees had come in to build the camp and to make a fine airstrip replacing the narrow and bomb-cratered blacktop strip the Japanese had built on the north island of Roi. This they did by dredging out from the lagoon vast amounts of living coral sand, spreading it out to make a generous runway and spraying it for days, as they rolled it smooth, to keep the coral alive long enough so that the particles bonded into a dense and firm stratum.

It was reasonable that we should arrive from Tarawa early, but we were not early enough. Marine squadrons of day fighters and dive bombers arrived a few days before us; their task was to protect against enemy attack and to harass Wotje and some other nearby atolls that U.S. forces had leapfrogged, so they couldn't function as submarine supplied bases for Japanese attacks on U.S. bases. The day fighters weren't a good defense since the Japanese by early 1944 could no longer mount a daytime counterattack. At Tarawa the Japanese had to do what damage they could at night. And about a week after Kwajalein was taken the Japanese sent a night flight of bombers that did a great deal of damage, killed many marines, and wounded many. That's when they sent for us.

Japanese intelligence was good enough to know about us, listening to our radio communications. We had taken to flying night patrols, no longer operating, as at first, with planes ready for takeoff at the sound of alert. Patrols were scheduled two planes at a time for two-hour stints, and we spent our time doing make-believe night interceptions, one plane the target, one the attacker, sharpening our skills, and also the skills of the fighter directors who controlled us. In the weeks that we "protected" Kwajalein no Japanese attacks took place.

As I reflect on it, I think we were doing some good flying. The F4U was a joy to fly, once in the air. You had to zigzag to see your way when taxiing because of the nose-up attitude, and the beginning of every takeoff was blind for a few moments. (One of our casualties was a takeoff that got out of control.) Landing was blind too, if you came in straight, so the proper approach was to make a descent in a fairly tight 180 degree turn and at the end of the turn straighten out, cut power and stall, landing tail wheel first. This is standard carrier procedure, of course, but the carrier pilot has the landing signal officer to help him control speed and attitude. We did this at night, and if our landings were not always soft, at least we never had a crash.

Flying solo over a wide ocean needs some reasonable care for navigation. Under usual conditions the ground radar kept track of us if we didn't know ourselves where we were; we didn't assume that we could rely absolutely on that radar, so we carried kneepads where we could record the vectors and times in some attempt at navigation. Ground radar was indeed unreliable; we lost Lieutenant Don Spatz because he was not properly tracked and did not know where he was when he flew out of radar range.

We were pilot and navigator in the Corsair. We were also radio operator and radar operator—which could be more than turning the set on and off, because the radar was rather primitive and quixotic. And we were gunner and bombardier. There was some strong opinion (not among us, but elsewhere) that to ask one person to undertake all these duties was too much, and so the third generation marine night fighters (the first was the PV-2) was the F7F, a twin engine plane carrying a radar operator in a tandem cockpit. The downside of that was, of course, the reliance on intercom communication and close cooperation between the two.

We were given and took credit for the peace on the atoll after we came. We were like a "fleet-in-being," to use the term some admiral used to describe the mere presence of powerful armament. That didn't satisfy our people; defense is alien to the marine elan. We were impatient for action, unsatisfied to serve by waiting. Possibly our superiors, concerned for morale as much as for effectiveness, thought of something for us to do. Wotje and other atolls had shown some signs of activity following their neutralization. So we undertook to do some glide bombing and strafing to damage again the runways that the small garrisons had been repairing.

Most of us had training in dive-bombers after our Pensacola careers. But this was not dive-bombing and the F4U was not a dive-bomber. Lowering the landing gear served as dive brakes, but we thought not for vertical dives. We sent planes out by twos, we attempted to surprise the Japanese with power-off glides, and we sometimes saw the enemy scurrying for cover. We did help by keeping the runways pot-holed, and escaped what antiaircraft fire we met. But we were amateurs trying to avoid boredom.

There were two marine squadrons based at Majuro after we left that were assigned the duty of harassing these islands where the garrisons were so persistent in their attempts to serve the lost cause. They learned that F4Us could do real dive-bombing, and they kept it up long into 1945.

South Pacific Hot Spot

By Robert A. Kilgore

I was stationed at El Toro, California, flying F4U Corsairs in 1943. After two months of intensive training we received orders to proceed to the South Pacific. This turned out to be an eighteen-day sail on a very old liner. We were unescorted and arrived in Numea, New Caledonia.

A few days later it was on to the island of Efate where we became part of a replacement pilot pool. About fifteen of us were to go to the island of Bougainville to join the fighter squadron VMF-215. It was a

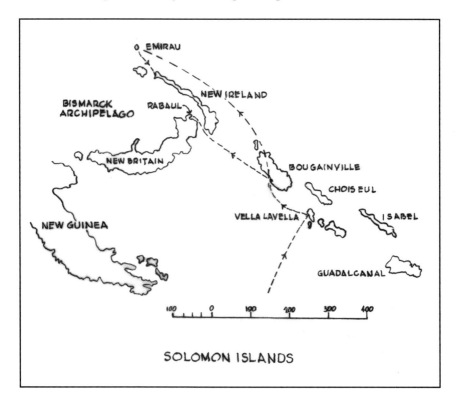

very large island in the Solomon group and the Americans had only a small beachhead with three airstrips separated by strips of jungle.

We arrived in a transport plane, only to find the airstrip being shelled by the Japanese, so we diverted to the island of Vella LaVella. After the marines came in and enlarged the perimeter on Bougainville, we returned.

Our main target was the large Japanese base of Rabaul, located at the eastern end of the island of New Britain. We pounded this base almost daily, and while most of their aircraft had been destroyed shortly before, there was enough antiaircraft fire to make it interesting. Another assignment was to keep the enemy from reinforcing their troops with barges.

One day while returning from a strike on Rabaul, four of our aircraft spotted two PT boats, one of which was stuck on a reef. When they dove down to investigate, the PTs opened fire on them. There were no flags or other identifications on the boats. It's hard to imagine anyone in the Pacific not recognizing the Corsair's distinctive bent wing configuration, which is unlike that of any other aircraft.

The flight returned to base and rearmed. They returned to destroy one of the PT boats. It didn't take long to find out that the boats belonged to General MacArthur's forces.

The result of this unfortunate incident was an order for all of us to ride on the navy's PT boats during their nightly raids on the island of New Ireland. At the time we were based on the tiny island of Emirau. It turned out to be a trip of almost 100 miles each way in a rough sea at 50 miles an hour in a relatively small plywood boat complete with fireworks. I don't think any of us would ever fail to recognize an American PT boat again.

A Summary Court Martial

By Edward Anders Sovik

The old timers in the Corps said they expected some thievery in military life; there always had been. Nevertheless, it goes absolutely against morale and comradery that anyone should steal from anyone in his own outfit. There are always some people who don't get the word, however.

There was a crap game in the head in one of the barracks at Cherry Point that brought those dicta to my attention. It happened the evening of payday, and a corporal who had not yet sent a remittance to his young wife (and baby) at home in Georgia was the chief and very heavy loser. A sergeant was the big winner. He had a bunk not far from the corporal, and he carelessly left his wallet in an open locker when he went to the head before going to sleep. The next morning a big part of his currency was gone. Suspicions were immediate; proof was not. The story went to the first sergeant and from him to the executive officer of the group, namely, Iron John Harshberger. (This was at Cherry Point in early 1943.) There ought to be a summary court, but to organize a trial where the evidence was uncertain, and where the circumstances of gambling would almost surely emerge as evidence, was troublesome. (Crap games were against the law in the USMC.)

Iron John thought of a ruse. The first sergeant would pass the word quietly that fingerprints had been found on the wallet and that it had been sent to Washington to get identification.

The corporal was not a hardened criminal and unsophisticated in matters of detection, and he probably had a troublesome conscience.

He came to the first sergeant and admitted the theft (of what he wanted to think was still his own money).

That made it easy. There was a brief court martial. I was made the recorder, Captain Tom Mount, our adjutant, the defense. I had the curious duty of talking to all the witnesses to go carefully over the evidence to make sure that there would not be a single reference to the crap game in the head. The evidence, after the recording of the guilty plea, was presented by the defense with the intent that the sentence should be gentle.

The trouble with being the senior member of a summary court is that the sentence must be irrationally heavy so that the commanding officer, when he reviews the case, can demonstrate his deep concern for his men—even those who err—by reducing the sentence of the court. And when the record goes to the judge advocate in Washington, he too should have a little leeway to reduce the sentence further, thus demonstrating that the commanding officer is not really a pussycat, but a real disciplinarian.

Unhappily, the senior member of this court was a powder-puff. He was so moved to pity by the arguments for clemency that the award was a very light sentence. This gave the commanding officer too little room, which, according to scuttlebutt, made him quite unhappy.

F6F Bolt Action
By Lyle Bradley

Our carrier had been damaged, we were returning to the states to reorganize, the atomic bombs had been dropped, World War II was over, and we were at El Centro MCAS flying F6Fs. We flew in the early morning and late in the day to avoid the heat.

Another pilot (Denny) and I took off on Sunday in our motorcycles for dates with two nurses we knew. We arrived back at the base Monday morning at 0615—we were scheduled to be on target at 0630 to practice rocket accuracy. The other planes were taxiing for take off as we approached the hanger and ready room. We slipped into our flight suits, wrote the numbers of the two remaining planes behind our names, and dashed for the flight line. Plane captains indicated the two aircraft were ready so we were taxiing in minutes, had clearance for take off, and arrived on target in time to take the last two spots for the first rocket run.

We watched the number five plane roll into his 60 degree dive. As he cleared the target Dennis called in, "Number six rolling in." I watched Dennis release his two rockets on the target and start his pullout at the bottom of his dive. Suddenly his plane came apart. The entire empennage tumbled crazily through the air while the fuselage, engine, and cockpit (with Dennis in it) went into a very tight spiral at a 45-degree angle aimed for the ground. I yelled at Denny to bail out but his plane was spinning so rapidly it was doubtful if he could move against the centripetal force on him. I watched helplessly as the plane crashed into the ground.

I radioed the other members of the flight. Only two of the other pilots had also witnessed the tragedy.

I radioed the flight leader that he should return to base and report the accident and I would circle the scene to see if Denny had made it out of the plane. It was obvious that he was dead. The F6F parts were strewn over an area the size of two football fields. I was sure parts of Dennis were also scattered.

When I returned to the base in 30 minutes the reports had already been filed and all the F6Fs were now grounded. The crash crew was ready to go to the site for their grisly job of picking up. I got the okay to join them and our four vehicles with at least 15 men started to the target about 15 miles away.

On the way the lieutenant in charge was filling in parts of the crash report that he needed from me. I gave him dive angle, direction, altitude, pullout altitude, and all the details on how the aircraft came apart.

At the site, the first activity was to stake a large marker so no other aircraft would use the target. Then the crew was briefed on the plan for the day. The lieutenant indicated that all the men had completed "crash school" but several had never been at a crash scene. He repeated twice, "It is so important to look close for details, little pieces of metal, a screw, torn fabric, a body part—everything important to find the answer to this tragedy."

A photographer was taking dozens of photos with two different cameras. Hundreds of bags were distributed to the men. I asked the lieutenant if I could help. His response was, "Absolutely. Walk around and write every thought you have about the accident and make sketches of what you see and remember."

Suddenly one of the men shouted that he had found part of the pilot. I gulped and walked to where he was standing. There was part of the leg from Dennis that only a few hours ago was straddling his motorcycle. His flight boot for that leg was about 10 feet away. Each part of his body was photographed and the position logged. Special containers were employed for body parts. Already I observed several men walk away and disgorge their breakfasts. The lieutenant asked how I was doing and I indicated that my biology background had given me a tolerant mindset on body parts.

It didn't seem possible that Dennis only a few hours ago was cheerful and full of zip—a superb pilot. Now here he was in pieces. For the flip of a number on the plane it could have been me. Dennis was one of the most experienced pilots in the squadron, had won a Silver Star in combat—but none of that expertise could help in a situation like this.

It was almost noon when a car appeared with lunch for everyone. I only saw three men go for the lunch. Another car came on the scene with several squadron pilots to check the happenings. A small crane mounted on the truck carefully picked up the larger aircraft parts. Each part was photographed and logged as to its position prior to loading it onto the truck. One of the field men called to the lieutenant to check something small, so both of us walked toward him as he pointed to an object on the desert sand. It looked like a broken bolt or small pipe. After it was photographed we examined it carefully. It was a bolt that had been broken, about a half inch in diameter. The lieutenant briefed everyone to start looking for the other part.

There were guesses where the bolt was located—no one knew for sure. I departed in the next vehicle that returned to the base. While riding I decided to stop in the overhaul hanger to see if I could check the skeleton of a plane to locate the bolt and what its purpose could be.

A squadron meeting was held about 1600 where the squadron CO gave as much information as possible. A week later we learned from the overhaul place near San Francisco that an error had been made—a small bolt had been used instead of the larger one required. At least a dozen other F6Fs had been discovered on the west coast with the same error.

Dennis had given his life to disclose the ridiculous error. Now many years later I read in my logbook for November 2, 1945, that Dennis was killed in a rocket run by an oversight. I can still see his plane, with him in it, spinning to the ground. The last word he heard was from me to bail out.

Accentuate the Positive
By Darrell Smith

In June 1945 when I was rotated from Okinawa back to the United States I was offered two choices for my next assignment. One was as a pilot in Air Ferry Squadron Three (VRF-3) based at Terminal Island near Los Angeles. The other was as a flight instructor at Pensacola, Florida, or Corpus Christi, Texas.

The Ferry Squadron sounded the most interesting. I would be checked out in a number of navy single engine aircraft that I would be flying all over the United States. Some would be coming back from over seas and destined for salvage, some would be sent to reserve squadrons being formed around the country, and some to navy blimp hangers to be stored for possible future use. What's more, there was extra travel pay for all our trips.

There were some ground rules. We could only fly from sunrise to sunset. Each night we had to send a message back to Terminal Island giving the type and bureau number of the plane and where it was. Once it was delivered we were on our own. They usually never heard from us until we picked up another flight or showed up back at Terminal Island. However, we were given priority clearance cards to ride on commercial airlines and navy transports, including what we called the "Admiral's Barge," which flew VIPs on DC4s between Washington, DC, and San Francisco, with a stop in Olathe, Kansas.

There was also an established route that we were to fly that reached from Seattle, Washington, down along the west coast to San Diego, then along the southern border of the United States to Florida and up the east coast to New York. Along this route there were a number of airfields that had refueling, maintenance and overnight facilities. Some had liaison officers who helped keep track of us. We often flew alone but sometimes in small groups when we had planes going to the same area. Basically we were transient pilots. It wasn't like being in a squadron where, when your ground crew said the plane was ready to fly, it was.

I learned this the hard way on one of my early flights. I had picked up an F6F at El Toro, California, that was going to Norfolk, Virginia. They cautioned me that it was beginning to take a lot of oil. I left late in the afternoon and wound up racing the sun to my first stop at Coolidge, Arizona, a small airfield near Phoenix. I was getting low on fuel. The F6F had two gas tanks, one in each wing, and one had a reserve stand pipe. For safety reasons we always took off and landed on reserve. When I landed, a fuel truck came out and the driver said he would fill the gas tanks. The oil truck had already secured, however, and he'd be out in the morning. I tied down the plane and left for the operations office.

When I came back the next morning there was no one around. I climbed up and checked the oil tank personally. It was full. I found a station keeper to man a fire bottle, got the engine started, went through the check-off list, taxied out, got a clearance, and took off. As I was climbing out and reached for the switch to go from reserve to one of the main gas tanks, I glanced at the fuel gauges—they both read empty! I called the tower and said I had an emergency and was coming back. They asked what the nature of the emergency was and I don't remember what I told them, but I don't think it was that I had been stupid enough to take off with empty fuel tanks. Luckily there was enough fuel left in the reserve tank to get me back on the runway.

It turned out that the gas truck driver had decided after I left that he'd come back in the morning when the oil truck came out. The oil truck got there before I did the next morning but the gas truck driver didn't. I certainly should have caught the empty tanks when I went through the check-off list but I was so sure the plane had been refueled the night before that I must have skipped right over that part of the list. If I had wound up among the cactus in the desert off the end of the runway that morning, I don't know how I would have explained what really happened to the Accident Board, but I learned a good lesson. Flying as a transient pilot was going to be a lot different than flying in a regular squadron!

Much of the time I was flying FM2s, F6Fs and F4Us, and had no trouble with them. But with the TBMs things sometimes got a little more interesting.

On one flight two of us were flown to Astoria at the mouth of the Columbia River, which ran along the border between Oregon and Washington, to pick up a couple of TBMs to go to Terminal Island. The other pilot had been in VRF-3 for a long time and was used to flying alone. He had been to Astoria before so he took the lead and I was flying a loose formation off his right wing. Somewhere south of San Francisco my engine started to lose power and I began to fall behind. I tried to call him on the radio but got no response. The TBMs had radios that could be tuned to commercial radio stations and he was listening to music from a local station. He apparently never looked back either because by the time we got to Terminal Island he was almost out of sight.

When I finally got there I called the tower for landing and said I was having a little trouble with the engine. They said, "Yeah, we already see you. You're trailing almost a quarter mile of black smoke. You're cleared for a straight in approach." I was in more trouble than I had realized.

The runway at Terminal Island was a bit of a challenge. To begin with, it was quite short. If you landed too long you would end up in the Pacific Ocean, and right at the approach end was a two-story wooden building. I was told the only reason someone hadn't already flown into that building was because our pay office was on the second floor. I suspect that more than one pair of eyes were watching my approach that day to see if I was going to clear their pay office. Fortunately the engine kept running and there was no problem.

Another time I was bringing a TBM from Sand Point near Seattle, Washington, to Terminal Island. This time I was flying alone. I don't know if all TBMs had autopilots, but this one did. It was a beautiful sunny day and I was cruising along at about 6,000 feet. This time I was listening to music from San Francisco and starting to get a little bored. Earlier I had noticed the autopilot switch and I was tempted to try using it but I had never been checked out on one and decided to leave it alone. Then someone came on the radio singing a popular song at the time that went, "You gotta accentuate the positive, eliminate the negative, latch on to the affirmative, but don't mess with Mr. In-between." I reached down and flicked on the autopilot switch.

That TBM immediately did its level best to do a snap roll to the right. By the time I got the switch turned off and control of the stick again we were upside down over the suburbs of Oakland. I managed to roll it on around to right side up again and started checking the flight controls. I wasn't sure that a torpedo bomber was stressed for that kind of maneuver. When I settled down a little, I was thinking that was about the dumbest thing I'd done in an airplane. I thought I heard the engine say, "I think so too!" I could swear it was grumbling the rest of the way to Terminal Island. After I landed I was told you had to bleed the autopilot on the ground before taking off if you planned to use it.

I had been flying in VRF-3 for nearly nine months and was having a great time. I loved being able to fly so many of the navy's best fighter aircraft. I liked the freedom of flying alone most of the time, of being able to make my own decisions, and the varying experiences of constant traveling.

However, by April 1946, aviation was winding down and one day I received notice that I again had two choices. I could stay in the Marine Corps and accept an assignment for occupational duty in China or I could resign from active duty. I knew this time would be coming and had already decided I wanted to get out and attend the University of Minnesota under the GI Bill of Rights. I gave them my decision, but as things turned out I had one last trip.

A Good Offense—the Best Defense
By Edward Anders Sovik

There is in the marine infantry at war a close association, a fraternal companionship perhaps, between the men and officers of a platoon or company. I think this doesn't exist in the same degree in an aviation unit. A squadron is made up of groups of varied specialists, the line crew who tend to the daily operations of the airplanes, the radio and radar people, the gunnery and ordnance section, the airframe people who do the repair and painting and metal work on the planes, and other groups. All of them have been through the boot camp that makes fighting men of them, but the daily concerns are different, and they are likely to be separated by the differences in their crafts. The pilots would tend to know them all, but perhaps none of them well; the pilots also have their particular craft, and pilots inevitably have a privileged position. They are officers—line officers—which gives them authority; they are also the "point of the arrow." The rest of the squadron is there to make it possible for them to exercise their craft. Their successes are everybody's successes, and their failures everybody's failures.

There is a kind of generous loyalty offered to these privileged people in whom the hopes of the squadron are focused. And the loyalty—"semper fi"—becomes a willing courtesy and a quick obedience.

A good officer took this loyalty and authority as a right. It is the necessary discipline of the Corps. Spit and polish disappears entirely in the field, but the real discipline remains. Of course, although the troops are tolerant, the pilot knows that if his performance fails, the loyalty erodes. And in the field the rigors of base camp discipline had best give way sometimes to common sense.

On a moonlit night at about three in the morning on March 8, 1944, a group of enemy planes was detected by radar at Engebi. A fighter on patrol was vectored out to meet the lead plane, but the interception failed, perhaps because of inaccurate altitude definition, which was the most troublesome problem of the ground radar installations. By ill fortune the first bomb that dropped landed close to the ground radar units and disabled them. For an hour Japanese planes came in dropping bombs and devices to confuse the radar of the F4Us in the air whose radar never fastened on a real target (not that that could have been expected without fighter direction). One of the enemy bombs hit an ammunition dump, and our own resources kept popping off, making us very wary in the interludes between the air attacks. Other than this, damage was less than we could have expected: one killed, several wounded, some destruction to installations, but no airplanes damaged.

Major Vaughan, our commanding officer (injured), and Captain Bedell, our executive officer, were both at Roi-Namur. The senior officer among us at Engebi, the north islet of Eniwetok Atoll, was Captain Warren Adams, our adjutant, who in real life was a member of the famous Adams family and a New York stockbroker.

Warren Adams had been up a day earlier among the men who had their camp across the runway from the officers' tents, and had observed that some men had not been taking good care of their rifles. So he had scheduled an inspection for the morning of March 8, and all the men knew that they would have to have their pieces cleaned and polished.

When the field was peaceful again and the fires out, with the sky becoming light, Master Sergeant Frank Sakert (the senior non-commissioned officer of the forward echelon) found me and asked me if I would arrange to have the scheduled inspection postponed, especially since the night had been so uncomfortable and routine had been so upset and there would be other pressures in the morning to be sure our planes and equipment were in order. He was somewhat embarrassed to make the request because the men knew that they had been derelict in not taking proper care of their arms, and because he had the sense that it would not be out of character in the Corps to be stiffly rigid in such a situation. I had flown a test flight earlier that day and a patrol earlier in the night, and like Sakert, I had spent the hours of the attack on the line, thinking that if a bomb were to drop or fire start close to our planes we might want to move them. I suppose Sakert knew that although Warren outranked me, I was really the superior officer (as squadron operations officer), so he came to me rather than to Adams. I thought for a short moment and told him to go across to the camp and get some sleep. And I went off to tell Warren that I had postponed the inspection. He wasn't sorry either.

A week later I was a passenger in a Catalina with the other pilots of my echelon back to Roi for our fortnight of patrolling there; then I flew a Corsair back to Engebi on March 31 for the second tour at the forward base.

On another moonlit night, in the early hours of April 14, we had another visit from the Japanese, flying out of Ponape (presumably). I was duty officer that night so was not scheduled to fly patrol. When the attack was detected we had two planes in the air; they had taken off not long before to relieve the pilots who came down from patrol and gone off to bed. We then had four planes on the ground. I immediately sent the next two scheduled pilots to fly the planes that had landed and been refueled.

The GCI controllers said that the attacking force appeared on radar to be a large group, and seemed to be circling and sending out the bombers to attack one by one. Of the two remaining planes, one was grounded for some reason that made it useless, and the other had not been scheduled because the VHF wasn't working. The low frequency radio was functioning, but low frequency communication wasn't normally usable because the Japanese jammed the airwaves with noise of all sorts so that communication, especially at altitude and at any distance from base, was practically useless.

I called the island commander and told him the story. We agreed that if the plane was flyable I should get it off the ground. I thought I knew the status better than the other available pilots, so I asked one of them (Thistlethwaite, I believe) to take over the duty and I took the plane up.

The fighter director who took me under control was Frank Mc-Clintock, an able officer from Tulsa, Oklahoma, and the son of a well-known banker and oilman. On takeoff he told me, "Vector two-seven-o, angels twenty, full speed, Bogey approaching." In ten minutes I was at 20,000 feet. Mac realized I wasn't hearing him well, so he kept talking from time to time. When I reported at altitude, I thought I heard him say, "Bogey ahead, clear to attack." The radio wasn't good, but the plane had a good radar set, and almost immediately I caught a blip on the little round screen. I called in my "Tally ho" to McClintock and thought I heard him say again in the cacophony of jamming noise that I was clear to attack. The target was above me, closing fast from about three miles. So I was able to make a textbook interception and found myself at the end of a 180-degree turn, less than half a mile behind the target and closing at a good speed as I climbed to 23,000 feet.

There were good reasons to make visual identification of a target, even though our radar and guns were bore sighted so that theoretically we could have fired blind. Our radar could bring a target as close as about 800 feet when working well. I suppose I took my eyes off the set at a little more distance than that, continuing to close, and flying so that the target would be above and to the right. On a clear moonlit night the sky is a little lighter than the ocean. I saw the target and recognized the contours of the dark shadow as a Japanese Betty, a twin-engine medium bomber. The image was clear, and I had switched on gun sight and guns. Our 50-caliber guns—we had three on the left wing and two on the right wing where the radar nacelle was—were loaded in sequence: armor-piercing, incendiary, and tracer, so we could see the trajectory. A short burst set the port engine of the Betty afire with scarcely any delay. Sliding over to the starboard, another short burst or two set the other engine afire.

I was at that point no longer overtaking the Betty, which began to lose altitude immediately, and as the engine fires grew and spread to wings and fuselage, the descent turned into a dive. I nosed down to watch, called to report the kill, and leveled out after losing some altitude. There was a window in the floor of the F4U. Looking down between my legs I saw the bright flame plunge into the ocean. It took several seconds to quench.

The episode had taken about thirteen minutes from takeoff, and I had used fewer than a hundred rounds of ammunition in the few seconds between the sighting and the destruction. Every aspect of the process (except the radio) went the way these processes were designed to go.

When I looked around again into the night I saw another flare a few miles south. Captain Bollmann had made an interception and destroyed another Betty. And when I landed I learned that shortly before, "Pete" Bonner reported what he thought was a kill. Unhappily the tail gunner disabled Bonner's F4U, and he had to bail out. His location was known and he was rescued from his raft by a destroyer at about nine in the forenoon. When he was delivered home he was sunburned red as a lobster.

Left to right: H. Bollmann, Joel Bonner and Ed Sovik on Eniwetok Island

It appears that we trapped the first three of the marauders, and those of us in the air continued to fly under controller's direction. Only Don Spatz was given a vector that might have been a bogie, but I think it was not. Rather, I believe it was some of the "window," the material the Japanese dropped to delude our radar. Spatz had been handed off to a navy GCI on Eniwetok Island, and whether by accident or ineptitude, he was allowed to fly out of range and was lost. We spent four hours and all five planes that forenoon in a search effort, combing the space where he was thought to have been, up to two hundred and more miles out.

The remaining planes in the Japanese flight didn't come close to the atoll. Presumably having lost the vanguard, they decided not to risk more, and went home. And that was the last attack made on Engebi.

As for Bollmann, Bonner and Sovik, the brass was so happy about the success that each of us was cited for a Distinguished Flying Cross, which may have been more notice than the action deserved.

The Distinguished
Flying Cross

A few months later when our squadron was back at Miramar in California, I had another conversation with Frank Sakert. We had been ordered back to the States in a hurry. The word was that we were to be trained quickly in a new plane, the twin-engined, tandem-seated F7F Tigercat, and sent out to the islands again. It was partly true; but we wouldn't see an F7F for four months, and some of us would not be sent out to the islands again. There were other rumors. Sakert approached me and said, "Lieutenant, the word is that 532 is going to be broken up into three squadrons with Vaughan, Bedell and Sovik named as squadron commanding officers. I would much appreciate it if, when that happens, you would ask for me to be your line chief." I said that would suit me.

His request surprised me as much as it flattered me. And I wondered whether it was the sympathetic officer who postponed the rifle inspection, or the pilot who studied his craft and made the quick and perfect interception, that impressed him. It wasn't that we knew each other very well, but he had a generous loyalty and we had shared two interesting nights. I can think of very few things in my life that have been more gratifying than that short conversation.

A Strange Encounter
By Carlyle Lageson

It was mid morning, September 14,1944, when an event happened that has long puzzled me. The previous day our squadron had been called down to Strike Command for a briefing. The target was Vuna-canau, a Japanese airfield and one of five airfields protecting Simpson Harbor at Rabaul on New Britain in the Bismarck Archipeglago.

We got a very thorough briefing as Strike Command wanted this enemy field neutralized. Involved would be two waves of SBD dive-bombers from VMSB-236. There would be a squadron of TBFs carrying 2,000-pound bombs flown by New Zealanders and fighter cover from another marine VMF squadron. I was to lead the second wave and my responsibility was to lead my wave into position to cover and eliminate any antiaircraft gun positions along the west side of Vunacanau.

The dive-bombers were to blanket the area so that the more vul-nerable TBFs who had been taking losses would have a better chance in their glide bombing attack. About one hour into the flight, while we were still climbing to altitude, a strange thought came into my mind—I was in trouble, and I must turn back. I checked my engine instruments and everything was reading normal. I hated to leave the formation. I had been briefed on my responsibility, and I knew how to lead the rest of my wave into the best position for their dive and then out to the channel between New Britain and New Ireland.

That first flash through my mind was final. I called the strike leader and informed him that I was having a problem. "Do you want an escort?" he asked. "Negative," I replied. After passing the lead to my wingman, whom I always briefed on my idea of the best approach, I pushed down and away from the formation.

I settled on a course of 150 degrees, which would return me to the bomber strip on Empress Augusta Bay, a small area held by our troops on the enemy-held island of Bougainville in the South Pacific. The rest of the formation was just out of sight when I noticed a nearly imperceptible change in the reading of the engine instruments. I had a strange feeling of being on my own over such a large expanse of water. I noticed the cylinder head temperatures were raised slightly, oil temperatures up a few degrees, and oil pressure decreased ever so slightly. I turned to a heading of 090 degrees to make landfall sooner, even if it was enemy-held territory, and cut back on the power setting to ease whatever was taking place with the engine.

As the mountains on central Bougainville appeared on the horizon, a speck of oil hit the windshield in front of me, then another and another. As I watched, the rushing air drew out the drops and strung them around to the side of the windshield. All this time the engine instruments were changing, indicating that internal problems were taking place rapidly.

As the coastline came into view, I changed my heading to parallel the coastline, but by now oil was streaming from the engine and I wondered how long the engine could take that pounding without proper lubrication. My forward vision was now completely obstructed, as well as the side of the canopy, so that I only had clear vision straight up, which wasn't much help. It was at this point that I realized that a previous decision now would probably save my life and that of my rear seat gunner.

It was a few months prior to this time, when a good friend with whom I had instructed in carrier tactics at Green Cove Springs, Florida, suffered a tragic death. Stu, like so many of the pilots, had gone "Hollywood" and was wearing only a baseball cap, sunglasses, and earphones, instead of the traditional helmet and goggles. Stu had taken a hit in the cockpit of his Corsair fighter and the shell had ruptured a hydraulic line, which was always under great pressure. The hydraulic fluid blinded him, but with help from fellow pilots they guided him back to base and attempted to talk him down to a water landing.

All went well, but the initial impact was too fast. Stu's plane porpoised, and the next impact was too hard. Stu's body was recovered, but a bruise on his forehead indicated that his head had hit the gun sight and he had been knocked out. I vowed never to fly without helmet and goggles after that tragic incident.

As oil covered the canopy, I knew I had to open the canopy to see. As I did, the oil flowed around the windshield and the wind whipped it around the cockpit. Soon I was covered with oil, but I could wipe the oil from my goggles with my sleeve and have some vision, even if it was blurred. As I approached Empress Augusta Bay, I decided to forego a landing attempt on the bomber strip and instead called the tower for the landing strip called Torokina right next to the water.

I advised them of my problem and requested that everything be cleared from the runway and that all airborne traffic be cleared from the approach end of the field. Gingerly I felt my way down to the ground. I finally touched down—long, but safely. I was saturated with oil and the plane was a mess inside and out, but the engine had continued to operate perfectly even if it was under stress.

For years I struggled with this incident and why it had happened. Why was I warned in such a positive manner? I kept toying with the idea that some kinetic energy of that throbbing engine perhaps sent a message to a pilot obviously "keyed up" and under some stress. However, there didn't seem to be any basis for such an assumption. I guess it was many years later that I finally admitted that some power beyond my own had warned me of the impending danger. Nor would I ever deny that the spirit of those who had fallen before still rode with me and every pilot as we headed out on each mission.

Eniwetok Interlude
By Edward Anders Sovik

Engebi, the northernmost island of Eniwetok Atoll, was taken on February 18, 1944, and the 22nd Marines moved down the atoll to take the remainder of the islands in the next few days. The attack troops were still present when on February 27 our echelon of VMF(N)-532 was sent from Kwajalein Atoll to Engebi with six planes. The other half of the squadron continued to patrol at Roi, and every two weeks until we were sent to Saipan, the pilots would exchange islands. A couple of days later half a squadron of SBDs joined us. Our GCI ground controller unit was flown in by transport with our ground troops.

Seabees were busy and had been busy night and day when we came. They had already built a strip and kept enlarging it. The gruesome remains of the battle were being buried and the debris of war, including a couple of enemy planes, was being disposed of. The devastation was everywhere, except where the Seabees had brought the new order. I had time to wander into the areas where the fighting had been acute and there, as graves were being dug, some of the 22nd Marines were grovelling among the corpses for souvenirs—Japanese swords, knives, flags, or even chopsticks—mementos of the day when they had once, or once more, eluded death. It was memorable; bizarre evidence of emotional intensity, a crisis passed, a way of coming out of fear, relief, and maybe retribution. Perhaps there is no way of clarifying what makes men so heroic and so mean. But it is a terrible part of warfare, and there was evidence that the same urgencies that seem so grotesque brought the same sort of actions among our enemies.

Emotional intensity endured long after the battle. I was with a cluster of our men who were quizzing one of the young privates who had been in the landing. His recollection was nervous and vivid: "We were moving across this place when all of a sudden there was a Jap. He comes out of the weeds like Jesus Christ rising from the grave, and before he could get his hands up he was cut in half by fire from all along our line."

At another time I was going somewhere a short distance from camp and saw the major who had the newly arrived SBD squadron and a couple of his men doing some work with lumber and an iron drum. They were building a framework to lift the drum overhead, along with putting other things in order. It was a shower, to be solar heated, and close by was a chest of drawers, a perfectly civilized piece of furniture right out of a bedroom. When I asked the major what he was doing he said, "This is my shower, and don't get the idea that you or anyone else is going to use it." Some time later I heard that this Annapolis man had been passed over for promotion; I thought it quite appropriate.

One of the surprises of the military is that a man keeps running into friends. For instance, of all the hundreds of marine pilots, how did two St. Olaf College men—Nolan Dugan and I—find the same squadron and stay together for three years? How was it that I was to become a classmate of Ed Dart at Yale, a man with whom I had a brief acquaintance when he was flying SBDs at Engebi (under the aforesaid major)? One day I flew down to Eniwetok Island and found Muriey Severtsen, St. Olaf grad of 1942, sitting in an antiaircraft gun emplacement. And among the company commanders of the 22nd Marines who came ashore at Engebi was a St. Olaf classmate of his, Maurice Amundson, from Cameron, Wisconsin.

There was a series of minor islands lying south of us on the eastern rim of the atoll—a chain linking Engebi at the north to Parry and Eniwetok Islands at the south. These minor islands had not been inhabited, but there was still a little question whether there might be some of the enemy who had escaped the battle to refuge on the islands of the chain. Amundson thought it would be good for his men to comb through the palms and undergrowth of the next island as a resumption of training. So he organized the foray and asked me if I wanted to go along to see how the company worked. I did, and John Thistlethwaite joined us also. A short trip in a landing craft; disgorging to the beach with weapons in hand, deployment in a line, and an advance warily and steadily for half a mile; then back.

The next I heard of Amundson was that he had been killed on Guam.

Severe Weather Flights

By Clyde H. Slyman

During a flight from Puerto Rico to Miami, Florida, after passing the equitime point (point of no return), severe weather was encountered.

The storm was penetrated at 6,000 feet MSL indicated altitude, where I encountered very strong updrafts and turbulence. Updrafts lifted the RC5 to over 10,000 feet MSL indicated altitude. At that point the airplane flew into a downdraft and descended to 4,000 feet MSL indicated altitude.

The updrafts and downdrafts were violent. The rain was torrential. The airplane was difficult to control. The airspeed ranged between 50 knots indicated and past the red line. Cylinder head temperature dropped below 100 degrees Farenheit. Remarkably the R5C withstood the structural loads. Thirty passengers were on board—most became "throw-up" sick.

Weather became a factor during another flight, this time from Itami, Japan, in an SNB-Twin Beechcraft to K-3, Korea. While over the Sea of Japan, severe icing and freezing rain was encountered. Ice was forming on the aircraft, the prop deicing fluid was exhausted, and wing-boot deicers were only partially effective. Airspeed was dropping and as a result we were unable to climb. Altitude could not be maintained. A water landing in the Sea of Japan seemed probable.

As the airplane lost altitude, the prop and wing ice started coming off. We leveled off about 100 feet above the Sea of Japan and continued to K-3.

Screw Up
By John Wastvedt

A couple of months after joining VMF-124 in November 1943, with about 70 or 80 hours in the F4U Corsair, I was assigned the task of picking one up at the North Island Naval Air Station, San Diego, which is about 100 miles south of Los Angeles. Mojave USMC Air Station, where I was stationed, was about 100 miles north of Los Angeles on the Mojave Desert, making a trip length of about 200 miles, less than an hour at cruising speed and three hours of fuel in the tank. One of the squadron pilots brought me down in a two-seat dive-bomber, and after completing the required paper work I took off for home base.

Prior to joining 124, I had flown dive-bombers out of El Toro USMC Air Station, just south of Los Angeles, for a couple of months and, with the time in Mojave, knew the area very well. I hadn't brought any charts along (big mistake!!) since I didn't think I needed them. However, smog covered the southern California area, and high winds over the desert raised dust, obscuring the terrain and limiting the visibility to about three miles along the route. If I had the charts, I would have been able to plot the magnetic course and used the compass and/or used the low frequency radio ranges for navigation. As it was, I estimated a heading and pressed on, thinking that once I got to the desert the visibility would improve and I would find my way. No such luck! I was lost. Fortunately just about then, I flew right over a military base with what looked like P39 Air Cobras. I decided to land, find out where I was, get some charts, and takeoff for home base.

On landing there was a very high cross-wind component requiring heavy braking on the right brake. I taxied in to the operations ramp, shut down, went in, found out where I was (Victorville Army Air Corps Base, about 50 miles southeast of Mojave), got some charts, jumped back in the airplane, started up and started to taxi off for takeoff. !?@#!! The right brake was frozen! This was not uncommon when a brake was overheated, and usually required a good jolt to break it free.

It was late Sunday afternoon and there was no way I could get any help from their maintenance until Monday so I shut down, called the duty officer at Mojave, told him I wouldn't be back until tomorrow, got a BOQ room, had dinner at the Officers' Club and went to bed.

The next morning, early, I had a plan. The Corsair was a curiosity to the Army Air Corps guys, its bent wing, tail hook and everything, so they were clustered around the airplane, maybe 20 or 30 pilots, examining the details, looking in the cockpit when I arrived. After answering dozens of questions I asked for six volunteers, explained the problem and my solution. I would get in the cockpit and they would line up on the left side of the fuselage as close as they could get to the tail. Upon my signal they would push as hard as they could, pivoting on the frozen wheel. They were told to keep pushing until it was swinging rapidly around. Then, when I judged the swinging velocity to be maximum I would step hard on the moving wheel brake, using no brake on the frozen wheel and, hopefully, the momentum would free the frozen brake.

It worked! So all I had to do now was start the engine. These early model Corsairs had cartridge starters. A cartridge similar to a shotgun shell, but somewhat larger, was inserted in a chamber containing a piston. The piston would be driven by the exploding cartridge and, connected to the crankshaft, would rotate it about half a revolution, much as the old Model T Ford was hand-cranked. This might or might not be enough to start the engine. An access panel inside the engine cowling contained a rack with six cartridges, now five, since I had used one the day before. Normally, a line person would insert the cartridges as needed while the pilot operated the engine controls and start switch, which fired the cartridge, from the cockpit. But none of these people had seen a starting system like this before so I decided I would have to do it all, which meant that, if it didn't start, I would have to clamber out and insert the cartridges myself.

It was January, and even on the desert it gets cold at night, so the oil was heavy, making starting that much harder. The crowd observing this whole spectacle had grown to maybe 50 or 60. I was apprehensive and would have to do it right or be forced, in front of this crowd, to admit defeat and slink into the operations building and call Mojave for help. Oh, the potential ignominy of it all!

So I pushed the start switch. Whoosh! But the engine didn't fire. I got out of the cockpit, installed the second shell, and got back into the cockpit. Whoosh! Same as the first shell. Now the third shell. This time, Whoosh! Whoosh! At least it fired. Two shells left. A silent prayer. This time it fired several times but then died. Now it was the last shell, a make-or-break situation. Another long silent prayer, then with fingers crossed, press the start switch and Whoosh! Whoosh! Faster and faster it went, then settled into a smooth rumble. Thank the Lord!! I fastened my seat belt, looked out at the crowd, who were cheering and waving, waved back, and was on my way.

About 20 minutes later I landed at Mojave, taxied in and shut down. As I walked into the ready room, the squadron duty officer told me that our commanding officer, Major Millington, wanted me in his office immediately. After a severe dressing down, with questions about my judgment in taking off with no charts, he assigned me as the squadron duty officer, an onerous chore, for five straight days, including my only day off during the week. A much deserved punishment, indeed!

World War II

Beginner's Hazards
By Edward Anders Sovik

Squadron VMF(N)-532 arrived on the atoll of Tarawa with our planes and the GCI (Ground Control) radar unit in the middle of January 1944. We had been transported on the CVE *White Plains*, a small carrier, from Ford Island. As we approached the atoll, the planes were catapulted off the deck and landed at Mullinix Field, a short and narrow strip built by the Seabees among the palm trees on the islet next to Betio, which had been the Japanese stronghold.

"Fales" had been built for us on the coral sand under the palms—square wood platforms on which pyramidal tents were mounted—with screened sides and screen doors. Despite precautions, many of us had bouts of dengue fever in the ensuing weeks.

The garrison of marines and navy people—and probably the island villagers too, who were engaged to do many of the chores such as clean up, laundry, and so on but whose village was still declared off limits—were reportedly glad to see us because the Japanese had been sending harassment planes over on most nights to do some haphazard bombing and perhaps strafing. Until we came the defense was by antiaircraft, with searchlights trying unsuccessfully to locate the enemy among the stars. The gunfire was aimed not so much at the marauders as at lifting morale, indicating that someone was trying to do something.

There was no good early warning, so aircraft noise was what set off the red alert, and we all scrambled to the personal foxholes we had been told to dig. We didn't get much of that experience, but had at least one night I remember because I lost my nice navy-issue sunglasses. They were in my shirt pocket by best memory; a late dusk

105

alert sent me in haste to crouch in the loose earth or coral. Somehow in the maneuver I lost the glasses. And though I could have surveyed them and got a replacement, I never did.

Our ground control radar, which served both as an early warning system and a means through which pilots were directed to the vicinity of enemy planes, took some time and skill to coax into an operational state. We pilots had flown about in the daytime to get acquainted with the atoll, the airstrip, and the ocean. A few days after we arrived the fighter directors were on the verge of being functional. We had, or the island commander had, the notion that our planes should be ready to takeoff immediately after an alert was sounded, so we had two planes parked and ready at the end of the runway. By chance, or perhaps because I was squadron operations officer, I sat in the first of the planes the first night when an alert came. All the lights on the island went out, including all the runway lights except for two hooded blue lights at the far end of the runway. The shell was in the starter. All clear from the plane captain…push the switch…engine catches…run it up…check the mags…stand on the brakes…rev to 20 inches…get off the brakes and full throttle. Off I went for a blind takeoff trying to keep the right heading. The long nose of the F4U—fourteen feet out in front of the cockpit and pointing up in the air until the plane was almost flyable—made the little blue lights quite useless as a directional target.

Things happen quickly. I was in the air in a few hundred yards—I know because quite unexpectedly I saw a little tower halfway down the strip go by an inch off my left wing, a little geometric shadow among the palm trees. The F4U, with its powerful torque, wasn't the easiest plane to keep on heading at takeoff; I had veered to port. I think that the tower crew, if there had been one, would have been blown out of the tower by the prop wash, after that narrowest brush-by of the wing tip.

Sovik on wing of Corsair.

That wasn't the last of an unpredictable evening. When I was safely aloft it became clear that the ground control radar was not yet operating. There had indeed been a bogie, and a bomb had been dropped into the lagoon, if my information was correct. The search-lights began their wavering and ineffectual search guided by sound. Unhappily the F4U is noisy too, and as I circled in the air hoping for instructions from the fighter director, it became clear that the search-lights were trailing me, and here and there antiaircraft shells were popping. This may have been comforting to the troops, but it wasn't to me. I headed out to sea, and complained on the VHF radio.

Things calmed down; no more bogies. Airstrip lights went on, and I landed, having been in the air for two hours.

Whatever troubles our people had were unimportant. The Japanese must have learned of Tarawa's new defenses, because that was the last of the enemy night attacks at that atoll after 30 attacks in not much over a month. On the following nights we changed our procedure and had planes in the air on patrol, awaiting the alert.

F4F Wildcat Plan to Kill Me
By Lyle Bradley

Besides the few holes I picked up in combat, my record was very good in not damaging aircraft in 25 years of military flying. There was an exception, however—the F4F Wildcat fighter.

When I look back on the 200 hours that I flew that plane—there seems to have been a plan to eliminate me.

It all started in May 1944 when seven of us fresh from flight school and new wings were given our first chance to fly a military fighter at Green Cove Springs Air Base in Florida. We talked to some of the pilots who had some hours in the airplane. We were warned about the ease in which the plane ground-looped, the cockpit heat while flying, the noise, how subject it was to electrical problems, and the unbalanced wheel oleos.

Our instructor was also a second lieutenant, but more experienced. He apologized for not having any combat time like the other instructors. I liked him—he was honest and didn't snow us with his instructor superiority. He gave each of us a blindfold cockpit checkout and asked many questions of our flight about the handbook and what we would do in emergency situations. When he was satisfied that we were okay for solo flying (only one pilot per fighter) he scheduled us to take off at 1300 the next day. He would be in the tower observing and be available for any questions.

The next morning we had another detailed briefing with many pertinent questions about safety, the cockpit, radio procedures, takeoff and landing techniques, airspeeds for maneuvers, and another walk around the plane.

We climbed into our planes at 1300, got clearance to taxi from ground control, and then received final clearance for take off from the tower. Each of us had carefully gone over the checklist and were now ready to take our first flight in a military fighter.

Already we could feel the temperature of the Florida sun, coupled with the heat of the 1500-horsepower engine in front of us. I got my plane lined up on the runway and received the "Cleared for take off" from the tower radio. I pushed the throttle forward and the engine responded with a roar, the wind tearing at my flight suit and helmet through the open canopy. I eased the nose down to get more speed and suddenly I was airborne.

The next step was to screw the throttle tight to hold full throttle, move my left hand to the control stick, and start to wind up the wheels with 26 turns using my right hand. About the tenth turn on the wheels my flight suit got hung up on one of the gun charger handles and the wheel lever got jerked out of my hand, causing the wheels to drop. At the same time the throttle started easing back (I had not screwed the throttle holder completely tight). Then it happened—I was flying through the top branches of a tree. My instructor told me later that he put his hands over his eyes and exclaimed, "Oh, no!"

After my tree-pruning episode on my first flight everything went well for a week. We were returning from a tactics hop and I could see the field in the distance when suddenly I heard a loud bang. It was behind me and at first I thought one of the others in the flight might have "bumped" me. Then Carl Miller said, "Bradley, you are on fire. Get ready to bail out!" Fire in an airplane is a real fear. Down below me was a huge swamp. The alligators, cottonmouth water moccasins, and other creatures didn't frighten me, but bailing out in a plane is always dangerous, so I asked if Miller could see any flames. He replied, "No flames, but much smoke."

We were now about five miles from the field so I called the tower for a straight-in emergency landing. They cleared the other aircraft from the pattern and gave me a green light to land. I kept bailout altitude until I was a mile from the field and then dove for the runway. The crash trucks were awaiting me. I landed the plane and immediately shut the switch off, clamped down on the brakes, and as soon as the plane stopped I was out of the cockpit and ran along the wing and jumped to the ground. Firemen surrounded the plane and we discovered the battery had blown. There was much smoke but no fire. I was happy that I had not used the "nylon letdown" (parachute) to bail out.

Another two weeks went by safely and we started gunnery practice. When we fired with live ammunition we went out 100 miles over the Atlantic Ocean. We took turns leading the mission.

On one mission I was leading, the day was very hazy. It was difficult to keep our flight and the tow plane with the target sleeve in sight. We were making vertical gunnery runs starting at 26,000 feet. Speeds built up very fast. It was hot work so to cool the airplane we opened the canopy about an inch to get slightly cooled. We had been warned about not making overhead runs with the canopy even slightly open.

On one of my runs starting at 26,000 feet, as I pulled out under the tow target I passed out. I came to at 6,000 feet with blood all over the cockpit and the canopy collapsed around my neck. I was concerned that one of the major blood vessels in my head or neck had been cut. On the radio I heard, "Where did Bradley go?"

I tried to reply but the canopy had also severed my radio antenna. We were about 100 miles at sea and I realized with the loss of blood I might not get back to land. We were flying out of Augustine Field so I used a compass heading of 270 degrees, pushed the throttle to full power, tried to get rid of the broken canopy to no avail, and probably said a prayer. By this time I realized my bleeding had been superficial with no major blood vessels broken. In 15 minutes the land came into view and then happily I could see the airfield. The tower gave me a green light to land as I wobbled my wings to indicate I was in trouble. The crash trucks were there in readiness as I reviewed the landing checklist and dove for the runway with my wheels down. The landing was good and I coasted to a stop. That's all I remember. When I awakened in the hospital an hour or so later my head was loaded with bandages.

My instructor arrived after the hop was over and greeted me with, "You stupid SOB! You forgot to close your canopy. You were damned lucky. We suspect that was the reason for several other pilots going into the water. Some guys don't come to before they hit the drink."

Today all pilots wear hardhats to prevent aircraft killing us in that manner.

With only one week to go before leaving the F4F behind in Florida, one of the pilots in our flight was Drury Wood from Atlanta, Georgia. He had relatives on a farm near Palatca, Florida, a few miles south of our Green Cove Field. On one of our last tactics hops Drury was going to lead us over the farm for a fly over. He asked me to fly the tail-end spot because it was the most difficult.

On our way back to Palatca he signaled us to get into a column. In this position each aircraft is tucked in tight under the tail of the one ahead. Foster (not our best pilot) was number six. Wood gave everyone room to maneuver by pulling out of the dive at about 500 feet. Foster decided to go much lower. Because I was keeping everyone in view, especially Foster who was directly in front and over me, I didn't realize Foster had dropped down to a dangerously low level (almost cornstalk height) and I was below him. Suddenly cornstalks were flying past my canopy. I could not climb higher without hitting Foster,

F4F Wildcat (with canopy open).

so I carefully slid out sideways, my wing inches from the ground. I was very mad and felt like chewing Foster's tail with my prop.

Upon landing, one of the plane mechanics wanted to know how all the cornstalks got into the engine. I explained that some of our low level tactics got a little too low. Foster and I, along with other members of the flight, had some nasty interactions after the flight. It was the first time profanity entered into our debriefings.

When we arrived in California two weeks later, Foster decided it was best not to fly with us. We never saw him again. I'm not sure if Foster and the F4F I was flying that day did not have a cooperative plan to kill me.

The Craft and the Equipment
By Edward Anders Sovik

The effectiveness of a night fighter squadron like VMF(N)-532 depended on two radar instruments and the people who maintained and operated them. One was set up on the ground; it was called a ground control intercept (GCI). This device sent out electronic impulses into the surrounding airspace and retrieved echoes from objectives as far away as 200 miles. The GCI amplified the faint echo and converted it to a bright spot—a blip—on a dark cathode ray screen. Distance and altitude of the object could be discerned. The GCI was our air warning device, signaling approaching aircraft. It was also the means of following our fighter planes as we navigated the skies around our islands. And the GCI made it possible for the fighter directors to tell the pilots where to fly to intercept attacking enemy planes. We used very high frequency (VHF) radios to communicate.

The second radar instrument was airborne, installed in our planes and operated by the pilots. An egg-shaped nacelle on the starboard wing of the F4U held a spinning transmitting and receiving antenna in a reflecting bowl about 12 inches across. The pulses that were sent out traveled through a conical space in front of the plane, repeating the trip through the space about every two seconds. The CRT was about three inches in diameter and was in the center of the plane's instrument panel. An echo from a distant plane appeared on the CRT as two tiny blips. If they were at the top of the screen the target might be three miles away. The blips might be to port or starboard, and if the right-hand dot was above the left, the target was above the fighter.

The fighter director tried to place the fighter behind the target and within range. If the airborne radar picked up the target, the pilot would proceed to pursue the target, watching the blips come down until he was close enough to take his eyes off the radar screen and try for a visual contact, trying to identify the target and destroy it if it was an enemy aircraft. It was possible to over run the target, to lose it, or to be seen by and made victim to a tail gunner.

The squadron to which I was assigned as operations officer had begun to fly Corsair F4U-1s in May 1943. But the planes were not yet radar-equipped. Modifying them to become F4U-2s was not done in the aircraft factory. But the navy had undertaken to do the work at the air station at Quonset Point, Rhode Island, in September 1943. Accordingly the next month Major Vaughan, our skipper, and I flew two of our Corsairs up to Quonset Point from Cherry Point with the intent that we would pick up two finished planes and fly back south. Then two more pilots would fly two more planes up in a few days and come back with two more finished planes, and so on.

The Spin-prohibited Corsair
By Clyde H. Slyman

In July 1944 I was a 22-year-old second lieutenant USMCR, who had recently completed operational training in the Corsair. I was assigned to VMF-924 Marine Corps Air Station Cherry Point, North Carolina, flying Corsairs.

I was "tail-end Charlie" in a six-airplane fight. We were in column formation (tail chase). The flight leader led the formation in a loop into an overcast sky. I got too slow and the Corsair stalled while inverted. This resulted in a violent spin. The rudder locked in the direction of the spin and the control stick was "thrashing wildly."

I tried to recover using partial panel (needle, ball, airspeed) but pulled so many Gs recovering from the dive that the Corsair stalled and entered a more violent spin. I decided I was going to bail out of the airplane as I could not control it and I attempted to, but the forces were such that I could not do it. I decided I was not going to die like this and grabbed the controls again and pushed opposite rudder and held the stick back until the rotation rate slowed. Then I pushed the stick forward, at which point the airplane was no longer spinning but in a very steep dive. This time I recovered from the dive by pulling back on the stick gently so as not to impose a high G-load on the aircraft, thereby avoiding a second high-speed stall and resulting spin.

The spin began at about 12,000 feet MSL and ended at about 4,000 feet MSL. During the 8,000 foot descent the airplane probably made 10 or more 360 degree turns.

Job Assignments
By Edward Anders Sovik

When I enlisted in August 1941 at the old Federal Building in Minneapolis I chose the Marine Corps aviation for several reasons. First, if I was going to volunteer it would not be a cowardly act—to escape the infantry, for instance—but the opposite. Second, I had two close friends who were already in flight training, having enlisted in the Corps. And third, there seemed the greatest likelihood, however scant, that along the way somewhere in the future I would find myself in China if I were a marine.

About the first reason nothing needs to be said. About the second, good and bad—one of my friends and I met briefly in Eniwetok, the other died in a crash as an instructor. In view of the third my mind was constant. Even though I had never studied written Chinese, I had voluntarily made some effort to learn, had continued desultorily in college and after, and some time in 1941 had subscribed to the Chicago Chinese Newspaper and begun to work at it with the help of a pocket dictionary. That continued for perhaps a year or two, including flight training in Pensacola.

We returned from the Central Pacific in early October 1944, I believe, and were sent to San Diego, where we went through training in twin-engine aircraft preparatory to flying the Grumman F7F Tigercat. We trained in the Martin Marauder, which was a good beginning as it was a "hot" plane. It was a slow process. My log says that from November 24 to December 29 I had two solo flights, along with some free days.

On some of these free days there was a chance to fly copilot with one or another of the instructors on their trips to Alameda. I had never been in Berkeley and on one of these trips I went on a walk around the University of California out of curiosity. On a sign at one of the buildings I read "Chinese Language Institute," and went in to learn what that could be. I found a door on the second floor and as I opened it I met a man who appeared to be leaving for lunch. But he stopped and said, "What can I do for you?" I explained my curiosity and my name. "Oh," he said. "My name is Pettis. I used to run the Language School in Peking; I know your uncle and I know of your father. What are you doing now? You should be here." I explained my status including the fact that because our F7Fs were late I would have, maybe, three months of leisure or not very purposeful employment.

"Well, spend the time here. The Marine Corps ought to take care to use your skills." "I would be glad to," I said, "But I belong to the Marine Corps."

"Come in," he said. "Maybe we can shake you loose." So we went back to his office; he picked up the phone and called the Marine Corps Personnel Office. "I have Captain Sovik here," he said. "He speaks Chinese. He says he has some months of waiting. If you give him orders he could study here which would be good for him, the Corps and the war." The authority at the other end of the line said it was a good idea, but that Sovik's group commanding officer would have to acquiesce. He would call Colonel Harshberger. He did. Iron John said, "Hell no. I want Sovik to be the G3 of the training group I am forming and we start in January." That was that. No China connection. That was the first I knew of Iron John's intention. But I wasn't about to object.

All the pilots of VMF(N)-532 were sent to Eagle Mountain Lake where we were occupied with preparing ourselves for going overseas with F7Fs, with giving instruction on night fighting to younger pilots, and with doing other duties in the group.

There came a time when our experience in F7Fs, their radar, and the radar operators, was sufficient. The colonel came to the flight office one day and said he was to select a group of pilots who were to be sent out to the Pacific. The colonel asked for volunteers. Everybody volunteered, as I remember it. How the ultimate selection was made I can't say, but Iron John, seeing that both Frank Lang and I were ready to go said to the two of us, "Sorry, but I can't spare both of you. You'll have to flip a coin."

We did. Frank Lang won, so I stayed at Eagle Mountain and he went to the Pacific. At the war's end Frank was among those who were sent to mainland China for a short stint. And so I missed by chance a trip to my native land. And he continued his career, distinguishing himself in due course by becoming the senior pilot in the Marine Corps, a senior naval aviator, and after a varied career in which he had flown every type of plane and helicopter in the naval aviation service, gained the rank of major general.

Palau Rescue

By Harry J. Goodyear

Warren Fisher, an experienced aviator who had served his first assignment in the marines on Guadalcanal as a fighter pilot, was serving his second tour as a division leader of four F4U fighter planes at Peleliu, with three first-tour pilots in the squadron. On November 15, 1944, Fisher's division, consisting of Cub Callis as wingman, Roland Helstrom leading the second section, and Harry Goodyear as tail-end Charlie (number four in the division), took off on a northeast heading up Babelthup Island. About halfway up the island Cub radioed that he had taken some fire, the engine was running rough and smoking, and he was going to make a water landing. Cub and Warren pulled up behind us a distance, and we banked and turned to the lee and started to protectively circle them as Cub descended to make his water landing.

The water was rough and had many swells—we knew it could be a tough landing. Cub was leveling out over the water and fortunately made his landing in one of the swells. The F4U stopped very quickly and sunk almost immediately. Cub went down with the plane; however, a few seconds later an orange blob came up and Cub was there thrashing around in the water.

We called base and told them we had a pilot down in the water and asked them to send a rescue plane. Base acknowledged the call and told us they were sending a Dumbo (a navy PBY Catalina amphibian airplane used for rescue missions) to pick up the downed pilot.

We circled Cub so as not to lose sight of him—he was hard to see bobbing around. We also had to start to strafe the beach to keep the Japanese from firing rounds and throwing mortars at him.

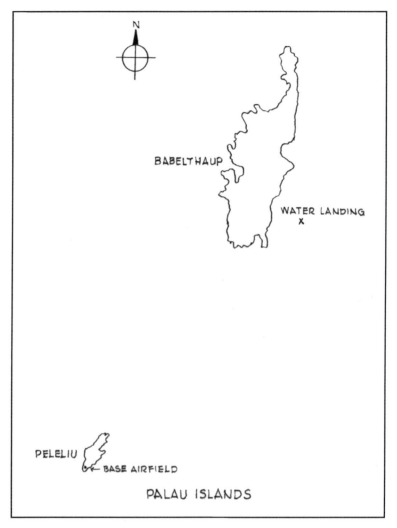

A few minutes later the Dumbo (PBY) showed up and spotted Cub in the water, then started its decent for the landing and rescue. The Dumbo landed and hit the top of a swell, bounced up, stalled, and hit its left wing in the water, which broke it off. The plane then swung around to the left 180 degrees and started sinking. Now we had Cub in the water along with the entire crew from the Dumbo, who had scrambled out of the PBY and climbed into their life raft. I think there were five in the raft and Cub in the water.

We called base again, described what had just happened, and asked them to send another rescue plane. They acknowledged, and we set up another Luffberry circle and strafed the beach to keep watch and to protect those in the water.

A few minutes later another Dumbo (PBY) came overhead and radioed that he had looked the situation over and would not attempt a landing because of the rough waters, so he shoved off.

With Cub and the Dumbo crew still in the water, we radioed base for advice. Taking into account the existing weather conditions, they advised us to try and contact one of the ships in a passing convoy to help in the rescue. We were advised that a convoy was passing a few miles to the east of us going in a northerly direction.

As tail-end Charlie, I was designated to go out and try to contact one of the ships in the convoy to aid in the rescue. Fortunately the convoy was spotted and a destroyer was on the fringe of the formation. I put my flaps and wheels down and flew about five feet over the port bow of the destroyer, flying off in the direction of those in the water.

Immediately the destroyer turned in the direction I was flying at full steam, and in several minutes it was nearing the men in the water. The destroyer, heading very close to the beach, started firing its guns. It quickly put its engines in reverse, put a boat over the side, picked up the men in the water, got the boat and the men aboard the destroyer, turned around, and headed back to the convoy.

Cub spent some time on the destroyer and some on R & R, so we didn't see him for about 10 days until he got back to the squadron and began flying again.

But all turned out well on just a routine patrol and barge sweep for VMF-122.

A First Time For Everything
By Carlyle Lageson

Don't you wonder sometimes how you get yourself into certain situations? Most of the time you aren't even aware of the consequences of your actions. The incidents I have in mind progressed to the point of no return. The first incident involved my good friend, John, and myself. What we did was not done on purpose, but the results were the same. We closed a naval training facility for one day during World War II.

It was November 1942. In September I had been assigned as a flight instructor to VND-16 at Green Cove Springs, Florida Naval Air Station. John and I, both marine second lieutenants, had returned from a movie in downtown Green Cove Springs. It was about 2130 hours, and we both had heavy schedules the next day. John suggested we have a nightcap before turning in.

The BOQ had a closed bar, but we retrieved the key, opened the door, fixed a drink, signed a chit, and proceeded to sing in quiet harmony. Soon there was a knock on the door, and we had a trio. Then after another knock, and we became a quartet. Our singing must have sounded pretty good because soon others straggled in and wanted to join us. By now we had a full chorus, and even the bystanders joined in as they poured out of their rooms to see what all the noise (music) was about.

Wouldn't you know, an important someone's sleep was being disturbed, and he walked in the door. It was Commander Shone, the base commanding officer. He had not taken the time to dress; he was in his bathrobe and slippers as he lived just across the street from the BOQ. I'm sure he wondered if all the officers were rioting. Our singing by now probably sounded off key, as I don't think everyone could carry a tune.

Since I had the tower duty the next morning (a pilot officer was required to be present in the tower during flight operations), I proceeded to my room to get some rest. It was reported to me the next day that Commander Shone had not exactly rushed off but had stayed and enjoyed the festivities.

Bright and early I went to the tower noticing along the way that the base was strangely quiet. There were no engines "turning up" and the usual activity was missing. I climbed the ladder to the tower and was met by the tower operator. "What's going on?" I asked. "It sure is quiet." The tower operator had the answer. "The Skipper has declared an M-Day (maintenance day)." I was stunned; I wondered if those one or two guys that made up the trio and quartet had said anything. As it was, I did not know them or their names. I wasn't too sure about John; he liked to talk. Later John and I went overseas together, and we often chuckled about how we had shut down a training base during war time. John passed away many years ago, so you will have to take my word on what happened.

Actually, we were flying seven days a week, and the weeks just blended together. I'm sure Commander Shone felt there was a reason that people were letting off steam, so he declared an M-Day.

I had been in the tower for maybe an hour when field maintenance called. They had a plane to test fly and I was to be the pilot. When I got to the flight line there was a small biplane. It was a Grumman F3F-3, the navy's first line fighter from the early to middle 1930s. I found the maintenance manual and proceeded to bone up on the basics I should know. I got the engine started, taxied to the flight line, and took off. Next I had to get the gear retracted. It was hand cranked to the retracted position, but it was a manual retraction and I could not budge the handle. Of course, I had not read that part of the manual. Then I noticed a pin in the center of the handle shaft. I released the pin, and after about 30 cranks as I wobbled through the air, I had the gear tucked away and proceeded with the maintenance check. I finished the check procedures and returned this wonderful little plane to the flight line. I wish I had taken the opportunity to fly it again but we were under pressure to train student pilots to complete the training syllabus.

The second incident that I must mention occurred in November 1943. I had shipped overseas in April 1943 and was assigned to VMSB-236. This was on the island of Espirito Santo, a marine training and staging area. It is here that the marine fighter and bombing squadrons were formed and trained and equipped for combat operations. This was one of the islands in the New Hebrides chain of islands and south of the Solomon group of islands where the conflict was very active.

Headquarters posted the list of names to form the forty pilots to make up Squadron VMSB-236. I was not on the list. I was at first disappointed, but then understood as I was assigned to Major Robertshaw. I was to train and schedule the incoming pilots from the States and make them combat ready for assignment and replacement in squadrons returning from combat. I enjoyed this assignment working with Major Robertshaw and was most pleased when I received a congratulatory letter from him later on, when he was a major general, after I was appointed to the rank of colonel in January 1964. The squadron deployed to Guadualcanel where they distinguished themselves in combat.

In November 1943 I was assigned to the rear echelon of VMSB-236. We were transported to the marine forward base on the island of Munda where we would be staging strikes mainly against targets on Bougainville, part of the Solomon group. Early in our tour we were assigned a target at Buka Passage, the northern part of Bougainville.

We launched 40 aircraft for this strike, but as we neared the target area we encountered alto cumulus clouds that towered above our approach altitude. The build up was scattered to broken, so the strike leader elected to continue the strike. In our near vertical dive, we were able to pick our way down the clear areas to the target. However, the whole air mass was moving, so I was soon forced off the target area. Now I was over water and forced to start a recovery at about 3,000 feet and under the cloud base. Suddenly I was surrounded with black puffs of antiaircraft shell bursts. I had no target, and this was no place to be caught by enemy fire. I did not want to jettison the 1,000 pound bomb, and I sure was not going to lug it back to Munda. So with 300 miles per hourspeed from the dive and under full power, I pulled the nose up and at the proper attitude I released the bomb, much like they do in slow pitch softball. I was aiming for a point of land ahead. On release, I pulled back and entered the overcast and went on instruments. I was not interested in being target practice for the enemy. It was later confirmed that I had hit a target area ahead of me.

I stayed on instruments, hoping no one else was in the area that I might run into. I let down over water and rejoined the squadron, returning to Munda. It had not been a good strike, but I realized I had accomplished something different. I was later to discover that I may have been the first person to employ the tactic of lob bombing. Later in the 1950s and 1960s the air force developed this tactic to deliver small nuclear devices to a target without having to over fly the target area. I do not know if it was ever used operationally, but the air force was able to deliver this ordnance very accurately. The combination of exact speed, angle of release, and distance would yield an accurate impact of the bomb while the plane could pull up and reverse course to be clear of the explosion. For me, that was a unique way to deliver my bomb, but I was getting shot at from behind.

Testing The Radar

By Edward Anders Sovik

The F4U-2 Corsair was the first U.S. single-engine military air-craft to become a radar-equipped night fighter. The radar equipment was installed at Quonset Point, Rhode Island, and Major Vaughan and I flew two planes up there to test installations that already had been made in other aircraft.

The major's plane seemed defective to him, so he asked me to fly it to check, and to stay while he took the acceptable plane home. I discovered the problem and stayed to have it corrected, thinking I would then take it to Cherry Point. Bonner, who delivered the next plane, said the major wanted me to stay up to test this next plane too. This went on unexpectedly until six of the planes were complete, and I had been in Quonset Point for five weeks with only what I brought in an overnight bag; I didn't even have my logbook.

The Marine Corps people decided that they could do the radar installation on the remainder of the planes at Quantico. So I moved there and continued the program. We got to the last plane when the radar people reported to me that they were short a particular piece of bent equipment and had no way of bending it at Quantico. Could I fly up to Quonset Point and pick up the piece so we could finish the job? It was November 27. I had flown two test flights that day and the planes had gone to Cherry Point. The weather, by evening, had turned cold and wet. The only plane I could take was the Corsair they had been working on, and the heater had been taken out so they could fit the new equipment in.

It was instrument weather; I had plenty of night flying but not any recent instrument flying, and if there had been a duty officer at the flight desk instead of a sergeant I probably would have been denied a clearance. But I filed an instrument flight plan and took off.

The weather got worse and worse, turning to snow. I flew the ranges up to where I tried to tune in to Hartford but found I couldn't. (Later I discovered that the Hartford range had been out of order for a few hours.) Nevertheless I got close enough to Quonset Point to catch a glimpse of some familiar red lights on a bridge, so I knew where I was. But they vanished in the mist and though I circled and descended as far as I dared, I never again saw them or any other sign of the earth. I turned back, heading for my alternate airport, Floyd Bennett Field in Brooklyn.

That leg was even colder and windier, but I had no trouble finding the field. It was snowing and the field was white, but the lights of the runway in use were a welcome sight. The trouble was that there was a considerable crosswind from the left, and as I set down a gust got under the exaggerated dihedral of the F4U and lifted the left wing. I pushed power up but it took time to rev up and the right wing kept going down and down until I thought that precious radar nacelle near the wing's tip was sure to scrape the ground and I would end in a catastrophic ground loop. But the engine torque did work, and I did come to a stop, turned around, and taxied in to the ramp. It was 0100. I had the plane tied down secure.

When I walked in to the flight desk the duty officer said, "Am I glad to see you! Hartford radio has been wondering where you are for an hour." I asked to have a marine guard put on the plane because of the secret radar on it, and was never happier to get a bed in the BOQ.

The morning was very cold and the snow was four or five inches deep. When I walked out to my plane I found a shivering marine on guard who wouldn't let me come close to it until I brought the officer of the day out to verify who I was. The weather was still bad at Quonset Point, so I flew to Quantico. Then I took the train to Philadelphia and the navy yard there. How I found my way to the right place, I don't remember. It was in the bowels of a factory. A worker there knew what I needed and supplied it.

Ten days later we left for the Pacific.

World War II

Guardian Angels Or Just Luck?
By Herbert Pfremmer

One must ask whether a situation is just plain luck, or if there really are guardian angels that some folks are blessed enough to have, watching over them.

Was it just luck that on March 1, 1945, while stationed on the *Essex*, flying second section on the flight leader Major Don Frame with Lieutenant Kenneth Maust as wingman, that on a bombing mission against Naha Airfield on Okinawa when heavy antiaircraft fire was encountered, that just the flap on the right wing and a section of the wing itself was blown away? The navy TBF to the right took a direct hit and exploded. The twenty-ninth carrier landing was made successfully. Lucky?

Was it luck? The date was March 19, 1945. Since March 10 I had been assigned to join VMF-123 along with Major Don Frame, Lieutenant Victor Rusling and Lieutenant Arthur Kercoude. The mission, on a day designated as "Lucky + 1," was scrambled at 08:30 for CAP at 20,000 feet. Our flight encountered no enemy planes, although many were reported in the area. Early in the flight we discovered the belly tank was not functioning and lasted but one hour and fifteen minutes, resulting in the need to use the main fuel tank. Just before we were going to land, the fleet came under attack, and with approximately five gallons of fuel remaining, instructions were given to either parachute ahead of a DD or land in the water ahead of a DD. We were further advised that none of the ships would alter course to effect a pickup. As a water landing was being initiated, a message was received that the CVE *Belleau Wood* was to turn into the wind for a launch, and that

129

if a landing could be accomplished after the last plane left the flight deck, it offered a third possibility, and one preferred. A landing was successful. As the tail hook was retracted and the throttle advanced to move forward on the flight deck, the engine quit. The aircraft had run out of gas. Lucky??

Was it luck? It was March 26, 1945. I was sitting on the flight deck at 06:30 with rockets and a five hundred pound bomb. The primary mission was a strike against Amamio-shima to take out the heavy concentration of antiaircraft facilities. The Japanese had flattened the tops of some of their highest mountain peaks and set up large antiaircraft guns. While awaiting launch with fifteen other planes, we saw a Japanese plane dive on our ship. For some reason it neither fired a shot or dropped ordnance, and in spite of all guns being directed at the plane, both as it approached and retreated, it survived with no damage to either party. But it did bring to mind, vividly, what had happened just nine days earlier to the carrier *Franklin* when it was preparing to launch planes that were fully armed and with full fuel tanks. A single Japanese plane dropped two 250-kilo bombs that destroyed all personnel on the flight and hanger decks and ended the service of the *Franklin*, which laid dead in the water. The *Franklin* suffered 772 casualties.

When the firing on the Japanese plane had stopped, the launch was made with Major Frame leading a division of the flight to destroy the antiaircraft positions. Rockets were fired on the first run and hits were observed. On the second run, bombs were to be dropped. The bomb run was initiated and the bomb armed, but when the release button was pushed the bomb did not release and, as a sharp pull up was initiated, the engine quit. Although the airspeed indicator indicated well over 250 miles per hour, the altitude was less than 500 feet, and there was an armed 500-pound bomb a foot or two below the pilot seat. As the plane slowed it was discovered that the fuel mixture lever had retracted and shut off fuel to the engine. Full forward, the engine started, and a casualty was averted. Lucky?

Was it luck? The date was April 2, 1945. The mission, a strike against Kuchinoerabu, a smaller island just south of Kyushu, with a harbor for transports and radio installations. The return strike would hit Kikia, a small island just east of Amamio-shima. Kikia was a haven for kamikaze aircraft and was heavily fortified with antiaircraft. The strike against Kuchinoerabu was successful with hits on boats in the harbor and the radio installations. It was the encounter at Kikia that was exciting. Our flight damaged and destroyed many aircraft on the ground and attacked antiaircraft positions. The antiaircraft was intense, both large and small. As we were leaving the island after the last run, antiaircraft caught us. A 40 mm hit the right wing and made a hole large enough for a man to crawl through. One could see the ocean through the opening. More interesting was the fact that the huge hole was just inches from the right aileron. There were several other holes in our plane, one of which was eight inches behind the pilot's head. Luck?

Was it luck? The date was April 13, 1945. The new day began at 0300 with a predawn launch scheduled. The mission, target CAP (Combat Air Patrol) over Amamio-shima, with the main focus to locate aircraft and possible kamikaze activities. I'd be flying wing on George DeFabio today, rather than second section on Major Don Frame. Lieutenant Frank Kurchinski and Lieutenant Victor Rusling make up the balance of our division. Major Mobley, squadron commander of VM-123, was the mission leader of the eight plane group. DeFabio's division had all former members of the Mojave 213 and had trained together since the reorganization of VMF-213 in January 1944 at Mojave. George was an experienced combat pilot, having been with VMF-213 on Guadalcanal. Kurchinski and Rusling had both seen plenty of action since joining the fleet in January. I had been, while stationed on the *Essex*, three times over Tokyo, had supported the Iwo Jima landing, and since joining the *Bennington*, had supported the Okinawa landing 13 days ago. Plus, I had taken part in the regular strikes and CAP missions that happened daily while stationed on both carriers.

There is a string of islands south of Japan. Some of the islands had airfields that became launch sites for the kamikaze, and as American forces came closer to Japan, the more intense the concentration of kamikaze activity became. Antiaircraft guns needed to be silenced so that American planes could lend air support to the ground troops. Japanese airfields and aircraft had to be destroyed to lower the kamikaze threat. Thus, the mission to target Amamio-shima.

Three hours went by quickly, and after rejoining, the eight-plane group headed back to the carrier. With Major Mobley in the lead position, the return to the carrier was via the island of Kikia to confirm that there had not been further kamikaze build up and to destroy gun emplacements that could be found. Major Mobley's four planes strafed the field with our flight close behind. As we pulled up and headed out to sea, antiaircraft fire became intense. George DeFabio's plane was hit and the plane was on fire. In seconds he bailed out but was still under fire from the shore batteries. Then two more planes hit the ocean. Victor Rusling and Frank Kurchinski both perished. George was not able to free himself of his chute and was presumed drowned. From our division of four, only one marine returned to base. Was the only one who returned lucky?

Was it luck? It was May 14, 1945, on Mother's Day, off the coast of Kyushu, Japan. The weather was exceptionally good. It was morning, with a mission to strike Kyushu at the air and assembly plant at Kumamoto. It was an eight-plane flight led by Major Frame. This time I'd be flying second section with Lieutenant Lyle Bradley who had joined the squadron on April 17. My plane was FG-ID Corsair

#76506. For firepower I had four rockets, six 50-caliber guns in the wings with a 500-pound bomb.

There was heavy antiaircraft fire over the target. All of the rockets hit the target and the bomb hit the factory. Leaving the target, we headed back to the carrier. Just off the coast of Kyushu, our division intercepted a Japanese medium bomber. Being first to see the plane made it easy for us to reach the target and open fire. Firing while closing on the target, the left engine started to smoke, a fuel tank exploded, and the plane was burning. Wingman Lyle Bradley fired the first burst. By that time Major Frame was there to take a shot, but the Japanese plane was in the ocean. Splashed, one Nick night fighter. As we arrived back at the carrier we had to wait 20 minutes to land. When I finally got permission to land and headed into landing position, the engine quit—the plane was out of fuel and a water landing was inevitable.

Water landings can be hazardous to one's health, as evidenced by so many that had not survived. Downed pilots had died due to their inability to exit the aircraft, for one reason or another, after making a safe landing. For some it had been the inability to open hatches that had slammed shut on landing. The Corsair was a wonderful aircraft but it was not made for water landings, as they sank immediately. Several examples suddenly came to mind. On March 18, 1945, Lieutenant Tim Clark was hit by antiaircraft while on a strike against a Shibushi airfield on Kyushu. He made a safe landing but was unable to get out of the plane. On April 3, 1945, two good friends, experienced and accomplished pilots, perished when they could not open their hatches after water landings. Captain H. J. "Rusty" Deal, VMF-123, ran out of gas and made a water landing, but could not exit the plane. He drowned. Captain W. E. "Rocky" Roques was shot down over Ishigalu, headed for the water and landed, but could not open the canopy. On April 5, 1945, Lieutenant D. E. Erickson was shot down over Tukuno Airfield, Okinawa. He made a water landing but was unable to vacate the plane. It had also been reported that Lieutenant Spencer Weills, from the Wasp, did not survive a water landing, and near Honshu, Lieutenant Daniel Hayes made a water landing during which the plane sank immediately. He was not observed getting out of it. Water landings can be dangerous in a Corsair.

I was able to quickly open the hatch and accomplish a water landing without difficulty. As soon as the plane stopped forward motion, however, the water began to engulf the cockpit and made disentangling myself from the belts and straps of the chute very difficult. I tried to recover the life raft attached to the parachute, and although it was separated, the raft was still attached to the chute. As the plane sank, which took just a few seconds, the raft trailed the plane as it sank. The life preserver was immediately inflated. Within a few moments a raft was dropped by one of the planes. However, it was some distance away, and although it was sighted occasionally, the swells kept it out of sight most of the time. There had been little time to think about anything other than getting out of the craft, for it was known that Corsairs do not float very long.

Now there was time, and although I knew help was close, I had a strange feeling of being very alone. No ships were in sight, no land was in sight, and I had no map of the immediate vicinity. I wondered whether sharks liked to eat marines, but the water was not uncomfortable and I recalled seeing a memo from Admiral Mitchner that said, "Relax and enjoy the inevitable." That sounded like good advice. Though the time in the water seemed to be going very slowly, the DD *DeHaven* soon popped into view. Before long I received dry clothing, a look at a bruise or two from the doctor, and a repair to the small cut on my knee. There was also a steak meal and royal treatment from a great bunch of navy personnel. When the commodore posed the question of when there should be a return trip made to the *Bennington* I answered, "At once!" Love those Breeches. Lucky?

And so it may be for each of us to decide, is it just dumb luck, or is it possible that one's life might, for reasons unknown, be watched over, and that each of us has a specific purpose to fulfill. That unusual things, and yes, maybe even miracles, happen. For this marine, it is not just luck.

Observations At Saipan
By Edward Anders Sovik

From time to time, and especially in the early 2000s, the suggestion has been raised among Americans that Truman made a mistake in authorizing the atomic bomb, and I suppose it often is raised in Japan. I think that almost none of the marines who fought or others who examine casualty figures would be among the doubters.

When we got orders to move VMF(N)-532 to Saipan from Kwajalein, the distance was such that the Corsairs couldn't make the flight. They would again be transported on a flat top with the troops. But it seemed wise to someone to send a few people ahead to do some preparatory work. Major Vaughan chose me and ten men of various skills. We went by a transport R4D on July 5, twenty days after D-day but several days before the last battle, and some weeks before the last Japanese soldier was flushed out of the jungles or cane fields of Saipan.

I ran into John Ambler, a Pensacola classmate who was flying OYs and spotting artillery for one of the marine divisions, at the chow line at Aslito Field. John asked me the morning after a particularly troublesome engagement with the enemy if I cared to go up with him to see the results of the action (he was not on call for his work). We flew low, never quite up to the front lines, which were advancing north again, but over the area, now quiet, where the worst face-to-face fighting had been. The sight of so many fresh corpses, and especially, I suppose, so many marine corpses, was especially moving. Seeing enemy dead was disturbing; seeing American corpses was very painful.

We were all disposed to a distorted view of life's durability. At the most intimate, we set a limited value on our own lives. The hazards of flying itself—we all had friends or acquaintances who had died in training accidents or other flying mishaps. But having committed ourselves we ignored the issue. More than that, we adopted the posture of meeting danger eagerly whenever an occasion was offered, assuming it was not simply foolish. I don't remember that there was ever one of the pilots of 532 who turned down a chance to fly. And when in the spring of 1945 the commanding officer of the training group in Texas where the 532 pilots were called us together and said he wanted ten volunteers to go to the Pacific again in a new squadron, everybody volunteered. The only time I remember a conversation confessing fear was a late night when Pfizenmaier, after too much to drink, said slurringly, "Ed, someday I'm going to have a terrible time with that Corsair." He did. He was strong, but only about 5'5", and one night a Corsair got away from him on takeoff. He spent a year mending many fractures in a Philadelphia navy hospital.

If we set a limited value on our own lives it is not surprising that we valued the lives of the enemy even less (though the judgment of God would not agree). There was a young sergeant in 532 who probably regretted being in aviation rather than in an assault division; when we were in Saipan he would get up at dawn and go out looking in the cane fields and jungles for Japanese survivors, of whom there were a few. But we were not generally bloodthirsty, simply very eager for success. Furthermore, there is a kind of objectivity in aviation war, where one never comes face to face with the enemy. And I remember that there was neither pang of conscience nor exultation of accomplishment when I landed after sending a bomber crew to oblivion—only satisfaction that we had won the contest. The contest, as we took it to be, was much like a long athletic event; but we knew the stakes were high.

On another flight with John Ambler he set us down on a tiny strip at Marpi Point, the very north tip of Saipan. The American troops had pushed the Japanese troops and the civilians whom they forced to go with them, to the extremity, the irregular and rocky cliffs, and they were lodged in caves and ledges not readily seen or attacked. The area along and back from the cliff edges was occupied by marines. Other areas, near where we landed, were dealing with people who were surrendering. They searched them, supplied drinking water, and loaded them onto trucks. There were Japanese-Americans with distinctive uniforms, *nisei* or *sansei*, talking through blaring loud speakers, trying to convince those who were still alive among the enemy that they should give up, that Americans would not torture them but treat them well.

There was a little stream of people coming up through the cane fields that lay between us and the cliff edge. They were civilians, *Chamorrans*, almost all of them, of all ages and both sexes, bedraggled and emaciated, voicing a continuous whine, half unconsciously and without objective. They were not making a plea; hope seemed too far gone. One ancient among them carried a baby, obviously dead, over his arm. There were a few soldiers, little men in light uniforms. These were the remains of the garrison troops, the only Japanese army prisoners I had seen.

Not long before the assault there had been an arrival of a large force of very good Japanese troops brought in from Manchuria (it was said) to reinforce the garrison. They had made the battle costly and it was some of these whose bodies we saw as Ambler and I walked down through the cane to the edge of the cliff. They wore heavy winter uniforms and were, or had been, big and strong young men.

Sovik (far right) in Saipan.

When we reached the edge we found marines stationed every few yards keeping watch, both for those who appeared climbing up with the intent to surrender and for any sign of resistance from the soldiers who were known to be hiding along the craggy rim. While we stood we saw a few civilians moving about on an exposed shelf 100 yards to our left. A few of them, four or five, suddenly gathered themselves together in a tight embrace. Immediately they were blown apart, exploding a grenade to put an end to it. Whether from fear that, as they had been told, the Americans would kill them, or whether from a fanatic patriotism, they had decided against accepting the marines' invitation.

A few minutes later, a shout came down the line. Looking the other way we saw, one after another, a dozen almost naked men run out from shelter, leap into the water and set about swimming—apparently trying to get around to the other side of a projecting rock for some reason.

I was standing next to a corporal who had his hand on his rifle. The range was not great. "Lieutenant," the corporal said offering me the rifle, "D'you want to shoot a Jap?" I'm glad to report that I said "No," that my job was airplanes. There were several riflemen nearby, and none of the swimmers got very far.

There were about 3,500 Americans killed on Saipan and about 13,000 wounded; almost 31,000 Japanese died. The proportions were sometimes much greater. The Japanese killed 200 Americans and wounded 500 on the Eniwetok assault, but lost 3,400 dead.

If the atomic bomb had not been used, and it had been necessary to invade the Japanese homeland to end the fighting, it is likely to have brought terrible losses on both sides. And inevitably the Japanese lost in Hiroshima and Nagasaki would have been far outnumbered.

Shot Down Over Koror

By Harry J. Goodyear

On the morning of March 4, 1945, a combined air strike of squadrons VMF-114, VMF-121, and VMF-122 was ordered to attack Battery Hill at Koror, the headquarters for all Japanese Imperial Forces throughout Palau and Micronesia. It also had a concentration of Japanese antiaircraft batteries that had shot down many American fighters and bombers over the Palau islands.

On this mission Lieutenant Brown of VMF-121 was shot down because of intense antiaircraft fire. Lieutenant Brown, although badly burned and injured, managed to land in the water in Malakal Bay, north of Koror. He was rescued by Dumbo, a navy rescue flying boat. He returned to his home base on Peleliu Island for treatment of his wounds.

As a pilot with VMF-122, I flew on this airstrike. Lieutenant Brown was interviewed and quoted by Patrick J. Scannon, M.D., Ph.D., some fifty years after this airstrike.

Survival

By Edward Anders Sovik

Among the utility aircraft that we had at USMCAS, Eagle Mountain Lake, was a Beachcraft, a single-engine biplane, a so-called "stagger-wing" because the lower wing was, unconventionally, forward of the upper wing. The plane was not built for the navy, but for civil aviation, and accommodated a pilot and three passengers comfortably, plus some luggage, and it was fast for such a machine.

One afternoon I took the Beach down to the air force base at Lake Charles, Louisiana, on a mission to pick up some special ammunition, I believe. Two of the line crew who thought they would enjoy the trip came along with me, as well as the gunnery sergeant. The weather was overcast, but was not expected to go instrument. However, while we were on the ground the ceiling came down, so that I had to file an instrument flight plan to go home. Unhappily this plane wasn't equipped for instrument flight, it had only one radio instead of two.

As it happened, I recognized the name of the air force captain who had the flight desk duty when we checked in. It was Captain Mike Peinovitch, whom I knew from college days as a star on the Concordia College football team. We had a pleasant conversation, and when I asked him to approve the illegal instrument flight plan he did, as a gesture of friendship.

I assembled the men, started the engine, and called air traffic control to say we were taxiing out for takeoff and would want clearance. At the end of the runway the engine was idling, but then it suddenly cut out. Unexpected and troubling. Was the idle set too low? I had no trouble starting the engine again and tested it by running it up to full power. Everything tested out. So, back to waiting for takeoff clearance. Then the engine cut out again. I decided this time to do the prudent thing, and set out to return to the hangar. While I was taxiing, air traffic control called to give me takeoff clearance.

What the crew found when they examined the engine was a carburetor half full of red powder. A mechanic at Eagle Mountain Lake had used a natural rubber gasket at the gas tank cap instead of neoprene; the rubber had broken down in the gas and was intermittently clogging the carburetor.

I thought about how close we came to disaster. Survival, if we had in fact gotten into the air and the engine had cut while we were flying over the pine forests, would have been unlikely. (One of our strong F7Fs went down in those woods later, and Charlie Caniff, the pilot, emerged a paraplegic after a year in the hospital.) Shouldn't I have called the flight off after the engine died the first time? Was God saving me, as he had at other times of danger, for some good purpose? Or was he saving the passengers I had been so eager to bring back to our base? How come the engine didn't die on the trip to Lake Charles, and behaved until the plane was on the ground? What kind of trouble would Peinovitch have been in for signing the flight plan if we had crashed? I saw him many times in later years. He hadn't been aware that I and my men had stayed overnight instead of going home because he had been relieved as OD by the time I brought the plane back to the ramp.

Artillery Spotting

By Clyde H. Slyman

VMO-6 OE (L19) mission was forward air control airborne and artillery spotting. The aircraft were OEs (L-19) single-engine Cessnas. The aircraft were not armored and not equipped with weapons; OE speed was 80 knots.

On my second flight, three OEs were airborne. We encountered intense antiaircraft fire, probably 37-mm. One OE was hit and the crew bailed out. The second OE took a direct hit in the left wing. The airplane entered a violent spin and the wing separated from the airplane. The crew was not able to bail out. I observed the airplane spin into the ground.

Crewmen from the first aircraft were taken prisoner. Crew members from the second aircraft were most certainly killed.

Special Engineering
By Edward Anders Sovik

Memory tells me that Colonel Iron John Harshberger was an engineering graduate of Cal Tech. He was first of all an aggressive marine and a superb pilot, of course, but he had both the hands-on practicality and the impatient curiosity of the really good engineer. So it was not surprising that while he was commanding officer of Night Fighter Training Group 53 at Eagle Mountain Lake in 1945, he should have been pursuing the objective of developing a really effective exhaust flame suppressor for the R-2800 engines on the F7Fs. It was an elusive goal—to make the exhaust flare invisible to a tail gunner on a dark night.

The ground crew had mounted a set of newly configured flame dampeners on an F7F on the day of this story. To check them out Captain Jim Wehmer took the F7 up one dark night. We didn't have a plane that you could look backward from in any normal way, but Iron John figured a scheme. We had a JRF, the lumbering amphibian Grumman Goose, and people who were familiar with it will remember that there was a round hatch in the middle of the hold of the ship. The scheme involved removing the hatch while in the air and sticking an observer's head out the bottom of the hull to peer back into the darkness looking for the exhaust flare. Wehmer would get on the tail of the JRF and slowly approach, reading off the distances from his radar scope, and the observer, listening on earphones, would try to establish how close the F7 was when the exhaust flare was first discernable.

Iron John flew the Goose. I was the observer; he said I had better eyes. To get in a useful position I had to take off my chute, squeeze down through the hatch, and hang on my elbows in the 115-knot wind. No great privilege. But the really memorable part of the evening occurred when Wehmer gave everyone a thrill. He caught up with the JRF in a burst of speed and passed under us so close that his high tail fin cut a six-foot gash in our belly a few inches off the line of my head and a few feet aft.

I was glad to be alive, but seething. It was clear that we would get home easily, but Iron John tried to raise Wehmer on the radio and couldn't get an answer. As it turned out, the only damage to the F7 was the loss of the radio antenna, and Wehmer got back to base before we did. I was still seething and would have been happy to see Wehmer grounded, if not court-martialed. The colonel was simply happy to see him alive and to find the plane without serious damage.

Everything quieted down quickly. No accident report was required, just a few hours in the hangar to sew the Goose together again. I don't remember what I thought of the new flame dampeners.

The Last Flight That Wasn't

Darrell Smith

The day after I told the people at VRF-3 that I planned to resign I saw on the bulletin board in operations that there was a TBM at El Toro about 30 miles away that was to go to a reserve squadron being formed in Minneapolis. I basically begged them to let me have that one last flight. They finally agreed with the stipulation that I would sign the resignation papers when I got back to Terminal Island.

The following day I was at El Toro and had checked over the TBM and filed a flight plan. One of the operations people came running out to the plane with a young sailor who he said was trying desperately to get to his father's funeral in Des Moines, Iowa, the following day. They had tried every way they could to get him there but hadn't had any luck. I was his last chance. Would I take him along and drop him off in Des Moines? I wasn't sure I was authorized to take any passengers, and besides, I didn't have an extra parachute. He said they could take care of that. I looked at the young sailor and could see the pleading in his eyes. After a minute's hesitation I said, "Okay. Go get us a chute."

The TBM was a torpedo bomber and designed to carry a three-man crew. The pilot climbed up on the wing to get to the cockpit and the other two people entered through a small door alongside the fuselage that opened into the torpedo bay and on up into the seats behind the cockpit where they could see out too. There was no way to get from the cockpit to the back seats, but there was an intercom radio so we could talk to each other. I explained all this to my new passenger and had him climb up into the second seat where he would ride. When they came back with the chute I signed for it, had him put it on, and explained how it worked if he had to use it. Then off we went. We made two stops to refuel along the way with no problems. By the time we approached Fort Worth, Texas, it was near sunset and we had to stay overnight. I had learned not to leave anything that wasn't tied down in an airplane overnight and asked my passenger on the intercom to bring his chute with us.

When we landed I climbed out of the cockpit and jumped down off the wing. The door opened and a voice said, "Sir, I think I did something wrong." One thing I'd neglected to tell him was not to carry the chute around by the red handle. Sure enough, he had popped the chute and it was spread all over the torpedo bay. Now we had a problem. There was no place in Fort Worth that could repack a parachute in time for my passenger to get to Des Moines the next day. I was pretty sure that somewhere in the navy's files there was a rule forbidding anyone from flying in a TBM without a parachute. Though I knew what his answer would be, I asked my passenger if he wanted to fly without a chute.

TBM with popped chute inside at Ft. Worth.

The next morning we were on the runway at the crack of dawn. We arrived in Des Moines around 10 in the morning and the sailor grabbed a cab. I don't know if he made it to the funeral in time but we'd done the best we could. They wouldn't ship the popped chute back to El Toro from Des Moines so I took it to Minneapolis. On the way I realized if I went just a little way off the direct route I could fly over my hometown in western Minnesota.

When I had enlisted in the navy V5 program I had to have a recommendation from a VIP that knew me. About the most important person in my hometown was the man who ran our two grain elevators. When I asked him for a recommendation he indicated that he thought I was shooting too high in trying to become an airplane pilot and an officer, but he did give me a recommendation. I still don't know if he was belittling me or challenging me. I took it as a challenge and never forgot it.

Now I had a chance to show him he was wrong. The main road in that area went right through the middle of town, and the elevators were on each side of the road at the north end. That TBM wasn't a Corsair, but it would do. I started a high speed let down over the road about a mile south of town and went through town at treetop level and right between the two elevators as fast as that TBM could go. I believe I made my point—a kid from the country could fly airplanes!

When I got to Minneapolis they did have facilities for repacking the parachute and said they would send it back to El Toro. I don't know if it ever got back there. There was also an SNJ there that was to go to Anacostia near Washington, DC. After a two-day layover I was on my way to our national capitol. My first stop for fuel was at the Glenview Naval Air Station a few miles north of Chicago. While we were refueling I noticed some N2S primary trainers just sitting there. I asked about them and I was told they were going to Clinton, Oklahoma, to be sold or scrapped.

The SNJ was a very comfortable and relaxing plane to fly. After leaving Glenview I went south of Chicago and was following a major highway east. I was cruising along munching on some cookies when I glanced down and noticed there was no highway. It was just gone. I circled back and picked it up again and was watching closely when the road suddenly disappeared again! I circled back once more and this time I kept my eyes glued on the road and saw it abruptly end. Then I looked ahead for what looked like close to a mile and could see the road up ahead. It finally dawned on me that I had come to a long tunnel.

I was a little concerned about security measures around Washington, DC, but was cleared right in to Anacostia. I had never been to our national capitol so I decided to stay a few days for a little sightseeing. I also couldn't get those N2Ss back at Glenview out of my mind. I had taken my primary flight training in the N2S and it was the most enjoyable airplane I had ever flown. It was a biplane with two cockpits, and while in training when making some serious mistakes practicing acrobatics, I had learned you really couldn't tear one apart in the air unless you hit something. After a few days in Washington, DC, I was talking to a couple of pilots that were going to Chicago with a DC-3 and they said they would be happy to drop me off at Glenview, so I hitched a ride.

The N2Ss were still there and they said they would be glad to have me take one to Clinton. The N2S had only one small fuel tank in the center of the top wing and was not a long-range airplane. I had also been off the regular ferry route since I left Fort Worth with the TBM and was planning my own routes and fuel stops as I went along. My first refueling stop was at Springfield, Illinois. When I arrived there I was looking for an airfield with surfaced runways, but their airport was only a grass strip. That was okay for an N2S, but I wasn't sure they had the right fuel. It turned out they did. That was pretty much the situation all the way to Clinton.

I felt like a barnstormer in the 1930s—and I almost was. It was great fun taking off in the mornings with dew on the wings and the wind blowing on my face in the open cockpit. I was just flying along close to the ground, taking my time and watching the countryside going by. At some of the smaller airports they had never seen an N2S and I gave them cockpit checkouts. The N2S had no radio, so I avoided the large airfields when I could. One exception was an army airfield by Tulsa, Oklahoma. Since I had no radio they gave me a green light to land, but I was met by a military police jeep. I had become used to landing on small runways and by mistake had landed on one of their taxi strips. I think they thought I was showing off and they didn't appreciate that at all. After quite a discussion they did give me some fuel and sent me on my way. It was one of my most memorable and enjoyable trips.

When I got to Clinton I learned I could buy any one of the N2Ss for $200, or a Corsair for $1,000. I seriously considered an N2S but I didn't have any place to keep it or the ability to maintain it. I wanted to go back and pick up another N2S but I couldn't find any transportation back to Glenview and besides, I knew they would be looking for me back at Terminal Island. I got a ride to Olathe, Kansas, and took the Admiral's Barge (R5D aircraft) to San Francisco.

At the navy base in Alameda there was another TBM, destined this time for Bangor, Maine. Ordinarily the first stop along the ferry route would be Terminal Island. I had agreed that the next time I landed there I would become a civilian—but Bangor, Maine! I had never been that far north along the east coast.

I decided to take a chance and flew over Terminal Island and landed at the navy base on North Island near San Diego. I was on my way to Maine. That night I had to send a wire back giving the bureau number and the location of the TBM. The next morning I had a wire from Terminal Island saying something like, "You leave that airplane at North Island and get your butt back up here."

I rode the train back up to Los Angeles and along the way, as I gazed out the window, I began musing about the barefoot kid in coveralls in a small town in southwestern Minnesota making model airplanes out of wooden peach crates. A kid day dreaming about someday being able to fly and how that same kid wound up as a marine fighter pilot flying many of the navy's top fighter aircraft.

I decided that last trip was a fitting way to end my military career and I was ready to go back to college. I had no way of knowing that four years later I would again be flying combat missions in Corsairs halfway around the world in a place called Korea.

Into A Hurricane

By Edward Anders Sovik

If you were to look up the weather records for July 19-20, 1945, you would find that a small hurricane was hovering in the Gulf of Mexico off the coast of Texas. At the time, Lieutenant Colonel John Harshberger was spending some days at the Beaumont/Port Arthur tactical training base. He had been pondering a tactical question: Is it better, when night fighters are attacking a ship, for a flare to be dropped on one side of the ship and the attack made from the other, or should the flare drop and the attack be on the same side?

One night at a Galveston oasis Iron John got into a conversation with a tanker captain who was in port at Texas City. It occurred to him that he might work out a research enterprise to get beyond theory to experiential data. He persuaded the ship captain to agree to a rendezvous his first night away, worked out a radio frequency for air-to-ship communication, and made plans for two F7s to make the flight. Iron John was, of course, the commanding officer of the night fighter training group at Eagle Mountain Lake, Texas. He told me I should fly his wing, which was an interesting prospect.

I was at Eagle Mountain Lake on the July 19 when the colonel called to say the ship was to leave port that day, and I should fly down to join him. I said, "What about these hurricane reports?" We had heard that the army air force had evacuated their planes from Lake Charles and were planning to fly everything out of Kelly Field, too.

But the colonel said, "Here I am and it's not so bad, and we'll not have another chance like this." I flew down.

The ceiling was high enough to fly, the air was rough and wet; but I took a scouting flight out over the water and found nothing unflyable. After dark I flew out again, and it was still not impossible. The hurricane was turning east, and the threat to the coast was past.

The colonel had arranged to meet the tanker at midnight; the ship captain would be coming off his watch and could give us his attention. We set out accordingly. I flew a tight wing, sometimes losing the colonel's running lights momentarily in the scud. But we got where we intended to be. Then came trouble. The colonel tried to raise the ship by radio and failed. Again and again he tried. We concluded that the problem was in the transmitter and went back to base. I might have called it a night, but not Iron John. The line crew got the radio corrected and we set out again.

By now the ship had traveled two or three hours on its course, so our navigation was adjusted. We were moving farther into the center of the storm, and the weather was worse—surely the darkest, roughest, wettest night I ever flew in. We kept under the ceiling, except for scud, but as high as we could (un)comfortably be, which was, I think, a couple of hundred feet.

Quite suddenly we broke into the open, into the great and quiet core. There was a bright gibbous moon lighting the clouds that formed a tremendous out-sloping wall of infinite height around the open water. And there we saw on the shimmering sea the dark shape of a ship, which we took to be our quarry. The colonel tried to make contact without effect. We dropped a flare; no response. We waited and dropped another. We circled for minutes more, and then concluded that the ship captain had given up on us and gone to his bunk, or that the ship was the wrong one. We'll never know.

Plunging down into the weather again we flew home. My flight logbook says that the flight lasted 1.9 hours in F7F-3, number 80367.

Bombings and Beer in the South Pacific
By Harry Anderson

Orders came to go overseas. I was assigned to get all our gear aboard a Hunter Ligget ship located in San Diego. It was a crowded situation—six pilots per room. The enlisted marines were stacked ten high in the storage of the ship. We got to Hawaii and had to transfer to a smaller ship that took us to Efate, New Hebrides, which was our rear echelon base. In getting ashore we had to get on a landing barge and jump from the barge to the land and then to the jungle. The ride to our campsite was a muddy one. It was good to see Quonset huts ready for us. They housed four officers and were made out of plywood.

We had a small airstrip that we used to get in our flight time. We would often go up to 10,000 feet to cool off our beer rations, which were two cans per person per day. The beer was Lucky Lager and gave many of us diarrhea.

We had no idea where the three other squadrons of our group were sent. An air force fighter squadron was stationed near us. It was the 144 Pursuit Squadron of the Army Air Corps. They were called to go to "Cactus," which was the code name for Henderson Field located on Guadalcanal. We were called to go to Henderson Field December 1942. I completed 39 missions—everything from close air support to shipping and harassment. The enemy still maintained the area at the end of the runway at Henderson Field, so it was always dangerous taking off. We lost one pilot.

My highlight was a mission in support of the Third Marines making a landing on Empress August Bay. It involved smoke-bombing for the landing forces, since they were caught in a cross fire from an island that had been overlooked by intelligence.

My last mission was a strike on Masigetta.

Pilot For Top Brass
By Edward Anders Sovik

It is said that the difference between talent and genius is that the talented person learns quickly, and the genius already knows—the genius has some kind of native or intuitive understanding. We meet them rarely. I am reflecting on a trip between Eagle Mountain Lake and Cherry Point that happened in the summer of 1945; to be precise, three days that included the day the bomb was dropped on Hiroshima.

Congress was working on the budget, the navy was putting together its numbers, and the secretary of the navy for air, whose memorable name was John L. Sullivan, was wondering whether the marine night-fighter enterprise had enough merit to deserve continued financing. Someone invited Sullivan to take a look at how it was done, or perhaps he invited himself.

Colonel Iron John got a call from Washington saying, "Send one of your instruction SNB's up to Cherry Point with someone to demonstrate the night fighter operation for the Navy Department." The colonel told me to pick the plane and the crew and make the trip. One might suppose that the colonel figured that it was better to have a captain to blame it on than the commanding officer of the group himself if something went haywire. But that is an ungenerous thought, and he was a generous man. It was generous of him to trust me, and he guessed that it would be more interesting for me than for him. He had no particular stomach for the society at Marine Corps Headquarters.

But there was no assurance that things wouldn't go wrong. Those radar sets were willful as cats. It was a recurrent problem to get them operating with the range and clarity they were supposed to have, and just as much of a problem to keep them operating. There was Sergeant John Duvall of Albany, Kentucky, a farmer to begin with who as an 18-year-old won first prize in his state for his corn crop. Duvall was picked to go to electronics school after boot camp. By luck or by discrimination someone did the right thing. It was not that he had talent—he had genius. He had a sensibility, a perception, a sympathy for, a precocious understanding of those capricious catenations of wires, wave guides, condensers, shepherd tubes, and all the irrational bits and pieces on which our success depended. So I asked Duvall to come along, along with Sergeant Henneman, the plane captain, and Lieutenant Bill Franks, my R.O.

I had orders to report to the chief of staff at Cherry Point, whose name was Colonel Burke. I remembered him from Pensacola; he had been a marine major on the committee to whom I applied for transfer from the navy to the marines. In answering why I wanted to transfer I gave several reasons, the last being that I had a cousin who was a chaplain with the marines. Burke corrected me, "No," he said with more attention to alliteration than to theology, "the marines don't have any chaplains. We depend on the navy to lead our people down the primrose path to the pearly gates."

He didn't remember that meeting, of course. But he made us welcome, assigned me a jeep, and told us how important our mission was. He gave us the picture and put me in touch with a pilot to fly the target plane for the demonstration. He was on the phone with me every other hour, I think, for a couple of days.

An R4D came down from Washington full of stars, chickens, and J. L. Sullivan. The weather was heavily overcast and rainy, and Colonel Burke was worried about whether it would be too thick to run the demonstration for one thing, and for another, I think, whether this captain was to be trusted in bad weather with a cargo of brass that included, along with Sullivan, General Field Harris, the senior marine aviator. Frankly, it worried me too.

We had made a check flight late in the afternoon. Henneman had the SNB in good fettle and Duvall had both the radar sets tuned. We got the ground radar people and the target pilot in synch, and we found that the clouds were layered with plenty of room for the target to fly around in between the layers.

We waited, and between every course of their dinner at the officers club Colonel Burke called to say the decision about flying or not was mine, and asked what I thought.

We flew, Sullivan in the copilot's seat and General Harris and a couple of others looking at the second scope in the cabin, with Duvall doing the play-by-play there. The interception went perfectly. Sullivan said he was impressed with the system, and wrote a note I still have to say so. I was impressed with him too, and with the crew I had to take care of me. And Colonel Burke was so pleased that he rewrote my orders to include a two-day excursion to Washington as a reward.

Mountain Climber Syndrome
By Richard Hansen

May 20 was my last combat flight of World War II. Along with a number of other marine pilots, I was sent back to the United States for rest and preparation for the coming invasion of Japan.

The invasion was planned for November 1, 1945. Kyushu, the southern most Japanese island, would be the logical starting place because of its proximity to our main supply base, which was Okinawa.

However, in the first two weeks of August 1945 the atomic bombs succeeded in bringing World War II to an abrupt halt, along with the surrender of the Japanese forces on August 14. I was at the naval air station in New Orleans and got in on the celebration in the city. It was unbelievable. I don't remember too much about it except there were lots of girls trying to kiss everybody in a uniform.

The war is over, so what happens next? I was sent to the naval air station at Glenview, Illinois, to flight instructor school. It was a stopgap plan until they could figure out what to do with us.

We flew a total of about 40 hours during September and October at Glenview with my last flight on October 25. We were able to fly any airplane on the base. They had a TBF there, which I flew.

There was a golf course on the naval air station so we spent a lot of time trying to improve our games. We partied every night because we knew that we probably would never see most of these guys again. We did not know then that another war was over the horizon.

In December I received my orders to the inactive reserve at the Minneapolis Naval Air Station and arrived home on Christmas Eve, 1945. I was happy to be home with my family and girlfriend, but something was missing—the camaraderie of a squadron.

I was lost, as were most of us. The military life was very structured, and war was exciting. Now we were home with no schedule and nothing to do. The excitement was gone. Fortunately I had my girlfriend, so I didn't hang around the bars like most guys did. Still, I was missing the action.

Finally I went back to school and saw some of my fellow pilots from flight school and we all were suffering, because a book does not a battle make. Between classes we hung around the Student Union and talked about where we were in the Pacific War and who was killed, and so on. Weird, but we wanted to go back. We called it "the mountain climber syndrome"—the world was just no longer high enough or dangerous enough, and that lost feeling lasted a long time.

KOREA

Bail Out
By Darrell Smith

May 8, 1951, was a clear and pleasant but windy day aboard the USS *Bataan*, a "Jeep" carrier, as we prepared to launch aircraft in the Yellow Sea between China and Korea. I was a pilot in VMF-312, flying F4U-4 Corsairs. On this day I was to lead a two-plane combat air patrol over the carrier, which promised to be an uneventful three to four hours of simply boring holes in the sky.

Orbiting at 12,000 feet about two hours into the flight I began to sense a faint vibration that rapidly grew worse until the engine began missing, then cutting in and out, twisting the nose about two inches each time the engine cut in again. I called the carrier, declared an emergency, and said I was returning. At that time I intended to try to get back aboard the carrier.

By this time my wingman had pulled up underneath and said I was losing quite a bit of oil. I had already cut back to low RPM and pulled the throttle back to near idle, trying to reduce the forces twisting the nose. By then I knew I'd never get back aboard the carrier and called saying I intended to try a water landing alongside one of the escort destroyers. I'd always felt that in such an emergency, I'd try a water landing rather than bailing out over water.

By the time we got back over the ships in the task force I was essentially in a long glide and down to about 7,000 feet. The engine was still running, but cutting out more and more. At this point my wingman called and said I was on fire underneath and urged me to get out. Fire was a different story, and I gave up any thought of a water landing. We were now right over the carrier and I was afraid that if I left then, the plane might hit the carrier or one of the six escort destroyers. I knew the carrier was monitoring all transmissions, so I called and said I planned to go a couple of miles straight ahead and bail out. They responded, "Roger. Clemintine is airborne and on the way." Clemintine was our rescue helicopter.

At that moment my wingman called again and said the fire was getting worse and I should get out as soon as I could. I unbuckled the seatbelt, tightened both leg straps and the chest strap of the chute, and opened the hatch overhead. Oil suddenly started coming through the cockpit, impairing my vision before I got the goggles down. I also cut the engine switch because somewhere in our training we were told to do this. It was a major mistake. Next I tried to stand up to go over the side and was jerked back down in the seat. All I could think was, "This shouldn't happen. I must have done something wrong." Then I realized I hadn't disconnected the earphones.

By now I could sense the plane was picking up speed rapidly—cutting the switch had changed the trim and it was rolling over and heading almost straight down. I didn't realize what was happening but something in my head said, "Get out NOW!" I slipped over the right side, trying to grasp the trailing edge of the wing to pull myself under the stabilizer. Suddenly I was free of the plane and tumbling through the sky, still thinking I was somewhere around 6,000 feet. Instead, both the plane and I had been going pretty much straight down. I stretched out my arms and legs, which I'd heard somewhere would stop the tumbling. It did, but I was facing straight up, a bad position to pull the ripcord because the chute was under me. Then I rolled face down, a good position with the chute above me, but I could still hear the plane and hesitated to pull the ripcord because I'd been told that if you can still hear the plane, don't open the chute because it might catch on the plane.

Again something said inside of me, "Pull that ripcord NOW!" So I did. The chute opened, I swung up once, then hit the water, coming down hard enough to lose consciousness. The cold water revived me almost instantly. I could see light above and came to the surface, but the chute was dragging me through the water. When I finally got it collapsed I was tangled in the shroud lines, having trouble staying afloat, and swallowing a lot of water and dye marker. The dye marker packet had apparently broken when I hit the water. (I learned later that the reason I was having trouble staying afloat was because the cartridges in the Mae West jacket were faulty and it hadn't inflated).

Suddenly I saw the helicopter coming, and waved, but they didn't see me and went right on by! My wingman, who had stayed right with me all the way down and was the only one who saw the chute blossom, kept me in sight and called the helicopter back. By then I'd gotten the chest strap and the right leg strap of the chute unhooked, but I'd pulled the left leg strap too tight before bailing out and my fingers were so numb I couldn't get it unhooked.

The helicopter dropped the rescue line to me with the harness open, but my fingers were too cold to get it around me and hooked. There was a lead weight a little smaller than a baseball just above the harness and I locked both hands around the line above this weight and they pulled me up, chute still attached. I got one elbow inside the door of the helicopter when the chute began to blow back towards the tail. They had to let me back into the water because they were afraid it would catch in the tail rotor. By this time I was exhausted. I still had my hands locked around the line and couldn't make myself let go, even though I was going under water when the peaks of the swells came through and up in the air when the troughs came through. I swallowed a lot more water and dye marker. The copter crewman climbed down the line to try to cut me out of the chute, but somehow got down there without the knife. Now there were two of us in the water.

Then I saw a destroyer bearing down on us. People told me later that it had taken off across the water like a scared rabbit the minute I said I was going to bail out, and it wasn't a moment too soon because by then I'd about had it. When I saw them throw a 10-man life raft over the side, I was able to let go of the line and wave the helicopter off.

The sea, which seemed reasonably calm, was too rough for the raft. Then I saw them put a lifeboat in the water. As they came alongside the two of us in the water, a big navy chief grabbed my flight suit by the back of the shoulders and the seat of the pants and heaved me, shroud lines and all, into the boat. I guess I felt we finally had it made because I lost consciousness again.

I came to, stretched out on a table in the destroyer's dining room where people were cutting me out of my flight suit and giving me oxygen. I rewarded them by promptly vomiting all over the table.

The most unnerving part of the entire episode came later in the day when they strapped me into a wire mummy basket and transferred me on a high line from the destroyer to the carrier, where they had better medical facilities. All I could think was, "If this line breaks, or I get dropped back in the water in this thing, I'm going to sink like a rock and won't be able to move even a finger." However all went well, and I was finally back home.

Later in the ready room where I was asked to review the experience for the benefit of others who might encounter a similar emergency, I ended up saying I'd made an awful lot of mistakes. However the CO said, "Well, you did a good many things right or you wouldn't be here."

A lot of other people did a good many things right, too. Especially my wingman, or I wouldn't be here either.

Being transferred from the destroyer to the carrier via highline.

The biggest lesson I learned is this: When I hear someone say what they would do in an emergency, I can't help warning them that they really don't know how they will react, or what they will do under dire stress.

Chosin Challenges
By Lyle Bradley

In combat we are forced to violate many aviation rules—this was one of the many necessary violations during the Korean War. This episode was my third combat mission in Korea and we had problems with weather, cold, and enemy forces.

Word from top generals indicated we would be home by Christmas. With these words of wisdom in mind our cold weather aircraft starting units (that we had in Minnesota) were not with us. On this below-zero day with falling snow, only two of us could get our F4U Corsairs started. A Chinese army had suddenly rescued the North Koreans and had surrounded the First Marine Division of 15,000 men. Generals MacArthur and Almond had violated normal military tactics by sending two divisions (one marine and one army) into mountains via small roads.

Our squadron was flying out of Yonpo Airfield near Hungnam, North Korea. We were about 50 miles from the marine division that was stalled at Yudam-ni near the Chosin Reservoir. The army division had already been badly mauled by the Chinese and the marines needed our air support because they were outnumbered.

The only way to get to the marine division was to fly up a tortuous mountain road. With the cloud cover down to 100 feet at times, it was difficult to keep the road in sight and avoid trees and rocks on each side of the road. We surprised some Chinese on the road and luckily they didn't have time to shoot at us—never expecting two Corsairs flying in a snowstorm at treetop height. We could hear some shooting but their surprised aim was not accurate.

As we approached the mountain pass, section leader Major Ken Reusser radioed, "In case we can't make any of the turns, we'll go high power, drop our load, and climb out on instruments."

"Roger," I responded. "We might slow our speed and drop flaps as we approach the first turn." My optimism of getting through the mountain pass was not high, as there were three strikes against us: low visibility, the winding road, and many Chinese troops in the pass who could enhance their promotions by shooting down a Corsair.

My four 20-mm wing guns were armed but on safe, and my four 500-pound wing bombs also were ready. It was doubtful if we would have a chance to use any weapons in this weather. My full concentration was flying wing and keeping an eye on trees and rocks that seemed to be within a few feet as we slithered through the narrow pass. I expected to hear bullets rip through the plane at any time, but the enemy probably did not expect two marine pilots to be flying in a snowstorm through the mountains.

Our Minnesota Reserve squadron had been one of the first to be called to active duty for Korean service, and within a few weeks I was part of Marine Fighter Squadron VMF-214. Minnesota pilots are accustomed to flying in winter conditions, but not with a ceiling of 300 feet while following a curving road. I put a great deal of trust in Reusser, even though we had known each other only a few days.

Suddenly, there they were—hundreds of vehicles and marines were bunched along a narrow road in a valley completely surrounded by snowy hills that disappeared into higher mountains. There were tanks, artillery, trucks, and many men in bulky clothing. It seemed preposterous that Generals Douglas MacArthur and Edward Almond had ordered two divisions (the other was the Army's 7th Infantry Division) into such a precarious area. Both units were surrounded by Chinese divisions clad in whitish uniforms and situated on the high ground.

We checked in with Dunkirk 1-4, the Marine air controller. Reusser gave him our mission and ordnance load. He had rockets, and I had bombs. Dunkirk's response was an excited, "We are happy to see you Corsairs. Please circle us as long as possible. You're our link to the outside world."

In order to circle over the position we had to keep our power high and flaps down 20 degrees. Those trees and rocky hills could be very unfriendly to an airplane even with a cushion of snow.

I asked Dunkirk if we could drop our external ordnance so we could reduce power and stay on station longer. Dunkirk responded by asking, "Could the plane with bombs drop them on an enemy mortar position behind one of the low hills on a course of about 320 degrees from the three tanks in the open?"

My first response was a rapid increase in heartbeat and metabolic pressures. We had only a few hundred feet of clearance, and the hills decreased that distance. Dropping bombs presented a new challenge. My radio response was, "I'll check it out, Dunkirk, to see if it is possible." Reusser gave me the okay, and I thought to myself that we've violated every rule of safe flying—might as well see if the Corsair can stand low-level bomb blasts.

I broke away from Reusser to get a closer look at the hidden mortar position. By tipping the plane on the left wing, I could get a closer look among the trees. It seemed that I was skimming the treetops when I spotted some tracks and then a human hugging a tree in a mustard-colored uniform. Two other whitish-uniformed people could be made out. My years of hunting and birding probably gave me an edge on observing details in nature that were foreign. A brief report was given to Dunkirk on the observation.

Dunkirk indicated that I was over the position. He cleared me to drop the bombs in that area parallel to the road.

Because of the proximity to the troops I repeated all instructions and told Dunkirk, "I will make one more dummy run over the position before the live drop."

Never before had I dropped any size bomb at such a low altitude. I calculated that my altitude at drop would be a maximum of 300 feet, so my idea was to use a hill as a reflective surface to protect the airplane and the guy inside. Reusser was on the opposite side of the orbit. I flew to the far end of the small valley, pushed the RPM to 2,500 and the manifold pressure to 50 inches. As my turn was shallowed the flaps came up, and bomb and gun safe switches were off. I could feel the nervous perspiration under my helmet and gloves. The canopy was then locked open for a fast low-level bailout if needed. I tilted the plane up one more time for a final check. Then I leveled the wings and in sequence dropped the four 500-lb bombs.

With the release of 2,000 pounds of bombs, the high power settings, and the blast itself, the plane wanted to climb. I pushed the F4U over because the hill gave some protection against the flying debris. The blast was so loud with the canopy open that I couldn't tell whether or not the plane was being hit. The controls were still working. Switches were then returned to safe as I rejoined Reusser.

Dunkirk's comments—"Looks like a perfect hit" and "We love you Corsair people"—were nice to hear.

During the next hour, Reusser got his rockets into suspected enemy sites and we both contributed some 20-mm wing gun fire where Dunkirk directed. Our effort to blunt the tightening enemy noose around the 1st Division apparently gave the ground troops a respite they sorely needed.

Reusser then radioed Dunkirk that we had to return because of low fuel. After an interchange of thank yous and encouragements from us, I tucked in close for the climb out through the "soup." At 6,000 feet we broke into the clear and flew toward our field homer.

Bradley (left) and William Holden during close air support at the Chosin Reservoir.

Reusser gave my plane a check for damage and indicated it looked untouched.

As the homer was passed, our let-down was commenced through the clouds until white caps on the Sea of Japan were observed about 300 feet below. Our return to Yonpo base was routine except for my concern about a possible damaged landing gear not perceived in flight. A thorough ground check after landing found no aircraft damage, so we dragged our tired bodies to the debriefing room. Several ranking marines were there to hear our detailed report on the status of the First Division.

At the debriefing we were given good news. Just as soon as the division was safely out of the Chosin trap, we would be evacuating this area of North Korea. Our planes would be flown to Japan and we then would be using the *Sicily* (CVE-118), under the command of Captain Jimmy Thach, as our base of operation. This was especially good news for me, after flying with VMF-123 off the *Bennington* (CV-20) during the battle for Okinawa in 1945.

This mission around the Chosin Reservoir was one of the most challenging that this aviator had in either World War II or Korea. I believe strongly that naval aviation prepared and continues to prepare pilots to be ready for any assignment, whether flying from land or a carrier, in rain or snow, close or high-altitude support, intercepting enemy aircraft, or flying a tortuous mountain road. My part in a military team where we learned to share, communicate, and sacrifice in order to keep our country strong has made this naval aviator thankful for the opportunity to serve.

At a history conference in Buffalo, Wyoming, in 1989, I met the marine who was Dunkirk 1-4 at the Chosin Reservoir. When he found out that I was involved in the snowstorm close-air mission, he hugged me and exclaimed, "You guys saved our fannies!"

Today, we both are part of an organization called The Chosin Few.

Risky Helicopter Evacuations
By Richard Hansen

World War II was over and we were in the inactive reserve. We could, if we wanted to, resign our commissions and be completely separated from the service; some did. The alternative was to stay in the reserve and join Marine Corps Reserve Fighter Squadron VMF-213.

We would fly one weekend a month at the Minneapolis Naval Air Station and spend two weeks a year on active duty flying out of Minneapolis or the Marine Corps air station at El Toro. We were paid for performing this duty and it didn't take us long to make that decision as we knew we would be flying our beloved Corsairs.

We started flying SNJs in Minneapolis on March 6, 1946. Our Corsairs came to Minneapolis in May and I had my first flight in the Corsair on May 12. The navy had two reserve squadrons flying the Corsairs also. Then in June the Marine Corps added another fighter squadron at Minneapolis.

Minnesota had more navy and Marine Corps pilots per capita in World War II than any other state, and the navy wanted to take advantage of this resource of trained pilots in their reserve arsenal.

It was great to be back in the air again and we took full advantage of getting to fly the iron bird again. We practiced bombing and gunnery over the northern bush country of Minnesota, but without live ammunition. There was one exception to this, when in early summer we dropped depth charges into the bogs to create wallows for the moose to help fend off the black flies.

When we went to El Toro we flew the planes there, and it was great, because there were other marine squadrons there and we saw a lot of our World War II friends. Again we partied pretty hard. At El Toro we used live ammunition in our training and found we were still proficient in gunnery, ground attack bombing, strafing, and rocketing.

This training went on annually until the summer of 1950 when the North Koreans invaded South Korea. Our squadron was called to active duty in August of 1950, four months after I was married. Many other marine squadrons were activated too. We were sent to the Marine Corps air station at El Toro for further assignment.

There was a lot of confusion when we arrived at El Toro because we suddenly had hundreds of pilots and very few airplanes to fly. Over the next few weeks the Marine Corps decided they would need helicopter pilots in Korea, Since very few were currently trained, they drafted a group of fighter pilots, including me, and sent us to

```
                MARINE AIR DETACHMENT
        MARINE AIR RESERVE TRAINING COMMAND
                NAVAL AIR STATION
        MINNEAPOLIS, MINNESOTA.     24 July 1950

    You are hereby directed to report to the Marine Air
Detachment for extended active duty on 1 August 1950.
You are scheduled for a physical examination at 0900
on that date.  It is suggested that you place your
personal affairs in order as quickly as possible.
                            R. K. ROTTET,
                Colonel, U. S. Marine Corps
                        Commanding.
```

Recall notice to Korea.

Quantico, Virginia, to the Marine Corps headquarters helicopter pilot school, HMX-1.

While waiting at El Toro to go to Quantico I did have two flights in the Corsair F4U-4, which was the fastest and most powerful fighter plane in the world at that time. The engine produced 2,450 horsepower. Late in World War II some marine and navy squadrons flew them, but VMF-224, my squadron, did not. This Corsair could carry 6,000 pounds of bombs, rockets, and bullets. The ground troops in Korea, both marines and army, loved this airplane because of the support it gave them in their battles.

In October 1950 I arrived in Quantico, Virginia, at the Marine Corps helicopter school, HMX-1. There was always much activity going on at the base, which was very spit and polished (meaning you looked and acted like a marine, including well polished shoes all the time when in a dress uniform). With the war on in Korea there were high-ranking officers from all the services and foreign dignitaries from our allies coming and going.

After a few weeks of schooling on the mechanics of helicopters I finally had my first training flight on October 16, 1950. I immediately discovered how different they were from fixed wing aircraft, and it would require a lot of training flights just to hold the helicopter stationary off the ground. We started out flying in a twin rotor helicopter, which is more stable than a single rotor machine because the rotors counter-rotate to help stabilize the flight. This helicopter, called the flying banana, was manufactured by the Piasecki Corporation. It was to be used as a troop transport as it could carry about 20 men. The marines did not use this helicopter, however, when I was in Korea.

After a dozen flights in the Piasecki we started to train in the Bell helicopters, the kind you see in the *MASH* films. We used this helicopter the most in Korea. It was a single rotor helicopter that could transport, under ideal conditions, five people: Three people, including the pilot, would be in the bubble, and two would be carried on stretchers outside the bubble.

While at Quantico I had a total of 67 flights in the Piasecki and 80 in the Bell. Only a few of these flights were over 60 minutes, and most of them less than that. I did take some high-ranking naval and marine officers to the naval academy at Annapolis, Maryland, and then to the naval air station at Mustin, New Jersey, in the Piasecki on January 5, 1951. Better than that, I flew Santa Claus into Washington National Airport on December 20, 1951.

My last flight at Quantico was March 21, 1951. I went home for two weeks and was then ordered to El Toro, and then San Diego, to the naval port of debarkation where I boarded a ship for the Orient. I don't remember where I disembarked, but I think it was Yokuska, Japan. From there I was flown to Seoul, Korea, and then in a Marine Corps DC-3 to the First Marine Division Command Post at Hongchon, Korea, on June 12.

The next day, June 13, I had eight flights and carried eight evacuations (wounded) to three different hospitals from three different command posts. I spent eight hours accomplishing this, and I said to myself, "What in the hell am I doing here?"

That night I walked over to a tent where the dead boys' bodies were in body bags, and as the tears welled up in my eyes I saluted them and I said to myself, "I will never complain again." I wished I was back in the killing game in the Corsair, but what I was doing was badly needed.

Besides the Bell helicopters we had two Sikorski H03S helicopters in our squadron, which they did not have at Quantico. On June 16 and 17 I flew the Sikorski on two medical evacuations. They were underpowered, as were the Bells, and to carry a litter we had to put it through the two side windows with the patient's head and feet sticking outside the machine. The general, whom we flew often, liked them because he sat behind the pilot, and there were three seats side by side. It was convenient for him to study his maps and converse with his field commanders that we picked up as we flew to various battle areas.

One other feature of the H03S was a cable hoist used to lift a person from the ground or life raft while the helicopter remained airborne on a rescue mission.

The workhorse, of course, was the Bell helicopter, which helped us evacuate over 10,000 wounded marines. When we were in battle we were generally fighting in the mountains, with the enemy on one ridge and our troops on another. When we went to get the wounded, the troops would level a small area on the ridge with their shovels so we could land for a minute while the wounded were put in the litters. We would hover just below the ridge, out of enemy view, until they were ready for us. Then we'd pop up and sit down on the leveled spot. While waiting below the ridge we were often mortared because the enemy knew we were waiting there but couldn't see us; on occasion mortar shrapnel would hit us.

While we were sitting on the ridge loading the wounded, enemy snipers would shoot at us, and our snipers would be shooting back at them, so there was always a big rush to get loaded and out of there. If there was only one wounded to transport, the medics would have to put a boulder in the litter on the opposite side of the helicopter to balance the weight. After the patients were in place we would rev up our engine and jump off the ridge into the valley between our lines and the enemy lines. We had to do this to pick up speed and altitude to get out of the valley as quickly as possible. We knew all hell would break loose; and it was always an exciting moment. We had to exit this way because the Bell did not have the power to lift up and back off.

In July, Errol Flynn, the movie actor, came to Korea with Delores Gray, an actress, along with some other entertainers, to put on a show for the troops. I was picked to fly Errol and Delores around to the various battalions that were not on the line that day. They both were very nice and it was a fun day. Delores sat between Errol and myself and, being the lover he was, Errol's hand was on Delores's leg the whole time. Delores responded by putting her hand on my leg, which was fine by me. When we parted, Delores put her arms around my neck, pulled me close to her, and gave me a first class kiss.

On August 10 I flew one of the Sikorski's to Pohang, South Korea, to await the carrier *Princeton* on its trip to Japan from its duty station off of North Korea. The next morning I flew out about 50 miles and rendezvoused with the carrier and went aboard. I was taking the helicopter to the navy repair facility at Yokosuka, Japan, getting some R & R while there.

Hansen (middle) with Delores Gray and Errol Flynn

I discovered some of my fellow pilots from VMF-213 were there, too, on R & R, so we spent a few days together. They were flying off of a carrier and kept kidding me how nice it was aboard the carrier with good food and nice beds, while I was eating outside in a chow line and living in a tent. I told them I had it pretty good, too, because I was with Errol Flynn's girlfriend, Delores Gray. I did not elaborate.

These guys were good pilots and good friends. In fact, we still meet once a month at the Fort Snelling Officers' Club and talk about the wars and our comrades. We were almost all in World War II and Korea. In Korea, fifteen of us went overseas and seven were killed, three in accidents.

On August 26 I was back in the war carrying wounded and flying the Sikorskis. The First Marine Division was then pulled back from the front to relocate the command post and VMO-6, our squadron, moved too. On August 30 I flew two helicopter mechanics up to the front and stayed there while they fixed one of our Bells. We were on the side of a hill, but the enemy couldn't see us even though we were only 300 yards from them. Later another helicopter came up and I flew the repaired one back to our encampment.

We operated out of the riverbeds as we had some OY observation planes in our squadron that flew over the front lines to observe the battlefields. These planes had a pilot and an observer, the latter generally being a line company officer. The observer was in contact by radio with the ground forces. These planes required a landing strip, and the only flat areas were in the riverbeds. I did check out in an OY in the event they were short of pilots and needed one, but that didn't happen.

In September and October the war continued at a quickened pace and we transported wounded constantly. One day a wounded boy who had been shot in the head had worked himself loose of the restraint straps on his litter while we were 1,000 feet in the air. He was sitting up, pounding on the side of the engine compartment of the helicopter. I had to land in a hurry in a rice paddy and put the straps back on him. Otherwise, if he had fallen or jumped out, the helicopter would have turned over in mid-air because of the unequal weight, and crashed.

We delivered the wounded to field hospitals where they were examined. If they were bad enough, they were transported by ambulance to the division hospital, or if it was too late, to the morgue. If the wounds were minor they were treated at the field hospital and sent back to their company. War is hell.

Pilot's Ready Room
By Lyle Bradley

Meeting Charles Lindbergh, playing a game of poker or bridge, planning a strike against the enemy, having a song fest, seeing tears in pilots' eyes, or listening to Tokyo Rose are activities I recall about ready rooms. It is a spot for aviators to relax, laugh, meditate, question, and plan for survival.

No one has ever designed the perfect ready room—it can be a tent, a spot under a tree, a room in an aircraft carrier, a building space at an airfield, or even a place under the wing of an airplane. It is a spot where pilots can mix, plan, review, question, swear, and feel happy or sad. Besides human voices of pilots there are other sounds with these areas such as radios, teletypes, and song records. There are also odors associated with ready rooms—sweaty flight suits, food, and a few medications.

Getting to learn voices of fellow pilots is important, especially when there is only one person in the plane. Carbon monoxide, hypothermia, illness, or injury will affect a pilot's voice. Knowing a voice well can make the difference whether another pilot can help the person in danger get to safety.

Some places, like the aircraft carriers, have minimum space for libraries or a reading room. Ready rooms are great spots for reading aircraft handbooks, aviation magazines, briefing reports, recognition manuals, and some good books that float throughout the area.

On the two aircraft carriers I lived on, the USS *Bennington* in World War II and the USS *Sicily* during the Korean War, pilots spent

Bradley (left) and Wally Jung, who was killed one week after photo, outside Ready Room in Korea.

more time in the ready room than in their rooms sleeping or in their planes flying. We flew about three days a week, then the ship had to refuel.

During briefings for missions, the ready room was quiet with attentive pilots. Briefings were given by senior officers, intelligence staff, landing signal officers (LSOs), division leaders, or squadron commanding officers. Maps were posted on the walls and used for briefings. Updates were given on survival, such as position of friendly submarines and destroyers for pilot pickups, current radio frequencies, and positions of enemy antiaircraft (AA) and aircraft. The latest recommendations on leaving a damaged airplane, as well as clothes best to wear for ground survival if shot down (aviators are not well liked by the enemy), are constantly discussed.

Engineering officers, crew chiefs, and experienced pilots update others on the best way to preserve fuel and care for the engine. Charles Lindbergh and other pioneer aviators helped our cause in World War II with their aviation experience.

There are kind words and caustic words exchanged between pilots. Because we never know who we will fly with the next day it is wise to respect and try to be friendly with all members of the squadron. At times a pilot's life might be in the hands of another pilot. The ready room is the spot to hash out problems in a tactful manner. There is no better spot to solidify the team effort and concepts than in the interactions that take place in a pilot's ready room.

An Orphanage in Korea
By Harry Anderson

I maintained my reserve status by flying and going to school in the Marine Corps. I went back to active duty as an assistant G-1 at the Naval Air Station in Glenview, Illinois, which was the headquarters of the Marine Corps Reserves. We were busy getting ready to go to Korea. We were sent to El Toro, California, to go into F4U close air support training.

As senior officer I was in charge of the twenty-fifth draft of pilots to go to Korea.

We were stationed at K-3 in Korea, which was the jet base for the Marine Corps. I was ordered to VMF-212, a Corsair squadron. Eventually I became the operational officer. Our daily flight schedules came from Strike Command in Seoul, Korea. A Korean group requested a meeting with a member of the "low-flying whistling death squadron." We were notified that our support for the ground troops was outstanding. They also told us that a plane could land on the beach at Chodo Island (located in the Yellow Sea north of the 38th Parallel) for a meeting. I took the mission and landed with no problem.

One of our strike orders was for 18 planes to go to the Manchurian border with bombs, napalm, and delay bombs to hit a railroad target along the border with North Korea. The mission was a success. The target was completely demolished.

One of the pilots checked the area north of the target while I circled to see what his intentions were. After repeated contacts, which had not been answered, I was running out of gas and decided to head back. The rest of the flight aircraft were long gone. Over Seoul, Korea, I ran out of gas and was over Kimpo Army Air Force Field. I coasted into half of the runway when the tower ordered, "Marine Corsair get out of the runway." After I explained that I was out of gas after a strike mission, a tow truck came to pull me to a refueling truck and I was on my way back to our home base.

After 101 missions I was assigned as the city engineer. This entailed all garbage, fuel, ordnance disposal, water works, 125 indigenous personnel, and general maintenance of all buildings.

A Catholic priest asked me to visit an orphanage near our base. The children had very little food, clothing, or heat, and the water was contaminated. With donations from various places, aid was given to these children. Doug Dreifus flew replacements into Korea on a regular basis. I called him in El Toro and asked him to bring me a case of Canadian Club Whiskey, as I found out from the major that he hadn't been home for two years and that he liked CC. That was also my bargaining chip to get unused cement from the army, which the Koreans used to construct a building to house the children. This was very much appreciated by the orphans and their caregivers.

Radio and Radar

By Sherman Booen

In 1946 I was commissioned Captain Executive Officer Marine Air Reserve stationed at the Naval Air Station, Radar Squadron 16. All squadrons were called to active duty in July 1950 and sent to Korea. I was assigned Communications Officer First Marine Airwing. The pilots of the Minnesota Marine Reserve went immediately to combat. Six pilots were killed flying ground support missions in the famous Corsair.

In October 1950, General Field Harris asked me to fly to Tokyo, headquarters of naval command, to determine why marine combat missions were not mentioned in news dispatches. I reported to operations and my airplane was an old TBM torpedo bomber. The pilot was Lyle Bradley of the Minnesota Air Reserve. I was settled in the bomb

Jim Christy and Booen (right).

bay where I could not see the pilot but heard him call out, "How the hell do I start this thing?" Lyle had never flown a TBM, but we got there anyway.

While at Naval headquarters I was assigned to the Armed Forces Radio Network Far East (AFRES). As operations officer I managed the radio station, 100,000 watts in Tokyo, and read the six o'clock news. I was responsible for news reports security and devised a manner of preventing premature news releases from reaching the enemy. The army awarded me a Commendation Medal ribbon.

Returning stateside I went back to WCCO-TV and also rejoined the Marine Air Reserve where I was assigned commanding officer of Radar 16 for a four-year term. During that time I helped design and build new and better intercept radar.

Booen with state-of-the-art radar equipment.

Close Air Support at the Chosin Reservoir
By Darrell Smith

One of the main missions in Korea for the marine air wing was close air support for marine ground troops. It was very effective in supporting the First Marine Division at the Chosin Reservoir. Following the successful invasion of Inchon on the west coast of South Korea and the retreat of the North Koreans, the division was taken by sea around the southern tip of Korea and up to Wonsan on the east side of North Korea.

Because of the delays they encountered, we were already flying out of the Wonsan airfield when they arrived and we had the pleasure of welcoming the ground forces to North Korea. They passed through the airfield in a long convoy to the only road that led to their assigned objective, the area surrounding the Chosin Reservoir, some 100 miles north of Wonsan. The first half of the road was fairly open, flat ground at sea level. The second half went into mountains as high as 6,000 feet. The road wound through the mountains and often along narrow valleys between the peaks. We were flying cover for them all the way up and were quite familiar with the terrain.

Meanwhile the army was moving north along the west side of Korea and the South Korean Army (ROKs) was moving north in the center. Back in Japan the high command was ordering all units to race toward the Manchurian border, assuring every one that the Chinese would not enter the conflict. The rumor was that we would all be home for Christmas.

The marine commanders, who were with their troops, were not so sure, and as they moved north they left some of their units at small

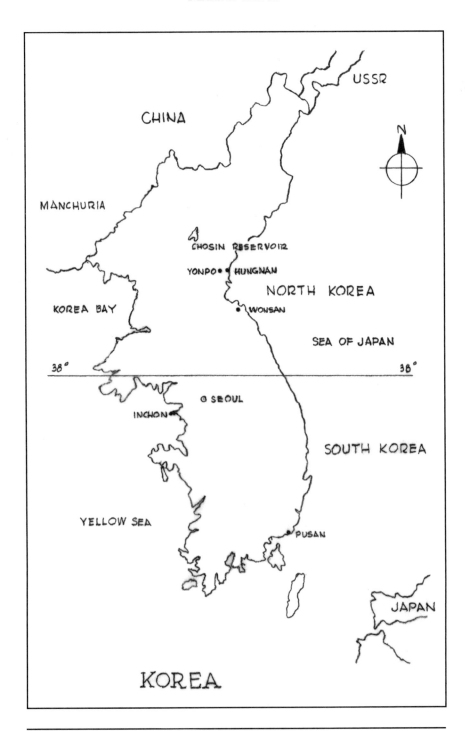

KOREA

villages along the way to keep the one road out of the mountains open.

In late November 1950, the Chinese did cross over into North Korea 300,000 strong! The army and the ROKs broke into a rapid retreat, leaving the Chinese free to swing east with the intention of eliminating the First Marine Division.

The key to marine close air support was a forward air controller (FAC), an experienced marine fighter pilot on the ground working directly with the division unit commanders. He knew exactly what the situation on the ground was and what our capabilities and limitations were for close air support. Each FAC usually had a jeep and was equipped with a radio that could be tuned to the same frequencies as our Corsairs. Any strikes we made, unless directed otherwise, were made under his control, and we almost always made a dry run, which he approved, to be sure we were on the right target.

On the day the Chinese appeared, the unit of the division farthest north was northwest of the reservoir almost 100 miles north of Wonsan. From the air their position looked hopeless. Chinese were everywhere, and I remember thinking they looked like a swarming colony of ants. When I returned from the first flight and debriefed, I had to say I couldn't bet a nickel on any one getting out of those mountains alive. I was wrong!

We were able to help the marines during the day, but during the night when the Chinese were most active, they were pretty much on their own. Each morning at the crack of dawn we would take off, fly up to check in with the FACs, fearing they had been overrun and there would be no answer. Each morning there was a response. They were still there and somehow they were holding their own, but we knew their situation was desperate.

The book for close air support called for the FACs to go through channels up to central command and down through our channels to the squadrons. This was to keep every one informed, but what was happening was that a call for help made in the morning would some times reach the squadrons late in the afternoon. That wasn't good enough. The FACs needed the support when they made the calls.

Then someone, or some group, made a decision that saved a lot of lives. One morning a marine R4D—a Douglas two-engine transport plane—appeared circling over the combat area. It had radios that could contact all the FACs and all our aircraft. As soon as our flights were in the air we could call the R4D, give them the number of planes in the flight (most of the time four, but sometimes only two) and the ordnance we were carrying, and they could send us right to the FAC that needed help the most. We could be over them in minutes. Soon we had flights on station with the R4D that could be sent as soon as the calls came in. We thought there was only one R4D but I was told later by one of the pilots that there were actually three, rotating to be sure one was always on station.

One strike we made still sticks in my mind. The marine convoy was stopped by a roadblock where the road ran along the base of a high ridge and was taking fire from a large group of Chinese dug in along the top of the ridge. They had to take that high ground before they could clear the road and move on. Our four-plane division was directed by the FAC to make our approach right over the top of the convoy and up the side of the ridge, strafing the area where the Chinese were dug in. After a dry run to be sure we had the right target, we went in one behind the other so we could see the planes ahead and avoid a mid-air collision.

On one of the early passes I could also see our people from the convoy running up the side of the ridge right under us. When the planes ahead would go over them and start firing, they would duck down and cover their heads, then jump up and start running again until the next plane went over, at which time they stopped and ducked again. I couldn't understand why they were doing this until some time later when one of them explained that when we started firing our six 50-caliber machine guns, the shell casings came raining down on them from the bottom of our wings, casings which were not only hard but also hot. We ended up dropping napalm at the top and our guys soon had the high ground. I'm sure this kind of action took place many times as the convoy fought its way out of the mountains.

Soon after the R4D appeared I landed at Wonsan from a late afternoon strike. The operations officer met me at the plane and told me to go get my gear as soon as the plane was refueled; I was to take it to Yonpo. All our planes and squadrons were being sent there because there were heavily trenched hills along one end of the Wonsan airfield and if the Chinese moved in there, we would be sitting ducks. Also, Yonpo was some 40 miles closer to the reservoir and on flat open ground that could be better defended. I had seen Yonpo on flights to the reservoir but it was only one surfaced strip with an oval parking area at the far end and no taxiways to get off the strip after landing. Yet some squadrons were already operating from there.

Although we never liked to send one plane alone, I was sent off as soon as the plane was refueled and armed. No sweat! Yonpo was only 40 miles north! But that flight turned out to be one of my most harrowing experiences. As I approached the strip it began to snow with dusk setting in. There were a number of planes, mostly Corsairs, circling the strip. Some were returning from strikes and low on fuel, some had been diverted from carriers where it was snowing too. All these planes were trying to call the tower, but the tower couldn't help because it couldn't see the strip or most of the planes in the air because of the snow. When I joined the traffic pattern, which was normally at 1,000 feet, we were down to about 600 feet trying to keep the strip in sight. Because of the snow no one knew where the other planes were and we were all funneling into a single landing strip, hoping no one was just above or below or along side us. We were also hoping that if we made the strip we wouldn't overrun someone ahead of us, or that someone behind wouldn't overrun us.

On my first final approach a Corsair suddenly appeared out of the snow to my right and slightly ahead. I knew he couldn't see me and it was too close for me to land behind him. I had to go around for another try. By the time I got around to the downwind leg I was down to about 400 feet and barely able to keep the strip in sight. On the second final I could barely see the strip and I knew I had to take a chance. I just went ahead and landed and got off the strip into the parking area as quickly as I could without overrunning someone ahead of me. As I shut down the plane another Corsair taxied out of the snow and stopped beside me. It was an old squadron mate from World War II that I hadn't seen since Okinawa. We closed the cockpit hatches and walked together through the snow for what seemed like half a mile toward some lights that turned out to be the damaged buildings I'd seen from the air. We agreed that we could both use a drink, but there was no bar yet at Yonpo.

The next morning there was a fully armed Corsiar laying on its back off the end of the strip. In the falling snow it had landed too far down the strip. We lost one airplane that night, but I was told that the pilot got out okay.

I don't know how the rest of the squadron got to Yonpo from Wonsan but they were there the next morning. It was now late December and it was getting cold enough so our ground crews had to start the engines during the night to keep them warm. If the engines got too cold they just wouldn't start. All the maintenance and ordnance people were working day and night outside, some days in subzero weather even at sea level, but each morning and throughout the day they kept all the planes that were flyable ready and armed to go. There was no

Corsair that was lost while landing in snowstorm at Yonpo.

complaining—they just did it because every one knew that 6,000 feet up in the mountains it was much, much worse.

The situation with the Division was still desperate but the convoy was slowly moving back down the only road out, stopped many times when they encountered strong Chinese opposition. But still they moved south. When they cleared the mountains and came by Yonpo on their way to the sea to evacuate, many of those who made it through stopped to thank us saying, "Without you and your Corsairs we would never have gotten out of there."

From Yonpo we flew continuous strikes every day except one because it snowed again and we couldn't get off the ground. We often stayed by the plane while it was refueled and rearmed and went right back up to the R4D for the next strike. Coming back from my last flight to the reservoir the engine began to miss. When I landed at Yonpo I went in to down the plane because of the engine problem. They told me the squadron was leaving that afternoon and I could either fly that plane to Japan or go out with the division. I learned that as soon as the planes could be refueled, a B-25 was going to lead the Corsairs across the Sea of Japan, and I decided to go with them. Probably not a wise decision with a questionable engine, but I wanted to stay with my squadron. As we flew toward Japan the engine seemed to gradually run smoother. Maybe it was just tired and needed a little rest, but I think it was just as glad to leave North Korea as I was. We didn't get home for Christmas but we did get back to Japan.

Being part of that effort to help get those people out of those mountains was the most satisfying part of my recall to active duty. We knew that we were helping them escape from a terribly desperate situation.

The Odenbaugh Affair
By Lyle Bradley

I met Tom Odenbaugh in the ready room of VMF-234 at the Naval Air Station in Minneapolis, Minnesota, in March 1949. We discovered that both of us were students at Iowa State University in Ames, Iowa. Our addresses at college were exchanged and we vowed to consolidate our driving to USMC reserve meetings each month.

Tom was an engineering student and I was a science student. His hometown was Ottumwa, Iowa, and mine was Dubuque, Iowa. He was married with a baby daughter and I was single. He smoked cigarettes and I smoked cigars. Both of us were second lieutenants. Over the next several months of driving the Iowa and Minnesota roads together, sipping beer or coffee and discovering common interests, we became close friends. Our interests in hunting, aviation, history, and women were parallel.

In July I returned from crop spraying to get ready for our squadron's annual maneuvers. Tom and I flew a fun tactics hop in Corsairs. We polished up on some formation aerobatics that both of us loved.

At the Cherry Point MCAS in August, we were assured by a USMC general that there was no plan to recall reserve squadrons for the Korean War that had started on June 25, 1950. We flew back to Minnesota after our two weeks of active duty and read in the Minneapolis newspaper that our squadron was being recalled. I drove back to my home in Dubuque and found my orders awaiting me. I had one week to prepare to go to war again. I sold my 1936 Reo auto that was in mint condition for $80. (Today because of its rarity it is worth about $300,000.)

Our Corsairs were left in Minnesota and all of us in our squadron were flown to the west coast. When I asked Tom how he felt about leaving his wife and daughter he replied, "If I don't return they'll be in better financial shape than they are now."

Our two-week trip to Japan on the USS *Antolac*, a troopship, was very relaxing. Tom and I got in several poker games, played chess, did some birding, talked aviation, and helped an artillery major train some new recruits.

We landed in Kobe, Japan, and were trucked to a World War II Japanese air base where we were put into a pilot pool. Pilots hate these pools because there is no flying and much waiting. A bright spot, however, was that it gave us an opportunity to visit Japan, a country that we had fought just five years earlier.

After a week in the pool a major announced that he was accepting volunteer pilots to join VMO-6, a squadron in Korea flying OY spotting planes for artillery and rescue missions. Tom Odenbaugh was the first to volunteer. He said, "Anything is better than this pilot pool." He departed the next morning to fly to Korea. When I shook his hand as he was ready to leave, I didn't realize that would be our last meeting.

About a week later I met a Captain Brown, a USMC artillery officer, at our officers' club. He had just returned from Korea for some supplies. In our conversation he gave me an update on the war. He also had close contact with the VMO-6 squadron. He indicated that they had lost two pilots in the past week.

When I inquired if he heard the names of the pilots, he checked his notebook and had both names—one was Tom Odenbaugh. He then relayed how Tom and an observer were giving his artillery unit information on how their rounds were targeting some North Korean trucks. Their plane was hit and started to smoke. The prop was windmilling and Tom dead-sticked the plane in a brushy field. The plane was immediately surrounded by a North Korean patrol. He had watched the entire episode with binoculars but could not fire weapons for fear of hitting Tom and his observer. The observer might have been killed because he never appeared to move. Tom got out of the cockpit with some effort as though he might have been hit also. He held his hands up, dropped his .38 pistol to the ground, and offered cigarettes to the North Korean troops. He was then led away with a North Korean soldier on each side of him for support and security. This took place at sunset. Next morning the plane and the men were gone. He finished his observation saying, "Im sorry about your friend and if I uncover any more information I will get it to you." With that we traded our current addresses and names and departed.

After Tom's departure for Korea I was assigned as a communication officer on the base headquarters. About 10 days later I received a letter from Tom's mother indicating she had received a letter from the defense department that Tom had been killed in Korea. She wanted me to get more detailed information on his death. I immediately sent her a return letter describing my conversation with Captain Brown.

She then called the defense department and all hell broke lose. I received a radiogram from Marine Corps headquarters in Washington asking how I could countermand their report. They instructed (ordered) me to get a signed statement from Captain Brown on all details about Odenbaugh's capture.

This meant I had to fly to Korea, find Captain Brown, and get the information requested by the Department of Defense. I checked out the only Corsair on our field, flew to Kimpo, Korea, checked out an OY aircraft, and flew to the VMO-6 area. I then took a jeep to where Captain Brown's artillery unit was located. It took me two days to find him and get the correct information along with his signature. The return trip was uneventful but it cost me two days of liberty.

Over the next months I received several letters from the Department of Defense. I felt like a terrorist or spy. Years later when I checked my file in Washington, DC, almost two inches of paperwork concerned that episode.

About a week following the letter from Tom's mother I was assigned to VMF-214 at Wonson, North Korea. We were flying Corsairs for which I had been trained. Within days we were helping the Marine First Division who were pinned down at the Chosin Reservoir by a Chinese army.

Tom never returned after the war was over. The POW lists never gave his name. We have wondered whether he was sent to Russia—there are no answers yet. About 1985 his daughter, now in her thirties, came to our home seeking information about her father whom she had never known. We traded addresses so that if either of us ever received any information about Tom we could pass it on.

Tom left a bright spot in my memory. He was very intelligent, an excellent pilot, a superb poker and chess player, a good officer, and a great friend. His name comes up frequently among his marine pilot friends.

Tom left a dark spot on my memory with his departure.

Called Back For Korea
By Darrell Smith

In 1950 I was flying Corsairs in VMF-213, one of two marine reserve fighter squadrons based in Minneapolis. Our two weeks of active duty that year were scheduled for August at Cherry Point North Carolina. Since we had more pilots than airplanes, about half of the pilots were assigned to fly the Corsairs down there and the rest went down on marine transport aircraft. Then the ones who rode the transports down would get to fly Corsairs back.

I had been married in June 1949, but because I had just graduated from the university and started my first job, I didn't get any time off for vacation. Now in 1950 we had our first two-week vacation coming and I was able to schedule it right after the two weeks of active duty. This meant a month away from work, quite a concession from my manager.

I was in the group that was going to fly the Corsairs to Cherry Point and we were able to arrange for Jeannette and the wife of one of the other pilots to drive our car down. Then Jeannette and I could drive from Cherry Point up the east coast to Maine and back along the Great Lakes to Minnesota. A great plan, including a delayed two-week honeymoon. Then things began to come apart, and for me the one month away from work turned into 10 months.

On the last day of our two weeks of active duty a general came down from Washington, DC, to brief us on current events that might involve the marines. Among other things he mentioned that there was some commotion in a place somewhere near Japan called Korea. They didn't think it would amount to much and he assured us that if we were needed we would get at least one month's notice. When the squadrons arrived back in Minneapolis the next day, orders to active duty for VMF-213 were already waiting for us. "Why us?" someone asked. "Because you are the most ready," was the reply. As young folks would say today, "Yeah, right!"

We were to be at El Toro, the marine west coast air station, in two weeks. I don't know if the general that briefed us back in Cherry Point the day before knew about this or not, but I'm inclined to give him the benefit of the doubt.

Meanwhile, Jeannette and I were happily touring up the east coast totally unaware of what was happening.

No one knew where we were! The squadron finally contacted my brother. He knew that if I was ever called back to active duty I would really want to go with my unit. He started calling collect (no charge in those days if you didn't get your party) any place along the east coast where we might stop—with no luck! He also called some friends in Cleveland, Ohio, where I told him we might stop to visit. We did, in fact, decide to stop there. When we arrived on Thursday of the second week our friends passed on the news. I called my brother right away and he told me VMF-213 was to leave Minneapolis, by air, for El Toro on Sunday morning. "You're kidding me," was all I could say. But he was dead serious.

We left Cleveland that night, drove straight through, and got to Minneapolis on Saturday. I packed my gear and trunk locker, which we were told we could bring, and was on one of the DC3s with the other pilots when it left Sunday about 2:00 P.M.. This left Jeannette pretty much high and dry, but I knew she had two brothers that could help her, and she could move back to her mother's house and she would be all right.

When we arrived at El Toro we expected to be activated as a squadron. Instead we found that the regular squadrons had been cut to half strength as the result of peacetime budget cuts and they were breaking up the reserve squadrons to fill vacancies in the regular squadrons. This was scary because some of the reserve pilots wound up in non-flying jobs; in fact, anywhere there was a position that needed to be filled. So much for all our efforts to stay with VMF-213—the squadron no longer existed!

When my turn came up for assignment, I could hardly believe what happened. I was put back in VMF-312 as a pilot. This was the squadron that I had flown with for nearly three years during World War II. It was now one of the regular squadrons that was being filled out. The downside was that it was to go over to Korea in just days, but I was happy. I was going to be flying. Even the squadron identity on my trunk locker was the same. They just tossed it on one of the trucks that was taking our gear to San Diego to be loaded on board a small transport carrier that was to take us and our Corsairs to Japan.

The carrier had been pulled out of mothballs up in Bremerton, Washington. When it arrived we learned that it was run on steam and had two evaporators, only one of which was working. Nonetheless we were loaded on board and started out for Japan. About 700 miles out of San Diego and about 300 miles off the coast of San Francisco the evaporator that was working decided to go out, and we were dead in the water. No showers or other unnecessary activities. We did have electricity and lights, probably from some generators. We expected to be towed somewhere, but instead they flew a repair crew out in a PBY and got the one evaporator going again. We thought we would be going to San Francisco for more extensive repairs. Instead, we took off for the Hawaiian Islands. I can only guess there were better facilities there for fixing the problem than elsewhere. Then again, what's wrong with the Hawaiian Islands!

We docked in Pearl Harbor behind the battleship *Missouri* and were given 24-hour liberty. Some of us stayed at the Royal Hawaiian Hotel at Waikiki Beach where we were privileged guests at $35 a day for two people. Nothing wrong with that. Two of us also rented a Piper Cub and flew all the way around Oahu. But most of our time was spent on the beach. After four or five days they had both evaporators on the ship working and we were off for Japan again.

The rest of the trip was pretty tame. We spent quite a bit of time sunning on the carrier deck and reading. Then one morning we woke up to find we were docked at Kobe, Japan, and they had already started unloading. Somehow I wound up all alone sitting on top of a truckload of crates that I was to guard with my 38-caliber revolver, a gun that I had not yet fired. We finally formed into a convoy and drove about 20 miles to Itami, the marine air base in Japan. We arrived there about noon and were told to drop off our gear in a small building that would be our quarters and go get lunch. While I was standing in line our operations officer came running up and said, "Go get your flight gear. I've got a one-hour familiarization hop for you in an F4U-4, but you have to take it right now."

We had flown the F4U-1D in World War II and in the reserves, but VMF-312 now had F4U-4s, a later version of the Corsair that had more power and a four-blade prop to harness that power. But more important, it had a totally different cockpit arrangement, one I was not familiar with and had never flown. I wasn't familiar with the area or terrain, either, and I had no map. I did have contact with the tower, however, so I flew around the area for an hour keeping the tower in sight. With all the changes, I was happy to find that the F4U-4 flew just like the F4U-1D. When I landed safely I was considered checked out in the F4U-4.

As I taxied up and shut down, the operations officer was standing on the ramp waiting for me and said, "Go get all your gear—you're going to Korea." I had been selected as part of an advance detail of four officers and about twenty enlisted men. In a quick briefing we were told that General MacArthur's invasion of Incheon, to be made by the Marine First Division, was under way. Their objective was to cut off the North Korean army that had already taken most of South Korea. As soon as Kimpo, the municipal airfield for the capitol city of Seoul, was taken, we were to occupy and hold an area that would already be chosen for our squadron. Of the four officers, two of us were marine reserve pilots who had combat experience in World War II, but no training in ground operations. The other two were regular postwar pilots who had never been in combat, but outranked us because the regulars had been promoted faster than the reserves. We were not exactly suited for the task at hand!

Nevertheless we were each issued some extra gear including, of all things, a World War II folding trench shovel. We then went aboard an air force four-engine transport plane with bucket seats and were on our way to Korea about 4:00 P.M..

Because the North Koreans had already taken most of South Korea, the air force pilots had been told to go to the southern most island of Japan, get a clearance from the people at an airfield there, then go around the southern tip of Korea and up the west side to Kimpo. By the time we got to the southern island it was getting dark and we were flying in a thunderstorm and heavy rain. When the pilots checked in by radio with the tower that was supposed to clear us on to Korea, they had no idea who we were or why we were there and refused to clear us.

It was finally decided that we should land and try to get things straightened out. Earlier I had been talking with the pilots and knew that the airfield was in a narrow valley surrounded by mountains. Now we were going to land there through a rainstorm, at night, on instruments, on a field they had never landed on. I said a silent prayer that we wouldn't wind up on the side of one of those mountains. When we finally touched down I began to breath again. By this time it was close to midnight and I remembered I had not eaten since breakfast on the carrier.

Around 2:00 A.M. we were finally cleared for Korea. We took off in the rainstorm, on instruments again, in the dark, through a narrow path between the mountains. I began breathing easily again after we cleared the mountains. By the time we went around the southern tip of Korea and up to Kimpo, it was just cracking dawn. I was standing between the pilot and copilot, talking with them as we approached for the landing, and could see a couple of trucks burning on the field. The runway was clear, however. Suddenly the copilot turned to me and said, "Go back and get your guys ready to leave. We just got word to drop you off and to take right off again." That should have told me something.

We stopped about halfway down the runway. With all four engines still running they opened the back door, dropped a rope ladder, and we all scrambled down the ladder while their crewman threw out our extra gear. They pulled up the ladder, closed the door and were gone. Almost immediately a group of flares went up about twenty feet from us and blossomed over our heads, really shaking us up until we realized what they were. It turned out that the marines had set out the flares during the night to alert them to any infiltration by the North Koreans. A stray dog had come over to greet us and had run through the trip wires, scaring himself even more than us. Before we recovered from that a marine major came roaring up behind us and said something like, "Who the hell are you and what are you doing out here?" We told him hurriedly and he pointed across the runway and said, "That's supposed to be your area—for God's sake get over there and dig in. We haven't taken this field yet!" The marines were on one end of the field and the North Koreans on the other, and we had landed in the middle.

We did have our trench shovels and we spent most of the rest of the day digging foxholes. Fortunately the North Koreans were on the run, and during the day the marines took the airfield. We, however, were not out of the woods yet and didn't get to sleep in our foxholes that night. During the day another advance detail from our air group arrived and about 4:00 P.M. called the four of us flyboys to a meeting. They told us that the ground marines were moving on to help take back Seoul, the capitol city of South Korea. They had agreed to leave two small tanks behind for a day because they hadn't had time to clear out a small village near our side of the field. There could still be North Koreans in there that would infiltrate our area. We were going to have to stand our own perimeter defense that night!

None of the four of us knew how to set up a perimeter defense. But we were given carbines and the enlisted men rifles and out we went. About half of the men were kids that had joined our air reserve squadrons back in the states. Some of them didn't know how to fire

Duplex foxhole at Kimpo, Korea, 1950.

a rifle or even how to load one. But the regular marines that were in our group did, and they did their best to check every one out.

The tanks were already set up about 75 yards apart and we were to cover the area in between. There was a small ridge running between the tanks about three feet high and looked like it had been bulldozed out when the field had been leveled. So we set up behind that facing the village. We had about ten positions of two men each spread evenly between the two tanks. The four of us planned to take turns moving during the night behind the ridge, between the positions to keep in touch with them and to check on how every one was doing. As it grew dark we sat and waited. This was a long way from flying Corsairs.

There was a clear sky and moonlight early, but later clouds moved in and it got very dark. We then began to find some of the men dropping off to sleep. True, they hadn't gotten much sleep the night before on the plane, they had spent a long day digging holes in the ground, and some of them were just kids. But this was troubling. Some of them seemed to have no idea that we could get killed out there.

Things stayed very quiet till a little after midnight. Suddenly a machine gun opened fire. Then another one. In the dark we couldn't see what was going on, but it seemed to be coming from the area where the tanks were. It turned out that we were right. One of them thought they saw movement and started shooting. It was the other tank. It fired back, probably thinking it was taking fire from the North Koreans. Fortunately our people were behind the ridge and not quite in the direct line of fire, but there were a lot of tracers flying by and we had a grandstand seat. It was frightening at the time because none of us knew what was going on. As far as I know no one even got hurt, but we didn't have any trouble keeping people awake for the rest of the night.

The Korean village on the edge of the airstrip
from which we expected a North Korean attack.

The next day more people and equipment came in and we were relieved from our perimeter defense. We got to sleep in our foxholes until some tents came in. Eventually our squadron and planes came in too, and we went back to flying Corsairs.

Foe To Friend
By Lyle Bradley

Two months past the start of the Korean War (June 25, 1950) found our Minnesota Marine Corps reserve Corsair squadron (VMF-234) recalled to active duty. Upon arriving in Osaka, Japan, we aviators were placed in a "pilot pool." This is not a good spot for those who opt to fly. I was snatched the first week to become a communications officer for which I had no training. The job was both fascinating and boring, along with great liberty—24 hours on and 48 hours off.

On a liberty sojourn to Nara, Japan (a beautiful city untouched by World War II), I was sipping tea in the rail station after a day of touring. Across the tea-bar was a Japanese man who glared at me. I was in uniform with my wings and I knew there was some resentment against aviators. When the gentleman got off his stool and walked toward me, I turned so he would not catch me off guard, especially if he had violent intentions.

About six feet from me he asked in perfect English, "What type plane do you fly?" I replied with a smile, "Mostly Corsairs." His response was quick, "Aso—Whistling Death—they are good airplanes. I was a Japanese pilot also." I continued, "What plane did you fly?" He responded, "Kawasaki twin-engine fighter." I told him that I was not familiar with that plane. We used nicknames for Japanese aircraft due to our problem with the language.

Next he asked me where I was going. When I told him Osaka, he looked at the schedule board and suggested that I take the next train and come to his house, which was only a few minutes from the station.

I hesitated for a moment before a Marine Corps adage popped into mind—*Can't live forever*. "Sounds good," I said. "Let's go."

As we walked to his home he told me he was a medical doctor for the Nara hospital and his father was the mayor for Nara. He was curious about my interests, family, and whether I had an occupation beyond military pilot. When I responded that my chief interest was science education he indicated that he could arrange for me to visit some schools if I was interested.

When we arrived at his home, he introduced me to his wife (she could not speak English). She was, however, a good hostess because within minutes, after we seated ourselves on the floor, we had rice cakes, peanuts, raw fish, and a bottle of sake in front of us. First on the agenda was a sake toast to each other. His name was difficult so I asked if I could address him as Dr. K. He laughed and said, "Please do."

He then reached up on the bookshelf for his aircraft recognition book and opened it to the airplane he had flown. There it was, a Nick—our name for his Kawasaki—the plane I had shot down near Kumamato, Japan, in 1945. My thoughts jumped—what should I say? Quickly I responded that a friend of mine had shot down a Nick near Kumamato.

He wanted to find out the date because he continued, "Our squadron was the only one flying that plane in southern Kyushu. Notice on this map how close we were to Kumamato."

I pointed to the approximate spot on the map where the Nick had gone down. The fact that the plane had gone down in flames and the rear gunner had hit my wingman was not mentioned. There was no question, however, that I had shot down one of Dr. K's squadron friends. He then proposed another toast of sake to all our departed pilot friends on both sides. It was a good toast and broke the stalemate of feelings.

As we nibbled on snacks and sake, Dr. K probably noticed that I had not touched the raw fish. He mentioned, "I'm the one who buys all the fish because freshwater fish are not safe in the Orient." He continued in a quieter voice, "I don't trust my wife to know salt from freshwater fish." I guess he anticipated I knew the danger of parasites in fish with my science background and parasitology courses.

Over a period of several months when I returned from Korea for R & R in Japan, Dr. K took me to his hospital, introduced me to several English speaking teachers in schools, and had a group of Japanese friends in for a party in my honor. He and I sang a Japanese song at that party. I found out he had majored in English prior to medical school, which explained his flawless English.

At one of our last meetings I admitted that I had shot down his squadron friend. He indicated that he had suspected it because I knew so much about the episode. He wrote the name of the pilot and the rear seat gunner for me. We then drank a toast to that duo of aviators.

I tried to communicate with him twice before leaving Japan for the States but to no avail. We did communicate by mail for a year after. When my address book was lost and his complex address was beyond my memory, our communications ceased. Our friendship was short but profound. I believe we both gained a greater understanding of the other's culture.

Of the three Japanese World War II pilots I have met, Dr. K was the most interactive. He had a superb open mind, was well educated and an excellent record keeper, had a good sense of humor, and was an outstanding communicator. We discussed the tragic war between our countries and the good relations we now have for each other.

This was one of the highlights of my 26 years as an aviator in the United States Marine Corps. Thank you, Dr. K, for your great interactions with me.

Command Decision
By Darrell Smith

About a week after our small group had been "dumped" off at Kimpo, two VMF-312 Corsairs flew in from Japan to see if they could find out what happened to us. About the same time air force C-54 pilots fresh from flying the Berlin Air Lift began flying supplies into Kimpo, including aviation fuel and ammunition.

The two Corsairs were fueled by hand from 50-gallon drums, and I and another reserve pilot from Minneapolis were sent on an early search and destroy mission into North Korea.

We were told that any motorized vehicles we came across were fair game, that the North Korean civilians had only bicycles and ox carts. We were also told that there were no friendly troops yet in North Korea. We were aware, however, that the North Korean Army was retreating north and that they may have some prisoners with them.

The maps we had covered only South Korea. North Korea was just a brown tint, which meant we wouldn't know where we were most of the time. But we knew we could always pull up, fly west to the Yellow Sea and follow the coastline down to Inchon and back to Kimpo.

We were following a gravel road northwest into North Korea at treetop level, hoping to slip up on some North Korean military vehicles. I was leading and my wingman was right behind. Up ahead the road curved north around a heavily wooded area. As we followed the curve we suddenly came up behind what I estimated was 100 to 150 troops marching four abreast, straight north on the road.

We were on them and over them in a flash, but we pulled up and around and came up behind them again, fully expecting they would have broken for cover in the trees. But they were still there, marching on as if we weren't even in the area. Something wasn't right! Who were these people? We flew over them again at treetop level. Still no response! Then we pulled up to about 3,000 feet over a fairly large city two miles ahead of them.

Near the center of the city was a large square building that seemed to cover most of a block. Painted on the metal roof was a huge Red Cross emblem that covered the entire roof. We were circling over this building, which I thought might give someone back at Kimpo some idea where we were, while I called in this information and asked if they had any information on friendly troops in the area. They didn't have any idea where we were but said once again that there were no allied troops in North Korea and these would be fair game.

While they were giving me this information I was suddenly startled to see a hole about the size of a soft ball appear in the right wing about a foot from the ammunition boxes for the guns, and even closer to the one locking bolt that kept the wing from folding. Up until that time we had no idea we were targets for antiaircraft guns located somewhere near the building we were circling. The only thing I could think of that would make a hole like that would be an antiaircraft round, since it went right through the wing but failed to explode.

I was really concerned that the locking mechanism might have been damaged and the wing might fold in mid air. I told Kimpo that we were returning. As we left I looked back down the road and the troops were still marching steadily north. I wondered—had we refrained from strafing some of our own troops or 150 some enemy soldiers that later could be attacking our people? I suspected we would never know.

Repairing Corsair wing at Kimpo, Korea.

While in Korea I had the opportunity to take about 200 color slides that I have shown many times to interested groups. Around 25 years after leaving Korea I was scheduled to show them to a group at the Roseville, Minnesota, VFW post. As I walked into the building carrying the projector and screen one of the people there came up to me before I could set them down and said something like, "I'm from Wisconsin and I came over because I heard a Marine pilot who was flying Corsairs in Korea was speaking today. I want to know if you were in one of the two Corsairs that didn't strafe us while we were being marched north."

I started to say no, I didn't think so—then it began to come back to me. I put the projector and screen down, sat down with him and started asking questions. He described exactly what I remembered except he said there were about 250 men in the group and they were being marched north as prisoners. Then he asked, "Why didn't you strafe us?" I replied, "Why didn't you break for the woods?" He said there were some pilots in the group and they started shouting, "Don't break! Don't break! Don't break!" I was stunned! We talked a few minutes more, neither one of us knew exactly where we were, or what day it was. But it's hard to believe two such incidents of that kind could take place in about the same area and about the same time.

I had a slide presentation to give so our conversation was cut short. At the end I looked for him but he was gone! I didn't have a chance to get his name or ask more questions or talk further about what happened to him as a prisoner in Korea. If anyone reads this and has information on who he was, I would surely like to have them contact me. (You can reach me at: Darrell Smith, 5258 Crestwood Drive, Minnetonka MN 55345; 952-935-2704.) If I never learn anything more, I sure feel a lot better about not attacking some 250 people that I now believe were our own POWs.

Between a Rock and a Hard Place
By Lyle Bradley

In August of 1950 our reserve squadron in Minneapolis was recalled to active duty for the Korean War. It was a dangerous place to be a pilot—eight of our Minnesota pilots did not return. I have a small rock in my display desk at home that almost kept me there permanently.

On a recon flight in April 1951, Joe McPhail and I discovered a huge cache of North Korean supplies on trucks at the bottom of a deep gorge. I had rockets and napalm on my plane while Joe had 500-pound bombs. I studied the target with binoculars and made our plan to strafe the trenches on the hillsides that were protecting the supply depot. Our plan was to strafe both sides simultaneously with each dropping a bomb or rocket on the way down. I would go all the way to the bottom to drop the napalm first.

On the Corsair, the trigger for the wing guns, bomb, and rocket releases are all in close proximity. We were both being shot at constantly, nervous perspiration was running down our necks, and I did a dumb, almost fatal mistake. When I hit the napalm trigger I accidentally hit the rocket release. In this deep gorge there was only one place for the rocket to go—straight ahead where I had to fly out of the gorge. The rocket exploded in the rocks at the same time I flew over the spot and I heard the splatter—I had been hit by the rocks from my own rocket blast.

I was heading for some trees and a cliff on the recovery. Then I realized the ailerons were frozen—direction control was lost and something had jammed it. My only chance was to use aileron tabs.

No one ever rolled aileron tabs faster or harder than I did in those few seconds. Joe yelled for me to turn but I was too busy to answer.

I barely missed the cliff but did brush the tops of some trees.

Back at the base before landing Joe flew under the plane to see if my wheels were down, locked, and intact. The landing was uneventful but discussions with the ground crew were not so uneventful. I had put 19 holes in the bottom of the plane. The armor plating had saved the engine and the cockpit. My concern with the aileron showed a small rock about two inches in size wedged into the left aileron. It took at least 15 minutes to dig it out. Today it is a memory of a very close call.

BETWEEN WARS

Special Weapons Delivery and Bird Strike
By Ralph A. "Lefty" Engelking

After World War II the armed services were experimenting with different ways and means to use, and deliver, atomic weaponry. The Marine Corps came up with a way to have attack aircraft, such as the propeller driven Douglas AD Skyraider, fly undetected to the target and deliver the bomb. The Skyraider could stay in the air for hours because of the drop tanks of fuel it could carry. They would fly at 50 feet over the water to avoid radar detection. When reaching the target, full power was applied with a 4.5-G pull. When nearing the top of the maneuver, at about 1,900 feet, you released the bomb, which would then lob to the target. The aircraft would dive back toward the water, rolling out on the path they had flown to the target, hopefully escaping from the bomb's over pressure, heat blast, and radiation.

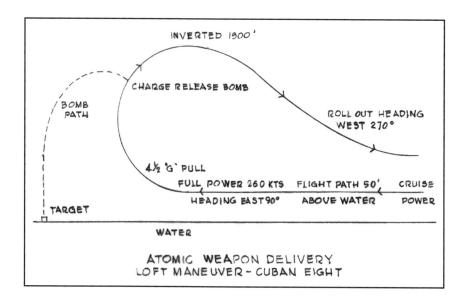

After completion of flight training and designation as a naval aviator in 1955 I was assigned to Marine Attack Squadron VMA-332. This squadron was the first in the Marine Corps to be assigned the mission of special weapons, or atomic delivery.

I was in a flight of four Skyraiders about 20 miles west of Marine Corp Air Station Opa Locka, Florida. The mission was to practice the "loft maneuver" at a target in the Everglades. I was making my run into the target with everything perfectly normal, when a large turkey vulture entered the cockpit. BANG!!! The slipstream from the propeller caught the bird and slammed it through the Plexiglas canopy next to my head. It knocked off my crash helmet, oxygen mask, and goggles, with the broken glass carving up my face.

Nose-up trim on the elevator saved my life. Regaining my composure, I noticed the Skyraider was in a gentle climb through 1,200 feet. I was covered with blood, feathers, bird guts and glass. Looking in the mirror affixed to the gunsight, I realized I had cut an artery above my mouth and cheek (what was left of it, anyhow). I knew it was an artery because the blood was spurting out with the heartbeats. I had my hands full flying the plane back to the base while trying to keep pressure on the artery to avoid bleeding to death before landing.

After landing, an ambulance was right there and I was in sick bay 22 minutes after the incident. After 42 stitches and a transfusion of three pints of blood, I felt ready for the officers' club.

The "dueling" scar on my face gave me the nickname Baron Von Engelking. Prior to my release from the Corps, I had plastic surgery in the Naval Hospital in Yokosuka, Japan. The navy doctor did one great job. I still have the J-shaped scar on my face.

Atomic Bomb Test
By Louis "Louie" E. Farrell

The following was an exciting experience flying in an experimental atomic bomb test, especially for a gung ho 23-year-old marine second lieutenant attack pilot. In reality, however, the event had a much more negative, and far-reaching impact, because of the medical damage incurred by both ground and civilian personnel located hundreds of miles away from the test site. (I recently visited the new Atomic Testing Museum in Las Vegas, Nevada, which covers all the testing done at the Nevada test site from the 1950s to the present controversial storage of spent radioactive material at Yucca Mountain.)

After the atomic bomb was used to end World War II, the United States government conducted many tests on how to apply this new technology using tactical warfare. The Nevada test site had been the Las Vegas gunnery and bombing range and was selected for atomic bomb testing. Nine hundred twenty-eight nuclear bombs were detonated from the early 1950s through the 1960s. After 1963 all were under ground, but for 12 years prior, 100 atomic devices were blown up in the open air, with 14 of them above what we called China Lake or Yucca Flats. My story is one of these 14 tests.

The name of this test was Operation Tea Pot, which occurred March 22, 1955. The purpose of the test was to see the results of the bomb's effect on a mock-up city with dummies, animals, equipment, and many other things. It was also a coordinated attack exercise after the bomb went off, with marine air, close air support rocket runs, and helicopters using vertical envelopment to drop troops in the ground zero area.

Four of us were selected from our squadron, VMA-323, to go on maneuvers to Marine Corp Auxiliary Air Station Mojave. One of the other pilots selected was Captain Rich Rawlings, who years later was a colonel in our Minneapolis Reserve Squadron. At Mojave we joined three other F9F-5 squadrons of four planes each to practice rocket runs and procedures for holding 16 aircraft on a marker beacon then rolling in for an attack after the bomb went off. We also received extensive training and briefing on the nature of an atomic explosion and emergency procedures. Extreme emphasis was placed on the brightness of the explosion. The plan was to have each division of four aircraft to be in a holding pattern at 1,000 foot intervals with the leaders flying instruments under a completely light proof bag. We wingmen would be flying formation with one eye closed from the count down of ten. It was stressed to us that the reflection brightness from a dark blue aircraft (with all light colors on the plane painted black) would be so intense that we would not be able to see for several minutes. It doesn't take a rocket scientist to figure out that in a single seat airplane you crash if you can't see.

In the pre-dawn darkness of March 22, 1955, 16 of us took off from MCAAS Mojave and arrived at Yucca Flats and began a holding pattern on a radio beacon placed five miles from ground zero. The atomic bomb was on a tower and was detonated exactly at sunrise.

The blast gave us a little bump, and they were right—the open eye we were flying with completely faded out all sight. We flew high-angle, six-inch HVAR (high velocity aircraft rocket) attack patterns with the other eye. After each rocket run we were instructed to check our dosimeter, which was a measuring device the size of a thermometer, to see how much radiation we were getting. Mine registered zero the whole time, although my film badge registered some, which was entered in my medical records. We returned to Mojave very low on

Logbook entry on March 22, 1955, for atomic bomb test run.

fuel. Atomic energy personnel went over the airplanes with Geiger counters on the end of the runway and released us back to the line.

The main reason for relating this story is to show how little our government and military knew about the long-term effects of radiation. When our airplanes returned to the line the plane captains were instructed to wash the planes down. They were the ones that received intense radiation—working over the "hot" wings—as you'll note from the following letter, written to me in 1981 from one of our plane captains. I've also included my response. Think of the hundreds of marine soldiers and helicopter guys that were tromping around ground zero and the medical problems they have since encountered. I did receive information that the plane captain finally received medical compensation from the Veterans Administration.

Albuquerque N. M.
February 3rd 1981

Mr Louis Farrell
% Republic airlines
Minneapolis airlines
Minneapolis Minn

Dear Louis

You Probably don't remember me, but I need your help. I have obtained your address from Lt Col Wally smith USMCR.

We served together in the marine Corp and I was assigned Col C. R Davis as Plane Capt. on 3-22-55 our unit VMA 323 MAG 15 went from El Toro Calif to Mojava Calif to take Part in an atomic Bomb test (Bee) shot teapot dome test series. Since that time I have devoloped cataracts on both eyes that my surgon feels were caused by radiation exposure. I filed a claim with the Veterans adminstration but it was denied because I could not prove any exposure to radiation. It seems the records were discarded after the test.

As I recall it our planes were airborn and took Part in the test. When they returne to base the planes were parked seperately and some unknown person in a space suit with face shield went over the planes with a geyer counter, that person declared the Planes to be very hot and my self and several other plane capts. were ordered to wash the planes with soap and water to decontaminate them. We were not furnished any film badges or any Protective Gear what so ever. I am trying to prove that I was exposed to an undetermined amount of radiation at this time in order to seek compensation for my eye injuries. I sincerely hope you can recall the event similar to my resume above. After getting out of the Corp I knocked around for a while, then became a police officer here in Albuquerque N.M. But due to my near blind condition I am being forced to retire, and needless to say I have three kids yet to put through school.

I hope I have not imposed upon your Privatacy by obtaining your address and making this request. I hope the Lord has been good to you, and will continue to bless you in all your efforts.

I remain sincerely yours

Melvin O Parker Cpt USMC
1461295
1700 Bonaguidi S.W.
Albuquerque N.M. 87105

P.S. a speedy reply is of the utmost importants. Please address the letter to Director of Veterans administration and MAIL to me at the above address. Thanks in advance Mel Parker

REPUBLIC AIRLINES, INC.

February 12, 1981

Melvin O. Parker, Cpt. USMC
1461295
1700 Bonaguidi S.W.
Albuquerque, New Mexico   87195

Dear Melvin:

In response to your February 3, 1981 letter, I do recall being a part of Operation Teapot. This is what I recall of that long-ago event, substantiated by my log book.

I believe four (4) of us were selected from our squadron VMA323 to fly close air support bombing runs immediately after the detonation of the atomic bomb. I am not absolutely sure who the other three (3) pilots were, although I think Col. Lund, the Squad Commander, was leading and Rick Rawlings (an attorney in St. Cloud, MN, with whom I still communicate) was on the flight. I was flying a F9F 5 Panther Jet, Bureau #126217, on this particular flight. After the detonation, we made several high angle bomb runs in the vicinity of ground zero which took us in and around the cloud. We all had film badges and dosimeters. We were instructed to continually check the dosimeters to monitor the amount of radiation we were getting. Upon landing at Mojave, specialists went over the airplane at the end of the runway to check the amount of radiation before taxiing back to the line. As I recall, my dosimeter did not reflect much radiation at all. The reading from the film badge was entered in my permanent medical records which I assume are on file in Washington. You have my permission to find these records and the amount of radiation on the film badge, if you need it.

If you have any further questions, please feel free to call me at my office, 612-726-7751.

Good luck in your endeavor.

Sincerely,

31 March 1981 Marine Capt Flemming Callus to Roland to Wanton My Permission to a page of Mourice Records to Parker.

Louis E. Farrell
Regional Director-Flying

LEF/jv

612/726-7411

7500 AIRLINE DRIVE
MINNEAPOLIS, MINNESOTA 55450

Jet Carrier Operations
By Andrew "Andy" W. Danielson

Aircraft carrier operations are always challenging. With the development of jet aircraft in the early 1950s it was found that the World War II and even Korean War techniques no longer were successful and often led to disastrous results.

With propeller powered aircraft, the landing was controlled by a landing signal officer (LSO) who signaled the approaching aircraft with paddles advising whether the aircraft was fast, slow, high or low. The LSO would wave the approach off if the approach was unsafe. He stood on a platform on the flight deck, port side aft.

With the coming of jet aircraft came the necessity for new procedures. The jets flew faster in the traffic pattern, causing it to be much

An old carrier with a straight deck. Note the flat landing pattern of the incoming aircraft. If you look carefully, you can see the LSO port side, aft, by the screen.

wider. It was very difficult to see the LSO, particularly at night. The old style of carrier approach was flat, meaning that the aircraft started the approach from a low altitude above the water. This resulted in many stall spin crashes and got worse with the later development of the swept-wing jet. These had higher stall speeds and greater sink rates. In the pattern around the ship you were flying only a few knots above stall speed, and the slightest mistake would set up a high sink rate. A high sink rate could result in a swim, or worse, a crash into the stern of the ship. Either one could result in notice to next of kin and was to be avoided.

Two innovations were developed. One was the angled deck carrier. The angled deck was set at an angle to the hull of the ship. This enabled pilots to land, add full power immediately and continue back into the air in the event of a broken arresting hook on the aircraft, missing the arresting cables on the deck, or for other possible reasons. The pilot would pull back on the power as soon as an arrested landing was assured. You could tell if the arrest was assured by the very sudden stop. The angled deck also allowed for aircraft to be launched from the bow end of the straight deck as aircraft were being recovered on the stern end of the angled deck.

The second development was the mirror landing system. This was developed by the British. A large gyro-stabilized mirror reflects a bright beam of light, which the pilot can see from well astern the ship. The approach is commenced from an altitude of around 500 feet rather than 150 feet. The pilot keeps the reflected beam in the mirror and lined up with a set of green horizontal lights on the mirror. This sets the glide angle. He then maintains the proper airspeed, which is critical, and lines up with the centerline of the angled deck. If he does all of these, he will touch down within a very small area of the deck considering the speed at which he approaches. If the approach is on the money, he will catch the number three wire. He then raises his hook, taxis out of the arresting gear so another aircraft can land, and be on his way to a hot cup of coffee. If he screws up, he is given a wave off and sent back up in the pattern for another approach, keeping a very close eye on fuel remaining. Now aircraft are equipped with air-to-air refueling to solve this problem. This was rare in the late 1950s.

The angled deck and mirror system were huge improvements. There were some other things that required adjustment. The superstructure on a carrier's deck is called the island. The island contains the stack from which smoke is emitted when under way. During flight operations the ship's crew sees that very little smoke is emitted. However, there is some. There are also hot stack gases. The two together cause some bumpy air and some restriction in vision. During the final approach the aircraft has to be flown through this area. It takes only a few seconds to pass through, but it occurs during a period of intense concentration during the final stage of the approach when airspeed is critical, along with lineup on the deck and maintaining glide slope on the mirror. Today the ships are nuclear powered so this may all be eliminated.

An angled-deck carrier.

So far I have discussed landing procedures. A jet cannot take off from a carrier without the assistance of a catapult (cat). The aircraft is taxied into position on the cat by a taxi director. The aircraft is attached to the cat via a connection under the aircraft. The launch officer gives the pilot the signal to run the engine up. The pilot checks his instruments, locks his left hand around the throttle and salutes the launch officer. A couple of seconds later he is on his way. This is great. The acceleration draws the skin and flesh back on the face under the oxygen mask. The bow of the ship comes rushing at you and in a second you are out over the water pulling up the landing gear, retracting flaps, and so on. It is a lot better than a roller coaster and does not cost a dime.

Writing about these operations brought back some memories that I had forgotten. I won't relate many but will tell of one showing that not all went according to the book.

I was flying the Grumman F9F-8 Cougar, which was a swept wing fighter and a good one for that era. We were based at the Marine Corps Air Station at Cherry Point, North Carolina, but were flying out of the Naval Air Station at Jacksonville, Florida. We had a little problem with the squadron's aircraft in that the tail (arresting) hook would not go to the full down position unless you pulled a circuit breaker in the cockpit. The problem could not be fixed readily, but the decision makers felt we could operate around it.

On the downwind leg and abeam the ship, procedure calls for you to drop the landing gear, flaps, and the arresting hook. My problem was that I have short arms. The circuit breaker panel was along the right side of the cockpit outboard of the pilot's right leg. There were many circuit breakers there so you had to count the number down and the number across to get the right one. I had to loosen my shoulder harness and stick my head down between my knees while feeling for the panel with my right hand. This meant flying with my left hand, no hand on the throttle, and with my head down between my knees. This was a little uncomfortable as the altitude would be around 500 feet above the water and the air speed a few knots above stall. It also meant that I had to remember to re-lock the shoulder harness before landing on the ship. If the shoulder harness was not locked the sudden stop would drive your head into the gun sight, which was in front of your face. This was very unpleasant as it guaranteed the need for extensive dental work and stitches. Those that had overlooked locking their shoulder harness were easy to spot in the bar at subsequent happy hours.

The best advice I remember getting about carrier flying came from a veteran marine pilot and ace from World War II. It was given to several of us during a briefing before going out to the ship for carrier qualifications. He said there is no man alive that could cause him to rush any part of the procedure, especially while getting ready to launch. Everyone from the ship's navy captain on down is in a hurry during the launching and recovery of aircraft. As a result, this advice is difficult to follow, but worthwhile to remember.

I would be remiss if I did not give great credit to the men and now women that work on the flight decks. Flight decks are very dangerous places. Jets are turning up, making it extremely noisy, along with high velocity jet washes behind them. There is at least 30 knots of wind down the deck during operations. It is crowded with aircraft, people, and equipment. If something breaks on a landing, aircraft pieces of metal can come hurtling down the deck in excess of 100 miles per hour. The pilots are actually in the safest place, sitting in the cockpit on the flight deck waiting to go fly.

Checking Out
By William F. Messerli

It was my first drill weekend at NAS Minneapolis after transferring from NAS Glenview where I was flying F9F-8s. A marine squadron in Minneapolis was flying AD-5s in which I had accumulated in excess of 500 hours while flying in Korea and Japan in 1955 and 1956. On October 1, which was a Sunday, I had my first and only FAM checkout ride in the AD-5. That afternoon the squadron CO asked for volunteers to fly two navy guys to Chicago. I and another squadron pilot raised our hands and in two AD-5s flew the two navy people to Chicago and then back to Minneapolis. There was near panic at Minneapolis while we were gone. It seems that I had not officially checked into the marine detachment. The detachment executives were not too happy with me, but happy that there were no accidents. Can't please everyone. The navy guys got to Chicago!

Dicey Descents
By C. M. (Tony) Plattner

Once I completed four years of active duty, I joined the Minneapolis Marine Air Reserves and flew Grumman F9F-5 Panther Jets and Douglas AD-5 Skyraiders. The AD (later designated A-1E) was a wonderful piston-powered, side-by side cockpit airplane, which was too late for World War II but did great work during the Vietnam War.

One drill weekend I was asked to fly to Casper, Wyoming, and return a needed part to the detachment. The weather was relatively clear but in the dead of winter it was below-zero cold and the ground was white with a recent snowfall.

I was flying contentedly along over South Dakota when the engine abruptly stopped. This sudden transition from powered to gliding flight is a silence that one never forgets since the AD's big Wright 3350 engine and 14-foot propeller normally made a noticeable impression in the cockpit.

I immediately took stock of my situation. On the downside, I was lightly dressed with a summer flying suit and leather jacket, and South Dakota in the grip of winter is indeed a bleak place with snow camouflaging hazards such as rocks and gullies that could have made landing precarious.

On the upside, I had some altitude and had the unexpected good fortune of being within gliding distance of a town with an airfield.

I immediately set up a best descent speed, pointed the airplane to where I thought the base was, found a frequency to call them, and received a vector to the base. I decided on a 360 overhead approach and was doing nicely coming into the final over the end of the runway when the engine sputtered to life.

Of course, I was skeptical of my good fortune and continued with the dead-stick landing. However after the rollout, the engine continued to run, so I taxied to the transient ramp.

After calling the detachment and discussing it with them, the most likely cause seemed carburetor ice, which melted during the glide. Preventing ice in the carburetor is fundamental to piston engine flying, but what made it unique in my case was that I iced up well outside of the handbook vulnerability temperature zone, possibly due to freak meteorological conditions.

I then refiled a flight plan and returned the airplane to Minneapolis applying ample carburetor heat enroute.

Later, I moved to California taking a job as a reporter with *Aviation Week and Space Technology* magazine.

This seven-year period in my career included a two-month stint as a combat correspondent in Vietnam reporting on the aviation aspects of that conflict. Interestingly enough, one of many combat missions I rode on was as a passenger in an air force A-1E during a strike in South Vietnam.

Another incident worthy of mention at Minneapolis occurred while flying the F9F Panther jet. It was on a local flight during drill weekend in the wintertime. After roughly an hour and a half, I decided to work myself into the pattern over the field because of deteriorating weather.

At 20,000 feet, where we would begin a special descent called a jet penetration, I could still remain visual but it appeared that conditions on the ground were getting bad. After reporting in, I was told that there were a number of aircraft ahead of me. The F9 gulped fuel at a pretty fast rate even when throttled back to the lowest speed possible so I waited patiently for my turn.

When the red fuel warning light came on at 1,000 pounds remaining, I again made approach control aware of my low fuel state but was told to wait for clearance. By this time, making it safely to an alternate field capable of accommodating the F-9 was no longer a viable option.

When I finally got clearance to begin the jet penetration—a teardrop descent at 4,000 feet per minute—I was down to 800 pounds. By this time, I was in dense clouds flying on instruments. To confound the situation, I had to make an approach to the east-facing runway because of wind conditions and there was no precision approach equipment available. And my IFF transponder was not working.

I was told by approach control that they would try to guide me in by monitoring me on their radar but they couldn't help me with altitude directions. During the procedure turn at about 10,000 feet, I received an unnerving communication that they had lost radar contact with me, meaning I was trying to execute a landing in instrument conditions without knowing where the field was located.

I immediately slowed the airplane to landing gear and flap speed and lowered both to provide a bigger radar target. By this time, I was down to 500 pounds of fuel—it should be noted that the gauging system of the F9 was known to be unreliable under 1,000 pounds.

Finally, the welcome voice of the controller came up and advised that he had picked me up again and resumed giving me vectors and distance to the field. I knew that I only had one chance to plant the F9 since a vectored go-around probably would have meant a flame-out, so I worked my way down toward field elevation.

When I saw the hazy outline of the large Washburn water tower on the left, I knew that I was heading in the right direction. Then the end of the runway appeared about one-quarter mile to my right through the blowing snow and I made a quick correction and landed at minimum visibility and ceiling. Back on the ramp at the Naval Air Station, my fuel gauge read less than 250 pounds and the peril of the situation became a reality.

I remain thankful to this day for having survived this and other such events, and I am humble enough to know that I wasn't alone through it all but was blessed by some power higher than mine looking over my shoulder.

Close Calls
By Lyle Bradley

Aviators like to compare close calls in training, combat, and even in routine flight activities. Close calls go with the occupation—some are interesting and some tragic. In my 26 years of military flying (including World War II and the Korean War) I recall 22 close calls. The following are three of the most memorable.

The Missing Cowling

My orders in August of 1944 read to report to the MCAS in El Toro, California, for transition to the F4U Corsair fighter. I had only seen one F4U to this point but was on cloud nine just thinking about flying one of the fastest fighters in the world.

After I had about 30 hours in the plane and my confidence was "hot pilot high," I wanted to see if I could get the plane close to the speed of sound. A fellow pilot, Walt Berndt, and I climbed to 44,000 feet, the highest I've ever been in the F4U. At that point I started into a split-S maneuver, rolling the plane and aiming for the ground. Within seconds the entire cowling of the plane peeled off, the canopy became fogged, and the plane started to vibrate. I quickly changed my mind about breaking the sound barrier, got the plane on an even keel, and started our return to base.

An hour later I was called into the CO's office to explain how I'd lost part of the aircraft. I told him it happened in a high-speed dive but did not tell him it happened over 40,000 feet.

Watching the Signs

In October 1943 I was flying an open cockpit Stearman biplane out of the Naval Air Station in Minneapolis, Minnesota. One morning a quick-forming fog trapped 20 of us doing practice aerobatics. We had no radio or other communications. This left us with two choices—bail out or let down through the fog until we spotted the ground or hit something. My decision was to let down slowly through the fog.

I slowed the plane to just above stall speed and entered the fog. My altimeter indicated about 800 feet. I looked ahead, then to the instruments—back and forth. Suddenly a big sign flashed by my right wing—it was a big number one, the sign on top of the First National Bank in St. Paul. Flying between the buildings in downtown St. Paul was not a comforting situation, so I added a little power and climbed a few feet, heading on a compass heading of 180 degrees toward Fleming Field. After two minutes I throttled back to decrease altitude and there was the Mississippi River. Another minute and I was on final to land at the field.

The bank sign Bradley barely missed in the fog in downtown St. Paul.

That big sign is still there today 66 years after I almost

hit it. I've stopped twice to thank them for their navigational sign that helped me in 1943.

Dunes and Deer

After Korea and a two-year stint as a flight instructor at Pensacola, Florida, I returned to Minnesota and rejoined my reserve squadron. In March of 1955 several of us reserve pilots were flown to MCAS Mojave, California, to check out the F9F Panther jets. We were to be the instructors for our squadron when we started to fly the F9Fs in mid-summer.

The F9F was a beautiful airplane but somewhat underpowered compared to other military jets. To overcome this weakness the plane had to be held in a low level position until a climbing speed of at least 300 knots could build up. Racing across the desert at 30 feet and going 300 knots was fun, and it was legal. In the Mojave Desert there were a number of small mounds from some geological past. These were nice to skim after take-off.

On my fourth hop (almost my last) I was getting close to the 300-knot climb speed and was heading for one of the mounds to skim. When I was about 100 feet from the mound, something exploded off the top of the mound—a large mule deer had apparently seen me coming and left his bed. He was almost in my windshield. I pulled up sharply and missed the deer by inches. I visualized the headlines in the local newspaper: "Two-legged dear meets four-legged deer with fatal results."

MARINE WINGS

Mud Marine Ohrn O'Dette
By Mac MacKechnie

There are some things a military pilot loves to do and there are some things a military pilot hates to do... and First Lietutenant Ohrn O'Dette, USMCR, experienced both on the same day in mid-1944, in the form of a Grumman F7F Tigercat.

Designed originally as a single seat twin-engine night fighter aircraft for the marines, the Tigercat contract was signed in October 1941 with the aircraft making its first flight in November 1943. Two F7Fs were shipped to NAS Patuxent where half a dozen USMC pilots were brought in to wring it out.

Pearl Harbor's aftermath found Ohrn O'Dette working in a munitions factory in Rock Island, Illinois. It was a dull, mindless routine that chafed at Ohrn's desire for action, so early in 1942 he enlisted in the navy's V-5 program. Training in Michigan, Livermore, and Corpus Christi, Ohrn was designated as a Naval Aviator with a Marine Corps option on October 20, 1943. He proceeded to Cherry Point MCAS, North Carolina, where he trained on PBJs (B-25s) in a squadron getting ready to ship out to the Pacific theater.

Shortly before the squadron left for the west coast, he and several other pilots were called into the CO's office and told they were being transferred to NAS Patuxent for "special duty," and indeed it was.

The half-dozen pilots were ordered to fly the Tigercats to their heart's content and do practically anything they wanted to the airplane, all in the name of test flying. They were to stretch the airplane to its limits, just to see how normal operation of the Tigercat affected the engines and the airframe. The six of them found some minor problems, but at least one major.

Lieutenant O'Dette loved to fly. He had never flown before joining the navy and now, in the Marine Corps, he was loving it that
much more. This test program was a dream come true. The six pilots
rotated through the two test aircraft, departing navy Pax for flights
over the Chesapeake Bay before returning to file a short report, then
more of the same.

Fly; report. Fly; report. That was it, until the one flight in mid-
1944. It was a cloudy day, some storms in the area, but the weather
was forecast to be good enough to get in the afternoon's first flight
and Lieutenant O'Dette was raring to go. Soaring into the wild gray
yonder, he put the aircraft through its paces for the better part of an
hour. The flight consisted mostly of low-level runs over a local radar
station at about 25 feet altitude, the radar crew using his airplane as
a target, measuring whatever radar stations measured as he worked
out the airplane.

Finally it was the last run, preceded by a dive at the radar station
and a wingover back over the station and on out over the Chesapeake
Bay. It was at the completion of the wingover, when he was out
over the bay, that he was introduced to one of the harsher realities
of flight, what goes up must come down—with or without engines
that work.

One of the unknown difficulties encountered early on in the
Tigercat program was that the engines had difficulty operating if
certain conditions occurred simultaneously. The aircraft had to be in
a climbing turn and the weather had to be just so, these conditions
combining to cause a vapor lock in the fuel pump system. At 25 feet
altitude, heading out over the biggest bay in the area, both engines
quit at the same time... this was not a good thing.

It was quieter than Simon and Garfunkel playing the "Sounds
of Silence," at least for the moment, before the wind rushing by the
airframe brought him out of his reverie. He got busy in a hurry. At

25 feet he wasn't able to do a 180-degree turn so he pulled back the stick to climb, getting what altitude he could to stretch out a glide. Too low to bail out, he would be riding it in…but wait! "What's that straight ahead? An island!" He was saved, so he thought.

It was an island with an open strip of land, one that would provide a landing spot for him (and the airplane) if only he could make it. Nursing, straining, milking it for all he was worth, the island grew nearer to him even as he fell nearer to the water.

There are some laws that are impossible to break and the law of gravity is one of them. He was about to encounter a science lesson firsthand and he was going to be ready for it. Realizing he was not going to make the island he braced himself for the impact. Seatbelt tight, feet braced. Lower and lower, almost to shore, almost, almost...

The Tigercat had large nacelles for the beautiful big Pratt & Whitney 2800 engines and when they hit the water, they threw up great plumes of spray, cascading up and over the engines, the canopy, everything. Ohrn was now a passenger on a soon-to-be winged boat and the cruise was going to be a short one, the ride down to the bottom of the bay was going to be longer than his short cruise across the water.

The aircraft hit the water "about a city block offshore." It didn't take long for him to swing into action. He unbuckled his seatbelt and popped the canopy seal, sliding it back to get out of the aircraft before it could sink in the bay and take him with it. It opened and he slid it back, all of eight inches!

The airplane started settling in the water. Ohrn fought the canopy as best he could but it would not budge. Time stood still. He unstrapped his chute, got up on the seat, and, somewhat bent over, tried busting it open with brute force. Unfortunately Lieutenant O'Dette was not much of a brute and, in spite of his fierce struggle with the recalcitrant canopy, he was unable to force the issue—or the canopy.

It was only after he had been struggling for some time that he realized he had been struggling for just that, some time, a time much longer than it would have taken to sink to the bottom of the bay. Suddenly it struck Ohrn that perhaps all was not lost, especially considering the fact that, glancing outside, the plane was not moving forward and, better yet, it was not moving down, sinking. The plane had stopped offshore but not far. The nose was buried in the island's mud bank and the bottom of the aircraft was submerged...in a foot and a half of water. It had sunk as far as it was going to sink and Lieutenant O'Dette had gone as far as he was going to go.

It took him a while to get the canopy open so that if an escape became necessary, he could leave. Radioing NAS Patuxent he was ordered to stay with the top secret aircraft, in the aircraft, do not leave the aircraft. He did just that, spending a cold, wet, miserable night guarding whatever it was the powers-that-be wanted him to guard. Islanders brought him food, so that was no problem, and a barge equipped with a crane came up from NAS Pax the next day to retrieve plane and pilot.

So the six pilots flew the remaining Tigercats until the end of the program. The pilots eventually went their separate ways, most to the Pacific, including Lieutenant O'Dette who went on to fly F6F Hellcats with VMF-541(N) until the end of the war. After the war ended the squadron (and Lieutenant O'Dette) went to China to fly "monitor" patrols (monitoring the advance of the communists against the Nationalist army) until the squadron's return to the States in late 1946.

Lieutenant O'Dette got to do what he enjoyed more than anything else, fly a great airplane to the edge of its envelope and a bit beyond. That one day though, the airplane fell out of the envelope and, for the short walk to shore when the airplane was hauled out, he too became a "Mud Marine."

Incidents Worth Remembering
By James C. Magnus

Don't drink too much orange juice and vodka the night before flying an F4U cross-country. One pilot did out of El Toro to Albuquerque and Minneapolis. The urge became critical and mandatory, so off came the flight suit. With no container handy, the enroute charts were used and thrown overboard. This caused a delay in Albuquerque to get the brown Corsair washed to its blue navy color.

The transition from F4Us to F9F aircraft was hazardous for the reserves as the fleet gave us tired old Grummans. One aircraft quit on takeoff and luckily landed on a frozen swamp. Another one quit on final and crashed into a house with fatalities.

On one summer in 1955 we maneuvered to El Toro for annual exercizes with the ground troops. My five-plane formation pulled up behind a Canadian Mil Dakota aircraft waiting for clearance, and was delayed. The tower advised us to make a 180-degree turn and get onto the runway via another taxiway. We were cleared to proceed. There was one problem, however. As five aircraft gunned their engines to turn, they blasted the DC-3's controls so badly that some of the controls left their aircraft. I returned to operations to prepare an accident report and sent the others on their way. The DC-3 crew wanted to stay in Minneapolis longer and really didn't care. However, when we returned two weeks later, they were still grounded and not very jovial. Incidentally, it took me five days to get to El Toro with problems in Minneapolis, Olathe, Kansas, and Albuquerque, New Mexico. As the saying goes, "Time to spare, go by air."

Lake Superior Bombing Practice
By Louis "Louie" E. Farrell

In June 1959 the Minneapolis Marine Air Reserves transitioned from flying the Grunman F9F-5 Panther jet to the Douglas AD-5N Skyraiders. The Skyraider is a single engine propeller driven aircraft with a Wright Cyclone R-3350 engine that produces 2,700 horsepower. It is so powerful that it can carry the same bomb load that the four-engine B-17 did in World War II.

Normally our annual two-week active duty training period was conducted at Marine Air Base El Toro, California, on the west coast, or at Cherry Point, on the east coast. With the transition period of checking out in a different aircraft, it was determined that our squadron would conduct training at our base in Minneapolis, Minnesota, with ordnance loading at Duluth National Guard Ramp. The target areas were about 50 to 80 miles northeast of Duluth in designated danger zones over Lake Superior.

Several of us pilots had flown the ADs in Korea and Japan; therefore we were designated as instructors or flight leaders. If we were on an ordnance mission, we would fly a four-plane division to the Guard base at the Duluth airport, refuel, and be loaded with rockets or bombs for target practice in the restricted area. On one of the many sorties we flew in July 1959 1 had an incident while leading a flight of four ADs.

After takeoff from Duluth we would rendezvous and check in with the air force radar control unit for vectors to the target area. When reaching the danger area we would peel off from 10,000 feet with an overhead roll into a 45-degree dive to the target. The leaders on all these flights had a smoke bomb that would be released on the first dive. It would float, giving off smoke, and would be the target we would aim at. The shooting aircraft would release his bomb/rocket at 1,500 feet above the water so as to pull out of the dive by 1,000 feet. The next aircraft in the bomb run would see the impact of the bomb or rocket and call the hit by the clock position and estimated number of yards from the target.

On this particular flight I rolled into the dive and dropped the smoke bomb, pulling out with the normal 3.5 to 4-G pull to zoom up as high as possible, with METO (Maximum Except TakeOff) power to get to 10,000 feet for a tight pattern to start the next bomb run immediately after the number four aircraft. After pullout from the

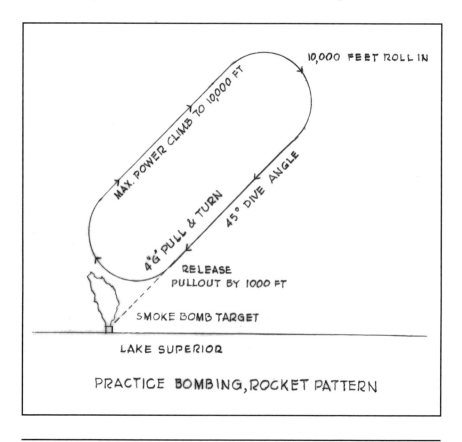

PRACTICE BOMBING, ROCKET PATTERN

second run my engine began running really rough, coughing and back firing. I zoomed as high as possible and called Mayday to the rest of the flight and radar control, who immediately gave me a vector to the Duluth airport. I was able to keep the engine running by adjusting the throttle, rpms, and mixture control, but could barely maintain altitude at about 4,000 feet. I really didn't want to ditch the plane in Lake Superior with the water temperature in the 30s. We had survival suits on (called poopie suits) which reduce your chances of getting hypothermia while getting into the life raft. That old engine kept sputtering all the way to Duluth Airport. I was cleared for an emergency landing straight in to runway 27, which is 11,000 feet long. I picked a spot about one third the way down the runway and immediately upon reducing power the engine quit and I dead-sticked it in.

A tug with tow bar was by the crash crew as they towed me into the Guard ramp. The maintenance and ordnance crew stationed there for the maneuvers opened up the cowling and spark plugs fell all over the place. This plane had just come out of a maintenance check and someone had failed to torque all of the plugs; some were only finger tight. I was really fortunate that the whole engine hadn't caught on fire. In each piston there are two spark plugs, so if one is missing the other fires the fuel air mixture and the fire blows out of the missing plug hole. Most of the wiring in the engine was badly burned. Lucky Louie!

A few days after this event, we were refueling and getting ordnance again at Duluth, when one of the master sergeants asked if some of his ordnance enlisted men could ride along to witness the bombing runs. We said of course, although they had to bring along barf bags in case they got airsick and finish the run, no matter what. We had to complete the mission because we didn't want to return and land with armed ordnance on the planes. The AD-5N was configured with a radar operator's seat beside the pilot seat.

The corporal that was riding with me was a very nice, typical marine. We talked and kidded around on the way to the target area. I rolled in on the first run and released the smoke bomb. After climbing up to 10,000 feet I noticed he was getting a little pale. After the second or third run, out comes the barf bag. You can imagine what it's like throwing up and pulling several Gs. I asked him how he was doing and he said he'd hang in there. Rolling in on the last run, I got squared away on the 45-degree angle. I looked over at the sick corporal, who gave me a salute and said, "Goodbye, Sir!"

He had hung on until the last, and was fine once we returned to base. Our marines are tough!

Flying The F4D-1 Skyray
By Andrew "Andy" W. Danielson

The F4D was designed by Douglas pursuant to the navy's request for a fighter capable of high-speed flight, along with the ability to climb rapidly to intercept enemy fighters and bombers flying in excess of 500 knots at an altitude of 40,000 feet or more.

Douglas delivered. In 1958 at Point Magu, California, the airplane set a world time-to-climb record of 50,000 feet in two minutes and 36.05 seconds. It also held the world closed course speed record of 728.11 miles per hour and was the first navy fighter capable of level supersonic flight.

All of the above was interesting bar talk, but what was it really like to sit in the cockpit and drive the machine? I flew it while a member of VMF(AW)-531 during the spring, summer and fall of 1958 while at MCAS Cherry Point, North Carolina.

The Douglas F4D Skyray

The aircraft had some flight characteristics that tended to make it unstable, particularly at low airspeed. Unlike many jets, use of the rudder pedals was required, particularly in the pattern. It also had bad spin characteristics that made spinning a prohibited maneuver without a spin chute, which we of course did not have. Inadvertent spins were problematic and were to be avoided. The spin was violent and often inverted. Spin recovery had to be done on instruments, as the pilot would become disorientated quickly. If a flameout occurred, the best procedure was to eject due to the extremely high rate of decent with a dead engine. It was not considered likely to successfully flare the aircraft and land safely. The high key position for a flameout approach (if one was to be attempted) was 10,000 to 12,000 feet. This illustrates the high rate of decent.

For training in 1958, you read the handbook, took a simple test on emergency procedures, and then went out and flew. In other words, the pilot knew very little about the flight characteristics of the bird he was about to fly. We learned mostly from experience. I recently read a cover article in the July 2006 issue of the *Smithsonian Air & Space* magazine. It described the test experience at the factory and at Pax River. I learned more from that article than I knew when I flew my first hop at Cherry Point. We were forming the squadron with some pilots fresh out of the training command while I was on my second fighter tour. Putting first tour pilots into the F4D was not a great idea, but what the heck, they had wings so they were supposed to be able to fly anything. Right? Sometimes wrong.

One interesting event would occur on takeoff. With the afterburner on, the aircraft would accelerate very fast. You had to pull the nose up to 45-60 degrees or so and retract the gear fast so as not to overstress. When retracting, each of the main gears rotated 90 degrees and then folded forward against the slipstream. The problem was that they did it one at a time. This would throw the aircraft into a hard skid.

In fact, it would almost turn the plane sideways if you didn't feed in heavy rudder.

I suppose some reasons for the above flight characteristics were related to the unconventional control surfaces. It had no horizontal stabilizer and no flaps. It had leading edge slats that came out when the airspeed got below a certain speed. They were held in aerodynamically. The plane was not fly-by-wire like most subsequent aircraft, including current ones. Control was not done with a black box (computer), which is now the case. When you moved the controls in the cockpit, the flight surfaces moved accordingly without any intervening input from a black box.

I have related some of the idiosyncrasies of the aircraft. Despite these, it did the job it was designed for. It was fast, it flew high, it got there in a hurry and it could turn. What more could a fighter pilot ask for? General Marion Carl was quoted that if he had the Skyray during the Korean War, he would have been able to pop off MiGs—one, two, and three. I consider it a privilege to have flown the airplane.

Why Favorites?

By Lyle Bradley

The Corsair took me through two wars and the SNJ took me through two years as an instructor. I survived both, and therefore, these are my two favorite aircraft.

The Corsair has received many plaudits from almost every pilot that has ever flown it, but the SNJ (AT-6) has received fewer, so here goes for this bird.

I was not happy when I returned from Korea and was assigned as a primary flight instructor to Whiting Field in Pensacola, Florida. We had been told that as a reserve pilot recalled to Korea we would have our choice of assignment upon our return. I had requested a jet squadron, but my request, obviously, had not been granted. My attitude was not good when I reported. I was in a pouting stage and was seriously considering a request to return to civilian life.

A navy commander in charge of the Pensacola training program told me that if I still desired to become a civilian after a week of training my first three students, orders would be cut for that purpose. That was fair. I reported to Whiting Field, met my first students, flew the first week, and reported to the commander that he could forget my orders to civilian life. My life had been turned around.

For two years I instructed cadets at that field and loved every minute of the program. I could see why we had lost almost 30 percent of the cadets when I went through the program in the early 1940s. Now the loss record was four percent. We were still using the same airplane, but the program had slowed and more details of learning had been added. In the two years of instructing, every one of my students soloed. I even picked up several students that other instructors had given up on, and got them to solo. The problem in most cases was that the instructors had done most of the flying instead of letting the students fly. A few instructors were actually frightened to allow students to fly.

The SNJ was a perfect training aircraft. It was easy to fly and usually forgiving for some of the common learning errors. It was a plane that was used by all the aviation services for at least two decades.

My life was changed when I started to instruct in the SNJ. I didn't realize teaching was my field until the military pointed it out to me. I was not happy at first to be an instructor for those cadets starting the program, but I learned with them, and they taught me some aspects about myself and teaching. I doubt if I would have ended up teaching and administering science for over 30 years in public schools if the SNJ and the Naval Training Program had not entered my life.

I have only one regret. I would like to remember the navy commander's name who was so considerate and understanding of me when I had a very poor attitude. He, the SNJ, and most of my students turned my life around.

Today there are still hundreds of SNJs flying in air shows, movies, and for private transportation. The few thousands of hours that I spent in the F4U Corsair and the SNJ (AT-6) Texan influenced my life favorably. Thanks to the manufacturers of the planes and their engines and to the USMC for placing me in their cockpits.

Boxcar Blues
By Myron H. Engel

Two C-119 aircraft were dispatched to MCAS Yuma, Arizona, for annual active training duty. On August 12, I was the aircraft commander and Lieutenant Kispert, my copilot, took off for a passenger trip from MCAS Yuma to MCAF Twenty-Nine Palms, California, to MCAS El Toro, California.

We stopped at MCAF Twenty-Nine Palms to drop off and pick up passengers. I was flying on takeoff. At the first reduction of takeoff power to climb power I turned off the water (ADI) and the left engine failed. I turned the water (ADI) back on and we were able to gain a little more altitude. I started to turn downwind and saw a group of base housing ahead.

We weren't that high off the ground so to avoid the houses, and because the engine was at maximum temperature, I made a 90-270 degree turn back to the runway. We dropped the landing gear and flaps as we approached the end of the runway. We landed and were able to stop the aircraft.

I believe that without the ADI for extra power on the good engine, we may not have made it back to the runway.

My crew did a marine-trained job of watching and helping me as well as keeping the passengers calm.

I was awarded a Certificate of Commendation from the commandant of the Marine Corps. Lieutenant Kispert and the rest of our crew were awarded a Certificate of Commendation from the commanding general of the Fourth Marine Aircraft Wing.

My commendation follows on the next page.

The C-119 Boxcar

United States Marine Corp Certificate of Commendation

     The Commandant of the Marine Corps takes pleasure in commending Captain Myron H. Engel, United States Marine Corp Reserve, for meritorious achievement in Aerial Flight while serving with the Marine Transport Squadron Two Hundred Thirty-Four on 12 August 1966. When the left engine of his aircraft failed during takeoff, he took immediate corrective action, and by his exceptional ability and presence of mind prevented the loss of an aircraft and possible death or injury to the embarked forty-seven passengers and crew. Captain Engel's conduct reflected great credit upon himself and upheld the highest traditions of the United States Marine Corps.

    Dated 22 APR 1967
Wallace M. Green, Jr.
Commandant of the Marine Corps.
Respectfully Submitted,
LT/COL USMCR Retired

A Flight to Remember
By Harry J. Goodyear

At Camp Ripley, Minnesota, in 1940, I was an enlisted private in Marine Reserve Squadron VOM-6R on a two-week annual duty tour. The duties during the encampment for enlisted men were military drills, KP duty, police duty (known to pick up and clean around the tent area), and learning to live like an active duty member of the regular Marine Corps. We also cleaned, gassed, and prepared aircraft for flight.

One day while I was assisting in preparing an aircraft, I was fortunate to be given the opportunity to fly in the rear seat of an SBC4 aircraft on a practice dive-bombing mission. The entire flight was exciting and eventful for me as my first flight in a military aircraft. The pilot was Colonel Melvin J. Maas. He was the congressman for the fourth district of Minnesota for eight terms, served in World War I and World War II, and was one of the founders of the Marine Corps Reserve Officers Association. He retired as a major general of the Marine Corps Reserve.

Truly a flight to remember!

Flying With Champagne, Cigars, and Ice
By Lyle Bradley

As a USMCR bachelor aviator, I was asked to fly hurried trips for our Minnesota squadron to deliver or pickup airplanes. In 1965 a squadron pilot, Tom Nystrom, and I were ordered to pick up two F9F Panther jets at the USMC air station in California. Our orders read to fly Western Airlines to Salt Lake City, change planes for Los Angeles, and then call for transportation from MCAS El Toro.

We met at the Minneapolis Terminal at 1700 on Friday, boarded the Western aircraft and waited for takeoff. This was a champagne flight so we had a bottle placed in front of us. Neither of us had eaten since breakfast so the champagne took effect quickly. A man in front of us was smoking a cigarette and neither of us were cigarette smokers. Tom indicated that he desired the guy to stop polluting the air. I volunteered to light up one of my cigars and blow the smoke at him. "Good idea," Tom exclaimed. So I did.

The smoker didn't notice the cigar smoke, but a stewardess did. She jumped on me and loudly said, "You can't smoke cigars in this plane!" When I complained about discrimination to allow cigarettes but no cigars, she responded that if I didn't stop she would tell the pilot. She begged me one more time to put out the cigar, so I dutifully responded.

The flight to Salt Lake was routine, but when we departed the plane the same stewardess who chewed me out handed me at least 10 Webster Fancy Tail cigars, which cost about five dollars each. "Just so there will be no hard feelings," she quietly said with a wink.

We arrived in Los Angeles and were picked up by a USMC car at the airport and spent a restful night at the air station.

On Saturday morning we signed the papers for the Panthers, gave them a good preflight check, and took off for Salt Lake City. We had filed an instrument flight plan because the weather was marginal. Our landing at Hill Air Force Base at Salt Lake City was uneventful. We refueled, filed the flight plan to Denver, Colorado, checked with the weather people for any indication of icing, and took off.

We were only about 400 feet off the runway when we entered the clouds. Our flight controller had told us again no icing could be expected. Icing for many planes is of little concern, but our aircraft had no deicing equipment.

As we were passing through 16,000 feet I made a quick check on Tom to insure he was still close on my wing. At that precise time both our blue airplanes became white with ice. We were covered. Almost instantly I could feel our climb speed slow so we nosed over to maintain the 300-knot speed. I communicated our icing situation to the controller and asked for verification that we could break out on top of the clouds at 26,000 feet. As we passed through the 20,000-foot level our angle of climb was decreasing and our climb speed was down to 260 knots because of the ice. It would be a difficult decision to return to Hill Air Base among the mountainous terrain. We decided, along with the controller, that we would nurse the planes for the last few thousand feet.

Suddenly we broke out of the clouds, and when the sun shown on our blue jets the ice started to peel off. In 10 minutes the ice was gone and our climb speed was back to 300 knots with our jets leveled at 30,000 feet. The reminder of the flight back to Denver and then to Minneapolis was routine.

Tom and I have chuckled over the years about our "routine" champagne, cigar, and icing flight to California and back. It was all part of the fascination of flying—never a dull moment.

Cross Country Navigation Training the Hard Way

By Andrew "Andy" W. Danielson

In the spring of 1962 the Marine Corps Reserve Command thought it wise to convert our two previously designated fighter-attack squadrons to transport squadrons. This was a bit of a shock to many who had previously looked down with disdain at anyone that needed two engines to keep a winged machine in the air. We were fighter pilots.

This re-designation meant that VMA-213 and VMA-234 would become VMR-234. It also meant the arrival of the dreaded R4Q, or as the air force called it, the C-119. How could they do this to us? Many thoughts went through our minds, none good. However, once we transitioned and learned a head full of new terms, we found that the C-119 could provide its own brand of thrills and chills. There were plenty of hours of boredom but many moments of stark terror, too.

The following mission took place during a NAS Minneapolis based ATD, a two-week period in which reservists sharpen their skills.

Four of us decided to sharpen ours by taking two boxcars (we will henceforth refer to the C-119 as a boxcar) to the island of Kodiak, Alaska, via Whidbey Island (Seattle), Washington. This took a bit of doing as special permission was required from on high. The entire plan had to be submitted to Glenview, Illinois, which was then headquarters for the Navy and Marine Air Reserve Training Command. I am not sure how we got this one through.

I should not go further without naming the guilty parties. Louie Farrell was a pilot with North Central Airlines (later to become

Republic and still later to merge with Northwest Airlines). Tom Nystrom was a physicist with 3M. Bill Messerli was an attorney, as was I. Bill and I were in charge of keeping the others out of jail. I don't know who was in charge of keeping us out.

We departed NAS Minneapolis on August 24, 1964. The flight to NAS Whidbey Island took about nine hours. It was uneventful but long. The evening was spent at the club playing ship captain and crew. Any marine is familiar with this game and should require no further explanation.

Because the next day would be a killer we chose not to get much sleep so as to be fully alert. We arose well before dawn, had the traditional fighter pilot breakfast of a cigarette and cup of coffee (we were still thinking fighter pilots) and were off.

The plan was to check our fuel in the area near Juneau and if tight, go on to Anchorage, refuel and fly down to Kodiak. The weather at Kodiak was often marginal as was the field due to the mountainous region. We would not have had enough fuel to take a missed approach at Kodiak and make it to Anchorage. There were no alternates, and swimming was not an option. The flight up the coast was a challenge due to clouds, ice rain, and stuff I choose to forget. Whenever there was a break in the clouds, the coastal peaks would appear to our right and sometimes above. The boxcar was a low flyer so we would then edge further out over the water. Also, the airways were via the old radio ranges rather than VOR. Some of you might remember the N and A quadrants. You young folks won't know what I am talking about. Take my word for it. It was interesting.

In the area of Juneau we elected to go to Anchorage for fuel. Seattle to Anchorage was eight hours plus. Refueling took at least an hour after which we took off for our destination, Kodiak. The sun sets late that time of year so we got to Kodiak right at sunset. This was after eleven or so difficult hours in the air.

Let me say a few words about the Kodiak naval and coast guard station. The longest runway was okay but sits in a valley enclosed on three sides by mountains, with one end at the water. The mountains are marked with white Xs in memory of those who attempted missed approaches. Landing was a little like flying into a horseshoe football stadium. At GCA (Ground Control Approach) minimums you had to land—there was no getting out of the canyon.

We checked into the BOQ (Bachelor Officer Quarters) but certainly not to sleep. We had to find out what the locals did for nightlife, so into the town of Kodiak we went. This was within a year or so of the great Alaska earthquake and there were still fishing boats sitting on the dirt main drag. The nightlife left a little to be desired. There was beer and a pinball machine and we learned a lot about gutting and canning salmon and king crab. We didn't want to spoil our edge by sleeping much this night either.

One of the rules we had to follow to make this trip was that we could stay out of the continental United States only one night. This rule was probably made by the same desk jockey that approved the trip. Since we now had our one night out, we had to take off before sundown. Salmon fishing was on the agenda so we got poles and lures from special services and headed for the soon-to-spawn fish. We caught lots. Special services was supposed to pick us up toward mid afternoon, but the earthquake had disrupted the landscape so at high tide the roads were under water. This put us in a time bind because we had to clean and ice the salmon, along with king crab that we had gotten, courtesy of the cannery. We also had to file the flight plan and get in the air all before sundown.

We got it all done and were set to takeoff for our eight-hour flight to Whidbey just as the sun was sinking into the Pacific. One big problem then arose. We could not use the best runway toward the water due to the wind. This meant takeoff toward the mountains with a full load of fuel, fish and people. This was the biggest challenge so far. Louie and Bill went first. They started their roll with the boxcar booms hanging over the water. We watched and watched and watched. They got off, made the turn, disappeared between two mountains and we finally spotted them out over the water. We did the same, but it was easier not having to watch, hoping those old 3350s would hold together just one more time.

We arrived at Whidbey just before dawn, but we had to takeoff right after refueling because of our load of salmon and crab. No sleep, but right back into the air for the eight to nine hour trip to Minneapolis. We were tired, so to stay awake across Montana and North Dakota we flew formation, and I mean real formation, not just two aircraft traveling in the same direction and in the same general vicinity. We were still trying to be fighter pilots. Our crews enjoyed this because they had never seen another aircraft in the air so up close and personal.

Bill, Louie, Tom and I have talked and laughed about the trip many times. It was probably best that this account not be published until now. I will let you compute the number of hours we were in the air with little or no sleep. All statutes of limitation have expired so we are safe. We did receive great cross-country navigational training but it came the hard way. Most importantly, we stayed out of jail.

Flameout!
By John Wastvedt

During the 1950s, after release from active duty during the Korean War, many of us continued on as pilots in the USMC Ready Reserve. We were required to report for duty one weekend a month and two weeks annually for training. The goal was at least 100 hours of flight time, preferably 150 or 200 hours annually. Accordingly we were encouraged to fly during the week but received no extra pay. By the mid fifties our Corsairs were obsolete and we were now flying Grumman Panther jets, single engine, single seat, day fighters that had no landing lights. Nevertheless, they were routinely flown at night, pilots soon becoming adept at using the runway edge lights as reference to judge height above the runway when landing.

To keep from getting rusty I would very often come out to the naval air station during the week after work to get in a few hours of flight time. These flights would generally be short cross-countries, simulated instruments or tactical work if other pilots were flying at the same time I was, which wasn't very often. Almost always these flights would conclude with four or five "touch and go" landings where the pilot would land, then immediately add throttle, take off, stay in the landing pattern, and land again.

On Thursday night, March 15, 1956, my wife was invited to a baby shower in her honor, expecting our fourth child in a couple of months, so I scheduled myself for a flight at the same time. Leaving work about 5:30 P.M. I arrived at the air station at 6:00 and was in the air by 7:00. After a short cross-country to Duluth, Fargo, and back, I requested several "touch and gos" from the Minneapolis tower, which were approved. The runway in use was 29L, to the northwest, which has a small lake off the end, frozen over at that time of the year. A road ran along the edge of the airport between the end of the runway and the lake (Mother Lake).

After two or three uneventful landings I had just made another takeoff and was in a left turn about 400 or 500 feet above the ground when all of a sudden there was a deafening silence—the engine had failed! The landing gear was retracting and from that point there was only a second or two to react—no time to think beyond "Don't Stall!" Seeing the lights of the city of Richfield immediately to the south and southeast, I pointed the nose toward Mother Lake, established an airspeed of 120 knots, well above stall speed, and rode it down. There were no landing lights, so I wouldn't know when or if I was going to hit the lake and wouldn't be able to flare and lessen the impact. As I was approaching the road, which had a large ditch alongside it just on the edge of the lake, the lights of a car appeared and it seemed I was going hit it, or the ditch, or both. Flinching, waiting for the crash, a fraction of a second later I struck the surface of the lake—I had cleared the ditch and auto! The impact must have been cushioned by the slightly extended landing gear that cut into the ice and kept the aircraft from careening across the lake. Even so, I saw stars.

Immediately after stopping I unbuckled the parachute, hopped out of the cockpit and ran a dozen yards in case it exploded. Now the silence was broken only by the hum of a few cars passing on the road I'd just missed. Then the faint sirens in the distance as the tower had alerted the rescue crews. In the few seconds after fleeing the aircraft and now awaiting the arrival of the rescue crew a feeling of exultation flooded over me—Oh my God, I'm alive!

A few minutes later the rescue crew and ambulance arrived along with a navy vehicle carrying maintenance personnel. The maintenance officer in charge ignored me as he strode immediately to the fuel port with a measuring stick in hand. I could read the disappointment on his face when he found plenty of fuel and couldn't blame the pilot. Now it was his problem.

The ambulance brought me to the navy sick bay for a check up and X-rays of my spine. No crushed vertebrae, fortunately, but for a week after I couldn't move without pain. Then the TV reporters and the station commanding officer showed up and it was a couple of hours before I got away and went home.

Meanwhile, at the baby shower, one of the husbands had been watching the news on television and saw a shot of the aircraft that "crashed" on Mother Lake. He knew that I had gone out to fly that night but no name had been mentioned. Finally the word came that the pilot was okay, so Laurene, my wife, was informed of the accident and that I was all right.

In the aftermath I realized how incredibly lucky I had been. The window of survival was no more than two or three seconds. A fraction of a second earlier and I would have hit the auto or ditch or both; two or three seconds later and I would have crashed into the residential area of Richfield. The odds of surviving either of these scenarios was extremely remote.

The inquiry by the navy into the cause of the accident was inconclusive. The engine was later examined and "run up"—no mechanical fault was found. It was surmised that maybe a slug of water had gone through the engine, but of course I had no time to attempt a restart to either prove or disprove this theory. One headquarter type claimed that I was operating on the "back side" of the power curve where the induced drag is greater than the available thrust. It was then pointed out to him that the thrust of the Panther engine was well above the induced drag even close to the stalling speed with gear and flaps down.

Many changes have occurred at the airport since the accident. The naval air station was closed sometime in the 1970s, the airport has much more traffic and has expanded to include another runway. But Mother Lake is still there, and every time I pass it on the highway to the west I think of that night fifty years ago.

I Married a Marine
By Laurene Wastvedt

I married a marine, John Wastvedt, the love of my life since I was age 15. We met while skating on an outdoor rink in the small town of Hawley, Minnesota, where we were born, and for 62 years we've had a fascinating and full life together. I married him when he returned from duty in the South Pacific where he had been flying Corsairs off the carrier *Essex*. After reading numerous books on the war, I give thanks to this day to still have my marine at my side.

The wedding over, we traveled to Jacksonville to report for duty after John's leave. We found a small bedroom to rent near the base. John left me to report in and said he would return in an hour. He didn't return. I waited all day and night. No phone call, no money for bus fare and nothing to eat, frightened by his total disappearance. The story: He was asked to fly a Corsair to a training carrier just off the coast, drop it off and return on a mail plane. "Shouldn't take more than an hour or two," he was told. It was Sunday, so there was no mail plane, and no phone call to me. My first upsetting moment!

The next move was to Sanford, Florida, this time to a rented motel room. Shortly, a serious hurricane blew in. The planes had to be flown to safe ground, leaving the wives to deal with the storm. We saw the streets turn into snake infested rivers with our cars under water.

The war was finally over, but my marine stayed in the reserves while attending the University of Minnesota. In 1951 John was re-called to active duty in the Korean Conflict and stationed at Cherry Point. We decided to join him there so that we could be together for the birth of our third baby. The navy doctor who delivered Jim was our

Laurene Wastvedt

next-door neighbor. He was a great support and friend to help alleviate the fear I had, as our first baby was brain damaged at birth. I was allowed one day for my stay in the hospital. The morning started with baked beans and fried tomatoes for breakfast, and then the navy corpsmen arrived in the doorway with numerous babies in their hands and arms, jokingly pretending they would make a football pass into my receiving arms.

Those in the marine reserves were not high on the list to receive housing, so we were told our time was up in the Quonset hut. We headed back to Minneapolis with the new baby, which had been misdiagnosed with malaria. Our trip to Washington to get me and our three babies on a flight to Minneapolis turned out to be hell. We were stopped by the police in a speed trap. We were herded in a caravan to a justice of the peace where we had to pay or go to jail. They wouldn't listen to my story of our sick baby or about having a flight to catch with little time to spare. We made it on time, however. I suggested getting something to eat for the babies, but John said we would get dinner on the plane. It was a very hot day and the air conditioning on the plane was inoperative and no meals were served. The stewardesses felt sorry for me and gave the boys all the cookies and milk they could hold. The plane was very late and my parents were to meet us but there was no listing of the flight on the airline schedule. My father thought they were covering up a mishap and the plane had crashed. What a relief for everyone when I arrived. I lost my voice for several days from the ordeal, but my parents were a great help. In terms of the baby's illness, it turned out to be all the chemicals in the drinking water at Cherry Point. Even though I boiled it for half an hour before using, it still made him sick.

Now I was home alone with the babies and very lonely. On New Year's Eve, during the day and without asking the boss, who was miles away, I ordered a TV set on the telephone and told the salesman to send the best in stock. It arrived the same day and turned out to be a lifesaving companion.

The Korean Conflict was finally over, but John stayed in the reserves flying jet fighters. On one of his night flights he crashed on takeoff at Wold-Chamberlain Field while I was at a baby shower celebrating the imminent arrival of our fourth child. The crash was all over the TV news but fortunately John was not seriously hurt. That baby was our first girl and is now a captain of an MD-11, thanks to the guidance of her flying father.

Our lives have been full of adventures related to being a marine's wife, including flying "space available" in huge military cargo and tanker planes across the Atlantic. Many times we slept on the terminal floor waiting to be called. Sadly, on one of the return flights, we shared the cargo section with many marines who had died in the bombing of their barracks in Beirut. The pilot of another flight asked if I would like to see a mid-air refueling. Of course I would! I crawled up a narrow tube and then laid on my back to witness the stars in their prime, along with the umbilical cord like tube finding its way into the fuel tank of a fighter. Then the pilot asked me if I would like to join them in the cockpit. What a thrill! Another journey was so cold in the cargo area I had to put my feet in a sack of wool yarn to keep them from freezing.

Our "space available" flights are now in the past. We enjoy the annual squadron reunion and renewing the important friendships from long ago.

Sunset Tactics
By Lyle Bradley

Would you like to fly with four beautiful F4U Corsairs, piloted by four marines who love to fly, getting pulled through the air by a huge prop attached to a 2,000 plus horsepower engine, on a late summer tactics flight? This hop was done on a perfect flying day with ground temperatures at 65 degrees, clear air, and an awesome battery of reddish alto cumulous clouds framing the setting sun.

The four pilots were John Wastvedt, Jim Bailey, Jim Levine, and myself. We each had over 1,000 hours of cockpit time in Corsairs in two wars (World War II and Korea), along with stateside training. All four of us had been division leaders in combat squadrons.

After takeoff from the Wold-Chamberlain Field (now Minneapolis-St.Paul International Airport) we rendezvoused as we climbed toward the tactics area about 40 miles west of the airport. John Wastvedt was the designated leader for the first series of tactics. We leveled off at 9,000 feet and he called for a tight division wingover as warm-up. The division is composed of two sections (two planes each), and tight means no more than space for one plane between each aircraft.

A tactics hop has much action and therefore must be done in an area where other aircraft are avoided. Everyone must still keep his "head-on-a-swivel" to insure air safety. Some of the maneuvers on this type of flight include aerobatics, tail chases, gunnery runs, barrel rolls, wingovers, and other wild ideas as defined by the leader. The leader is changed often to parallel the changing colors in the sunset. Yes, it is a perfect time to fly.

I was thinking that flying in heaven could not be better. Could pilot heaven (a spot we heard about many times in training) be as wonderful as this evening setting?

The four of us all thought that the Corsair was our favorite airplane out of the estimated 20 types that each of us had flown. We all loved to fly, which our logbooks, experience, and conversation proved. All four of us had complete confidence in ourselves and in each other. Our aviation experiences had been diverse and time proven.

As each pilot took the lead, he would call out by radio his choice of maneuver. It might be a division barrel roll, a tail chase loop, a section fighter weave, a flatside gunnery run, or a division Cuban eight loop.

Flying fighter planes is an exacting skill, especially when more than one aircraft is involved. Let's examine a simple maneuver like the barrel roll. Say we start at 8,000 feet at a speed of 220 knots. Our heading is 090 (heading east so no one faces the sun). All four planes are tucked in tight and nose over to exceed 270 knots. The leader then starts an easy climbing turn so that he will be 90 degrees off the start heading and have all four planes on their backs. A quick glance at his altimeter should indicate he is close to the start altitude. The roll is smoothly continued as the easy dive is turned back toward the original heading. The last part of the roll is an easy climb back to the original altitude, heading, and airspeed.

The barrel roll, and every maneuver, takes practice by yourself before trying it in a formation of aircraft. There have been accidents because one or more persons screwed up, whether it be in horse and buggy, automobiles, bikes, or airplanes. Overconfidence combined with little experience can result in tragedy with any vehicle.

Our maneuvers on this flight were limited. We did not chase tails close to clouds (one of my favorite activities), do overhead gunnery runs, snap rolls, spins, or extended inverted flight (flying upside

Corsairs in formation

down). Maneuvers taking excessive airspace or resulting in aircraft not under complete control every second were not practiced, because there is always a chance of crashing during such split-second maneuvers, even with extremely competent pilots.

After landing, with four happy and perspiring aviators walking to the operations office, Jim Levine expressed all our feelings. "Wow! That was one of the best hops I've had in years. Thanks, guys."

As it turned out, that was the last Corsair flight for two of us. Our Corsairs were at the end of their service tour and were being replaced with F9F Panther jets. Ten years later I sat in the cockpit of a Corsair in Oshkosh, Wisconsin, at the EAA (Experimental Aircraft Association) and felt tears trickling down my cheeks. Yes, pilots do get sentimental about airplanes, especially when one carries you through two wars, years of training, and fabulous memorable flights. Of the 22 military aircraft that I have flown, the Corsair is my all time favorite.

This perfect flight is one of those memorable ones. It took place 42 years ago, but it seems much more recent.

TRAINING

Whirlybirds
By Robert A. Kilgore

I was stationed in El Toro, California, in October of 1950 flying F4U Corsairs but getting very little flight time. One day there was a notice on the bulletin board noting that the Marine Corps needed helicopter pilots in Quantico, Virginia. Enrolling in a hurry, I was soon at Quantico not knowing what to expect.

My first flight was with an instructor in a tiny Bell copter that felt like flying in a fishbowl. We came skimming across the field and suddenly the instructor stood the copter on its tail, and we came to a stop ten feet in the air. As a fixed wing pilot, stopping while still airborne was not recommended, and I had serious doubts about my recent decision.

Another maneuver, known as auto rotation, was to be followed if the engine failed. It consisted of disengaging the engine from the rotor, allowing the rotor to freewheel. Inertia built up in the rotor on the descent and gave lift when you flared as you approached the ground, allowing for a soft landing.

We moved up to fly the Piasecki HRP, a much larger machine with twin rotors. It was underpowered, and every landing was like a controlled crash. After three months training, I received my helicopter license, number 321.

Shortly thereafter, a group of us were sent to Santa Ana, California, to start forming squadrons for Korea. We were now flying the Sikorski HRS, which were troop-type copters. We began ferrying them from Quantico to Santa Ana in groups of four.

On my first trip we ran into a terrific thunderstorm. When it became impossible to maintain visual contact, all four of us landed in

Kilgore in the Sikorski HRS

a farmer's yard. After his initial shock of having four large machines land in his yard, the farmer was very considerate and fed us lunch.

The trip took four days and consisted of seventeen hops of about two hours each. There were no altitude restrictions at the time so we spent some time at 200 feet. It was a remarkable way to see the country. Flying across the desert, the crew chief spent time shooting at jackrabbits with a .45. It kept him and a few others occupied, and there was very little danger to the rabbits.

One of our stops was at Wink, Texas. While circling for a landing, I saw a pickup truck from town headed for the airport. On landing, we found the truck driver was a girl who had a case of beer for us. The landing wasn't a total success as one of the pilots chopped off his tail rotor. After refueling we proceeded to leave the crew chief with the damaged copter. I found out later the crew chief married the girl in the truck, so the incident had a happy ending after all.

Carrier Landing Woes
By C. M. (Tony) Plattner

Flying experiences are like good wine—they improve over time with every flavorable sip of retelling. I loved flying but it was not without its risks, and there are a few memories worth recalling.

I had the good fortune to fly some of the great piston-engine airplanes as well as jet-powered aircraft. Additionally I cherished the great friendships and experiences that came about from being in the Marine Air Reserve.

I went on to accumulate 27 years of reserve time and over 2,500 military and civil flight hours before retirement. Although a lot of my reserve career was spent at other bases in California and Washington, Minnesota always remains special to me.

It all began in the middle of the Korean Conflict, within two weeks of graduation from Carleton College in June 1952. With my new college education as a background for tough decision making, I decided that getting paid while learning to fly in the premium aviation program of the time would be far more rewarding than learning to march and carry a rifle.

Prodded by the Draft Board in my hometown of Walker, Minnesota, who informed me that my college deferment was over, I sought out the navy recruiting office, signed up and almost immediately took a series of visual, physical, and mental tests at the Naval Air Station at Wold-Chamberlain Airport.

I passed handily and on August 30 I was at NAS Pensacola checking in as a naval aviation cadet. This would be my rank for the next 15 and one half months. It was somewhere in the no-man's land between enlisted and officer, paid $98 a month, and had few privileges early on, but the training was enjoyable and challenging.

Two experiences worthy of note occurred during training.

The first was on a Field Carrier Landing Practice (FCLP) hop from Baron Field in preparation for landing on the carrier at the finish of primary training. After entering the racetrack pattern, I proceeded from the 180-degree position abeam the field to the 45, all the while carefully controlling speed and altitude and trying to respond meaningfully to paddle controls of the landing signal officer located next to the painted outline of a carrier deck on the runway.

Suddenly, my engine quit. At the time, I was only a few knots above stall speed and about 125 feet above the scrub-covered terrain. This left little time for reflection since stalling out at that altitude almost certainly would result in one of those grim fatality statistics, so I dumped the nose hard. Setting up a glide and making a smooth landing from those conditions is difficult at best, and I hit the ground hard, cart wheeled, and came to rest upright.

The engine of the rugged North American SNJ trainer had come off, and after everything stopped it lay off to one side with a fire quickly beginning near the firewall—meaning a potentially explosive situation.

With the canopy already open I swiftly unfastened my lap and shoulder harness, jumped out of the stricken plane and started running with maximum dispatch to escape the anticipated explosion.

However, after running some 10 to 20 feet, I sensed that I wasn't making the progress that I should and looked down to see the parachute still attached to me by the leg buckles.

One of the checklist procedures prior to entering the pattern was to unbuckle the leg straps and prevent this very situation, but I had been hurried for some reason and neglected this detail.

In any event I soon distanced myself from the burning aircraft much faster without my clumsy attachment and waited for a helicopter pickup. Once inside the helicopter, the corpsman made available the standard medicine for an uninjured crewman—two miniature bottles of booze, which I quickly dispatched.

After a speedy accident investigation, I rejoined my flight, completed field landing carrier practice and flew to the carrier for my six traps and graduation from primary.

Another notable but less life threatening experience at Pensacola was at the completion of advanced training. It also involved carrier landings. This time the machine was the Grumman F6F Hellcat, which was a memorable airplane to fly. It was one of the truly great piston aircraft of the era, with an outstanding record in the Pacific during World War II.

I had decided to become a marine rather than navy aviator after primary training, and for single-engine (rather than multi-engine) types this meant qualifying again on the carrier.

It was during the final big event of landing the F6F on the carrier after field practice that it happened. Keep in mind that this was an era before modern aids, including glide-slope lenses, angle of attack indicators and canted decks, had been invented. The pilot was tasked with putting all flight variables together manually on the approach with direction from a landing signal officer waving paddles on the stern of the carrier.

I was in the first flight from shore to land directly on the carrier. I diligently followed the commands of the LSO, kept my airspeed, attitude and altitude in good shape, and in the "controlled crash" that was judged a good carrier landing, picked up an early wire.

As I followed the directions of the flight deck crewman to raise my hook and taxi forward, a stern voice came over my headset: "Iron 36" (my call sign). "You have just cost the navy $56,000."

To a young cadet who hoped to receive his aviator wings and second lieutenant bars within a few days and depart for home by Christmas, this came as a devastating and perplexing blow. Then came the wing fold, and I taxied to the elevator and was stowed below on the hangar deck. My directions were to wait in the ready room.

After one to two hours during which no one answered my question as to what was going on, the LSO came into the ready room to debrief the flight. When he finally came to Navcad Plattner, my anxiety had built to a fever pitch.

He said that a leather mallet had been forgotten in the nose air scoop during maintenance and that in the deceleration of the landing it had lurched forward, was caught by the propeller, and was skyrocketed upward.

The operations officer on the bridge mistook this for a ramp strike and assumed I had put on my brakes, nosed forward, and had hit the wooden deck with my propeller, causing debris to be thrown upward. The LSO asked if I wanted to get back into an airplane and continue, and I have never been so affirmative in a response.

At a modest 5'8" in height, the inlet of the F6 was beyond my jumping acumen, although I remember trying without success to look in the air scoop while preflighting the airplane. The remainder of the day was uneventful and after five more traps and a final cat shot, I flew to the beach and graduated with my flight.

Aerial Gunnery With Lewis Machine
By Goodwin Luck

One of the most interesting training exercises in 1936 at Camp Ripley, Minnesota, and at Duluth over Lake Superior, was aerial gunnery. The gunner rode in the rear cockpit of a Curtiss 02C-1 Helldiver and fired at a white cloth sleeve being towed by another aircraft. The machine gun was a Lewis 30-caliber model of World War I vintage. The shells were fed from a drum mounted on top of the gun. The drum held 99 cartridges, which had painted tips that would leave identifying marks on the sleeve when hit. By counting the number of the shooter's color in the sleeve the gunner's score could be determined.

PFC Edward Luck, USMCR, V06-MR, prepared for an aerial gunnery exercise at Camp Ripley, Minnesota, 1936, in Curtiss Helldiver.

A couple of junior officers decided to play a trick on the commanding officer by shooting a new sleeve on the ground with a full drum of bullets painted with the CO's color, not thinking that the CO would get any hits. They then bet the CO would get the most hits, which he did. The CO, however, managed to get some ten hits of his own, and the junior officers' game was over.

Gunnery over Lake Superior was very interesting. There was no horizon line where the sky and water met and vertigo for the gunner was common. Gasoline for our aircraft was driven to Duluth from NRAB Minneapolis by truck on old Highway 61. At night we slept in hammocks in the navy training ship *Paduka*, anchored in the Duluth harbor.

Learning to Tame the Iron Bird
By Richard Hansen

In World War II, all the armed services were in need of pilots. The navy program was available to high school graduates who were physically fit, could fit a height and weight parameter, had 20/20 vision, and could pass a basic intelligence test.

Those who qualified and were accepted entered a Civilian Pilot Training program at one of many local airports to determine their suitability for flying. I was assigned to take my training at South Saint Paul Airport.

While we were taking the Civilian Pilot Training flight course we also had some ground schooling and some marching and weapon handling training, and mine was at the armory at the University of Minnesota.

Preflight school at the University of Iowa at Iowa City followed. This course lasted about ten weeks, seven days a week, and included a physical training program and a lot of advanced ground schooling.

The physical program included swimming. The swimming instructor was a terror for people who didn't know how to swim. Fortunately I did, and I didn't have any problem with him. If you didn't you learned fast, because in his opinion, if you wanted to fly for the navy off a carrier you needed to know how to swim. The rest of the program was designed to get you in shape and included running and other physical exercises.

The ground school academic program included much weather data, navigation (including celestial), and dead reckoning courses.

Over the wall.

We spent a lot of time identifying friend or foe (IFF), memorizing airplanes and ships from both allied and enemy forces.

After the ten weeks we were anxious to leave preflight school and move on to the Minneapolis Naval Air Station to start training in the navy planes.

When we arrived at the Marine Corps base in El Toro, California, for fighter pilot school, there were all kinds of stories about checking out in the Corsair by pilots that preceded us there. Most of them pertained to the first takeoffs and landings.

The Corsair was a magnificent airplane powered by a 2,000 horsepower radial engine with two banks of nine cylinders each. This engine spun a 13-foot diameter propeller that produced airspeeds in excess of 420 miles per hour, both at full throttle and in war emergency mode.

Armament consisted of six 50-caliber machine guns or four 20-mm cannons, plus 2,000 pounds of bombs or napalm and six rockets. The Corsair was used for air to air combat and as a close air support plane for the ground forces.

I approached my first flight in the Corsair with much excitement and anticipation. We had been told to ease the throttle on and to ease the left rudder pedal down to counteract the tremendous torque generated during takeoff. They were right, and it worked; in 900 feet we were flying—and I was in love.

I flew around for about an hour, then came in and landed. I went right back to the head of the runway and did it all over again a few more times. The power of that bird was so different than what we had been flying, including the TBF, that there was no comparison. The engine in the TBF was 1,850 horsepower, but the aircraft was a lot heavier and the propeller shorter.

The next few days were all familiarization flights and I flew it upside down, looped it, rolled it, and pushed the speed up to over 400 mph. The plane did everything I asked, with more power still available.

For the next twelve weeks or so we flew every day, weather permitting, and by now we had tamed the iron bird. We no longer worried about takeoffs and landings as everything was now routine.

During this period we worked on gunnery, bombing, strafing, and fighter tactics. In combat formation we flew in flights of four whether it would be an air battle, bombing and strafing, or close air support. If it was a big bombing raid we might have 48 planes involved, but we always maintained the flights of four that made up the basic units.

Four planes in each flight was developed early in the war by a navy commander named Thatch. The reasoning for this is that in a flight of four, two of the planes can always cover for the other two planes. In air-to-air combat, the two planes could weave back and forth in a scissor fashion, watching the other two planes. This action was called the Thatch weave.

In gunnery practice we had a tow plane that pulled a cloth sleeve about 100 yards behind it. The individual planes would make four or five gunnery runs on it. The bullets we used were coated with a colored dye that came off on the sleeve as they went into it. Each pilot had a different colored bullet, and after the exercise the sleeve was dropped on the runway and retrieved to see who had the most holes in it. (Although Ted Williams of baseball fame was not in our group, it was said that he was always the best.) This was good training, and we learned how much to lead a target coming in from different directions.

By now we were well trained and were anxious to move on. Because of a paper mix-up, my orders to go to Mojave for formation of a new squadron with my best friend and roommate, Bruce Guetzloe, were sent to a different person by the name of Hansen. Instead, I was sent overseas as a replacement. I was very sad and upset for quite some time.

As it turned out, my friends that went to Mojave only saw one day of combat. They were aboard the carrier *Franklin* when it was hit by two bombs that killed about 700 men, most of whom were their squadron mechanics.

Cold Weather Flying
By Robert A. Kilgore

We had just finished preflight training in Iowa City and were sent to Minneapolis for basic flight training. The planes we flew were mostly the Stearman N2S fabric-covered biplane with two open cockpits. It was a wonderful plane for beginners, such as myself, with no bad characteristics. The only drawback was that it had a rather narrow landing gear, which led to ground loops (the aircraft going off the runway). It was December, and over half our group was from Minnesota, with the other half being from the south. Many of them had never experienced cold and snow. Needless to say they grumbled for three months.

Our daily routine was to don a fleece-lined leather jacket, pants, helmet, boots and gloves. Then we lugged our parachute and our instructor's parachute out to the plane. This outfit was not only heavy, it was extremely cumbersome. Sometimes we had to help push the planes out to the flight line.

When we first started flying, they suspended flight operations when the temperature dropped to ten degrees because of the open cockpits. It got colder, so they lowered the temperature to zero degrees. We weren't getting much airtime, so they lowered it again to minus ten degrees. We wore chamois facemasks, but at that temperature your nose drips and the mask ices up from your breath. Your fingers stiffen and don't function well after a few minutes. The planes were equipped with a relief tube (for urinating), but any thought of using it was out of the question.

Despite all the problems, we finished the program almost on time. When they announced we were heading south, I heard a weak cheer from our southern comrades.

Pheasant Catch
By Lyle Bradley

In September 1943 I had just soloed in the N2S Stearman biplane. The next stage was to work on our landings. At an outlying field near our Fleming Field there was an 80-foot circle painted on the field. We had to enter the landing pattern, cut the throttle completely, and glide the plane to the circle. Next we poured the power on to takeoff and try again.

One morning I was the first one to the field using the circle and did the normal power off and glide to the circle. When I opened the throttle, the sudden sound frightened a rooster ring-necked pheasant. It flew up in front of the wing, and since my speed was greater than his, we crashed together. He got caught in the right wing wires,

The Stearman biplane.

fluttered a little, and then went limp. I had bagged a pheasant out of season and he was staying with me. For the entire flight the bird hung in the wires.

When I landed at the home field the bird drew much attention. Thankfully no game wardens were among the admirers. One of the plane captains asked if he could have the bird, so I assume he and his family had preseason pheasant for dinner.

Uncertainties In Training
By Edward Anders Sovik

When we were nearing the end of our months at Pensacola those of us who had been accepted for Marine Corps commissions were asked to choose fighters, dive-bombers, or transport flying for operational training, the final phase. Most of us chose fighters, I suppose. But all of us couldn't be winners. How the judgment was made I don't know. I was sent to Opa Locka, near Miami, for dive-bomber training. There we did more formation flying, more navigation, a good deal of gunnery, flying SNJs with 30-caliber guns aiming at cloth sleeves trailed behind tow planes. I did well enough, with more hits than anyone else in our flight. We often had some leftover ammunition after the gunnery runs. Someone got the idea of dropping down to the ocean to see if we could shoot some sea gulls as they cruised the wave tops. We could. I missed some, shot one and quit the hunt. It was very dangerous, and when one of the pilots came back with his propeller tips curled from dipping into the water, the practice was banned.

For the dive-bombing exercises we flew an ancient airplane that had been retired from the fleet called the BT-1. It was a monoplane, designed, I think, in the early 1930s. It was a slow climber with engines that sprayed oil on the windshield, and old telescopic sights. My log says I made nine bombing hops, each with ten practice bombs. We climbed to 10,000 feet above the target, then came down one after another to drop the bombs and pull out; we then started the long climb up to 10,000 feet and did it again. I remember getting the hang of it, and on the last flight dropped all ten bombs inside the circle.

Training

But the flight I remember best from Opa Locka (we flew 65 hours solo and 10 hours in the back seat those six weeks) was a hop in another old scout bomber, the Curtiss SBC. It was a biplane and was not easy to fly; it landed very fast for a carrier plane, and its wheels were close together so ground loops were a hazard. We were, I believe, learning formation flying and navigation. Our hops were out over the water and as long as three hours.

An instructor led us out in six-plane divisions. As it happened one day our instructor left us early to land and I was at that time leading the first section as we approached the field. Which runway to use? (We didn't use radio communications with the tower.) I saw a nice plume of smoke from a tall stack perfectly parallel with one of the runways. "This is easy," I thought as I broke off, and I was perfectly set on what I thought was the downwind leg. I made a tight turn and made my landing. "Fast," I thought and suddenly realized I had landed downwind. The brakes and everything else worked, and as I turned off for the ramp halfway down I saw that the others in the flight had been smart enough not to follow me. One of them was on final approach coming in the right way at the other end of the runway.

The instructor was standing waiting for me as I taxied in and got out of the plane sheepishly, expecting some sort of discipline. "Stupid, wasn't it?" I said. "Sure was," he said, "but if you can land that thing downwind and get away with it, I guess we'll let it go. You won't do it again."

I've blessed that man often.

In January, Nate Bedell, John Thistlethwaite and I, who were the marines in our flight of fledgling dive-bombers, got our orders. We were to go to night fighters, a new venture in marine aviation. The training group was at Cherry Point, North Carolina, a place of which I had never heard.

Flying the F3F-2 Biplane
By Goodwin Luck

When I received my wings at the Naval Air Station in Pensacola, Florida, in 1939 I was anxious to be assigned to a marine fighting squadron, but I was assigned to Marine Scouting Squadron Two stationed at North Island. I flew Curtiss SOC-3 aircraft for a short time and then was transferred, along with two other SOC-3 pilots, to Marine Fighting Squadron Two, which operated Grumman F3F-2 fighter aircraft. At the time the F3F-2 was the hottest fighter in the U.S. Navy Fleet.

There was apparently some need to get us three new pilots carrier-qualified as we were allowed about 15 hours of flight time in the F3F-2 aircraft prior to landing on the aircraft carrier *Saratoga*. Most of our familiarization time was dedicated to field carrier landings. The *Saratoga* was put to sea off the California coast, apparently to permit us three pilots to qualify. We did this in spite of our apprehension, to put it mildly.

The *Saratoga* had a straight flight deck with a barrier fence made of several strong cables across the flight deck about mid ship. When a plane landed on the deck, a hook on the back of the plane caught a heavy cable to stop. The barrier farther down the deck was to stop any aircraft not initially "trapped" by one of primary arresting cables. The barrier was laid flat on the deck to allow aircraft that had landed properly to taxi over the barrier to the bow area.

After my final qualification landing I had just taxied over the barrier when I heard the crash warning sound. The aircraft that landed behind me did not catch one of the arresting cables because its landing hook was broken. Fortunately for me, the barrier came up in time to stop the aircraft, and no one was injured.

I was designated squadron navigator and flew in the number three position on the squadron commander. This was a "busy" job since the landing gear was operated by a hand crank. Staying in formation was a challenge, as was navigating the squadron, which was a big responsibility. Throat microphones helped lessen the problems. One of our main assignments was to fly high altitude (30,000 feet) "picket" flights over the fleet so as to intercept attacking enemy aircraft. The F3F-2 aircraft cockpit was not pressurized or heated, so the pilot had to wear winter flight gear to keep from freezing. Oxygen was supplied to the pilot by a pipe stem tube held in the pilot's mouth. This was a dangerous situation because if the oxygen tube was dropped at 30,000 feet the pilot had less than a minute to get oxygen flow stabilized again. Also, the cold temperature caused the lubricant to congeal on the two 30-caliber machine guns, which fired through the three-bladed propeller. The guns were controlled by gearing so as to miss hitting the propeller blades. At altitude we would manually lean the engine running with the mixture control and reduce the engine RPMs to 1500. This increased endurance considerably.

On one such picket flight on August 29, 1940, we had been kept on station for an extra long time. Apparently a Japanese "fishing" boat was too close to the *Saratoga* and one of our destroyers escorted it some distance away so it could not observe our carrier landings. This took some time, which used up extra aircraft fuel. The first twelve F3F-2 landed okay on the carrier. The engine stopped on 2-MF-16, the F3F Bob Galer was flying, and ditched into the ocean on its final approach to the *Saratoga*. After the aircraft sank, one of our destroyers picked up Bob, who was not injured. In about 1998, that same 2-MF-16 was salvaged from the ocean and restored at San Diego and

The salvaged F3F.

Pensacola. It is now on display in the Museum at NAS Pensacola and is currently the only F3F in existence.

Other flights in F3F-2s were familiarization, field carrier landings, instruments, gunnery (aerial and camera), homing, tactics, observations, formations, night tactics, bombing, takeoffs, navigation and utility.

Apparently the need to get VMF-2 completely carrier-qualified at an early date was changed because the carrier Enterprise with VF-6 attached received orders to Hawaii instead.

VMF-2 was designated VMF-211 and was transferred to Wake Island in 1941 equipped with a few F4F aircraft which replaced all the F3F-2s.

I was transferred to Naval Reserve Air Base Minneapolis, Minnesota, as a flight instructor in time to almost get frozen in the devastating November 11, 1940, blizzard. I continued there well into 1942 and had many students.

I crossed paths with one of my students, Ed Sovik, more than 60 years later at a Minnesota Marine Air Reserve meeting in 2005.

As we talked, we soon discovered it was a historic reunion. As the pages in our logbooks show for March 5, 1942, I was an instructor and Sovik was a beginning flyer, and therefore rode as a passenger. Sovik's record has two important lines; one shows me as the pilot, Sovik as passenger. The next line shows Sovik as pilot, flying solo. I had given Sovik a check flight after about eleven hours of instruction, and the logbooks imply that I gave Sovik an "up-check," warranting that he was ready to fly alone. We continue to have lunch together each month.

Luck's logbook for March 5, 1942 (top line), shows him as instructor for Sovik.

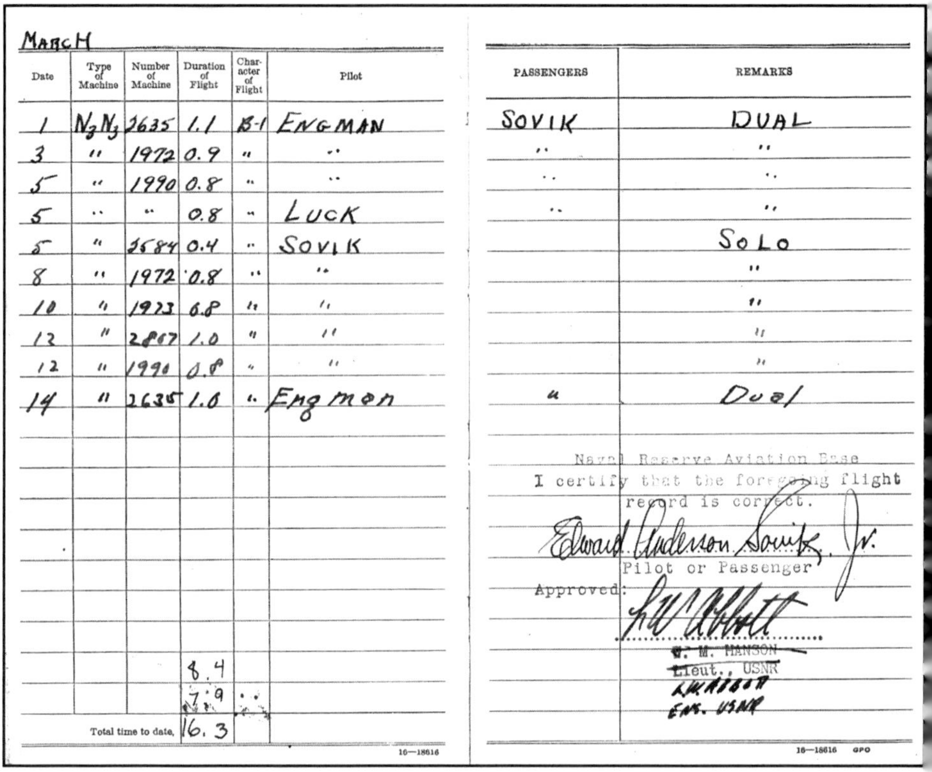

MARINE WINGS

Date	Type of Machine	Number of Machine	Duration of Flight	Character of Flight	Pilot	PASSENGERS	REMARKS
1	N_3N_3	2635	1.1	B-1	ENGMAN	SOVIK	DUAL
3	"	1972	0.9	"	"	"	"
5	"	1990	0.8	"	"	"	"
5	"	"	0.8	"	LUCK	"	"
5	"	2584	0.4	"	SOVIK		SOLO
8	"	1972	0.8	"	"		"
10	"	1923	6.8	"	"		"
12	"	2807	1.0	"	"		"
12	"	1990	0.8	"	"		"
14	"	2635	1.0	"	Engmon	"	Dual

Naval Reserve Aviation Base
I certify that the foregoing flight record is correct.

Edward Anderson Sovik, Jr.
Pilot or Passenger
Approved:
C. M. HANSON
Lieut., USNR

8.4
7.9
Total time to date, 16.3

Sovik's logbook on March 5, 1942, shows Luck as instructor.
The next line shows Sovik flying solo.

298

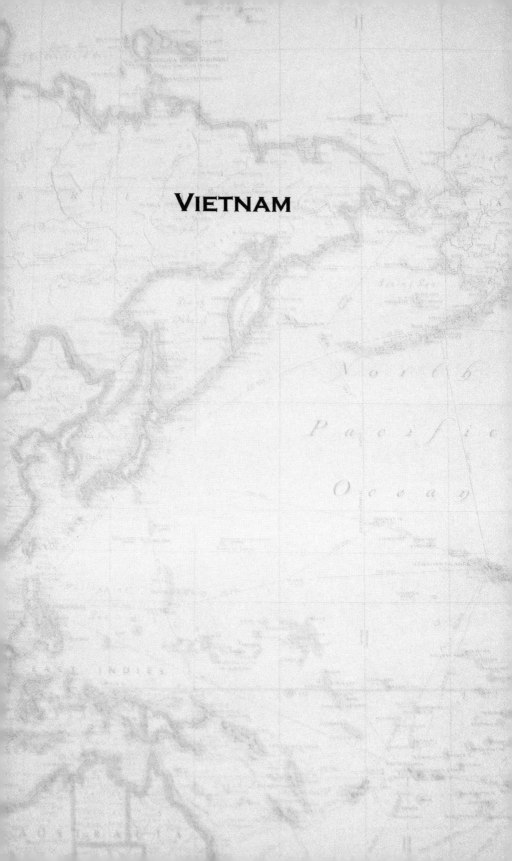

VIETNAM

Of Life and Limb
By Louis "Louie" E. Farrell

On December 10, 1965, Jim O'Neil and myself had a grizzly experience while preparing to depart NAS Minneapolis.

During the Vietnam War it was popular for church groups to collect soap for the Vietnamese people. The soap was transported by military air units on a space-available basis. Our group, VMR-234, flying C-119 aircraft based at NAS Minneapolis, flew many of these missions. Lieutenant Colonel Jim O'Neil and myself were assigned to active duty for three days to fly a load of soap to MCAS El Toro, California. Jim couldn't leave work early this day, and in order to save time he asked me to fly the first leg to Lowery AFB in Denver. At this time the aircraft were across the airport in hangers and had to be taxied to operations at NAS. I would complete the flight plan and aircraft preflight and pick Jim up at operations with engines running.

While I was preflighting the aircraft, the duty master sergeant asked if about 20 enlisted mechanics could taxi across the field in the C-119 with us for dinner at the mess hall. This would save them a long truck ride around the field. Of course, I approved, and we set out. It was a cold, dark, misty evening when we arrived at the operations building. Jim was approaching the aircraft when our crew chief asked a couple of the departing riders to pull the landing gear safety pins. The standard procedure of pulling the pins with the engines running, rather than waiting until the engines were shut down, was due to some electric and hydraulic problems with the C-119 aircraft.

I had the throttles back as far as they would go to reduce the wind stream on the troops. This was about 600 rpm. All of a sudden I felt a jerk, jerk, bang! I knew immediately that something had hit the right prop and shut off both mixture controls. I ran out of the plane and up in front of the right engine. I could see a body with Jim hunched over it in the shadow of the operations floodlights and the eerie red grimy propeller, still rotating. Jim was feeling for a pulse on a corporal's neck because the arm was laying about six feet away. There was a large gash through the coat and into the stomach area. There were intestine parts on the side of the aircraft where his body had been slammed, denting the aluminum. The base ambulance was there immediately with one of the base doctors. They took him to the VA hospital, which was only minutes away.

We decided to continue the mission as scheduled. Another aircraft was preflighted and fueled. The cargo was transferred and we were on our way to Denver in about an hour and a half. Before we were out of radio range with operations they contacted us and said the corporal was still alive.

Three days later when we returned he was still in a coma. By this time some of the details and reasons for the accident had been investigated. It was determined that the corporal (I apologize for not being able to recall his name) had been working on the helicopter line and was used to the wind, noise and rotor blades. The routine there was to pull the chocks and run forward, which he did in this case. He probably realized about the time of contact (it's 12 feet from the wheel to the prop) what he had done, because his arm was up with the pin when the first blade severed it and slammed the fist into his head. This caused the concussion. The next blade caught him in the mid-section and slammed his body into the fuselage. His coat cushioned the blade, although it still opened him up badly.

Now for the good news! He came out of the coma several months later, although he was not normal. We visited him in the VA hospital and he would talk goofy, like his hand (with no arm) was getting better, and not recognizing anyone. After several months he was transferred to the Philadelphia Naval Hospital. About one year later I was in operations and a corporal walked up to me and asked if I was Major Farrell. Yep, you guessed it—it was him, perfectly normal, less one arm. He was in the process of getting his medical discharge and going home to Duluth. In the Naval hospital he had popped out of the mental state he had been in and could recall everything up to the time of the accident. Not too many people have run through a propeller and survived.

Soap and Suds
By William F. Messerli

The mission was to fly the C-119 from Minneapolis to Denver for refueling and on to Las Vegas for a night on the town. Then on to San Diego to deliver a load of non-prescription drugs and soaps to the U.S. Navy for shipment with similar cargo from all over the United States to Vietnam. It was called "Operation Hand Clasp." The gifts were given to the Vietnamese families in Vietnam to assist in their every day needs. A worthy cause.

Dick Irgens and I took off with 8,000 pounds of cargo at approximately 3:00 P.M. on January 17, 1968. The weather was CAVU and it was an easy flight to the Denver airport for refueling. The weather in route to Las Vegas was clear so we filed VFR Denver direct to Las Vegas, which meant flying at 16,000 feet over the mountains. Take-off was about 6:00 P.M., which was twilight. An hour or so out from Denver the red light came on for the right engine and the oil pressure began dropping. The C-119 (commonly known as "10,000 buckets of bolts flying in close formation") was losing an engine. A quick calculation from the handbook told us that with the load on board, the C-119 couldn't maintain its altitude of 16,000 feet. It was pitch black, with no visibility to see the mountains on either side. Master Sergeant Moe, the crew chief, was told to dump the cargo as soon as possible. The flight center picked us up on radar shortly thereafter and gave us a vector to the Cedar City, Utah, airport, which was in relatively close proximity. In a matter of a few short minutes, the crew had dumped about a third to one-half of our cargo.

Landing was uneventful. The next morning we spoke with the station chief and told him of our flight and dumping the cargo in the mountains not too far from his airport. We pointed out the approximate location as to where we thought the cargo would be in order that his jeep patrol could try to locate it. I told him that in the spring, if the rancher's cattle were foaming at the mouth, that they should tell them not to worry; it was not a disease, it was just that the cattle had found the soap. Another plane picked up our onboard cargo and flew it to San Diego.

An engine was flown out and installed on our aircraft, but it took about three days. Dick and I played lots of pool. We never got to Las Vegas or San Diego. Probably saved a lot of money.

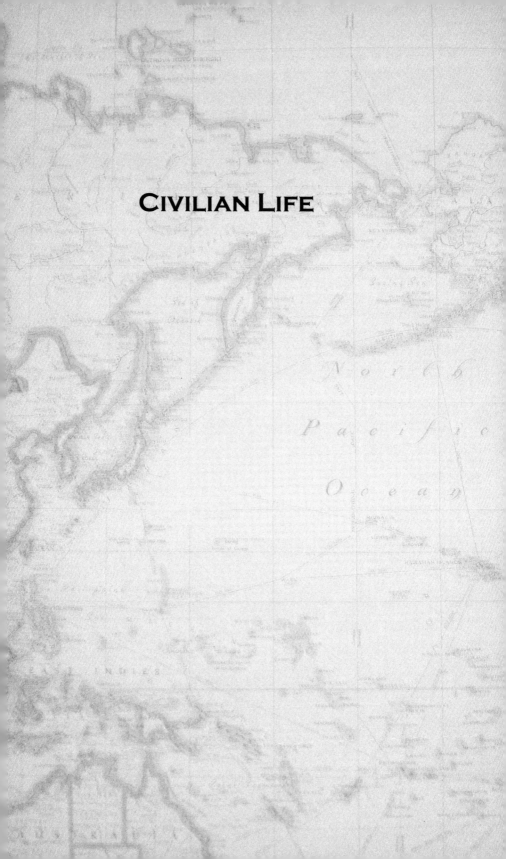

CIVILIAN LIFE

Collision: Airplane Meets Truck

By Louis "Louie" E. Farrell

It was the night of June 23, 1957, on the last leg of a DC-3 flight operated by North Central Airlines. The flight originated in Minneapolis with interim stops at Brainerd, Bemidji, and Thief River Falls, supposedly terminating at Grand Forks, North Dakota.

It was almost midnight on a dark, moonless night, when Captain Orlen Gudim "Goody" gave me the order, as copilot, "One-quarter flap, gear down." We were turning final to lineup on Runway 18 at the old Grand Forks Airport. I commenced doing the landing checklist and noticed in the far distance a semi truck coming from west to east on US Highway 2. This highway runs adjacent to the north boundary of the airport within 100 feet of the beginning of Runway 18. Goody called for half flaps, and after positioning them I looked up and saw that the relative position of the truck on the windshield was the same as before. Pilots know that if the relative position of two moving objects does not change, there's going to be a crash.

We continued on with the last order of full flaps. When I looked out again, nothing had changed—the truck was in full view directly ahead of us. As a new DC-3 pilot, I wasn't about to mention the truck in our windshield, especially when it was so obvious. Plus, I knew Goody was an excellent pilot, and that after his release from World War II as a DC-3 pilot he was hired by SAS as an instructor pilot before being hired at North Central Airlines. I also knew that depth perception in a DC-3 was entirely different from that of the fighter jets I was used to flying. Many times in my short, three-month airline career up to this point, I had been concerned about being too close to power lines, dikes, and other obstacles. The experienced North Central Airlines captains were always right. At least until this time.

Bang! Crash! Everything turned glaring white, then pitch black. White. Black. White. Black. When we hit the truck the aircraft pointed directly at the ground, and the bright landing lights in the wing reflected off the ground, which was very close, making everything white. The next oscillation pointed the nose straight up into the black sky. After a few decreasing oscillations the runway was straight ahead with an airspeed around 60 knots.

My impulse was to pull the power off and belly it in. I thought maybe the right wing was damaged or the right elevator gone, but it wasn't my call. Goody put full go around power on and called for gear up. I really didn't want to be any farther off the ground than I was at that moment. Flying the airplane, Goody could feel that be had adequate control. So away we went into the night. Goody's first statement to me was, "What does it look like out there? Have we got enough gas to make it to Minneapolis?" I shakily shone my flashlight at the right engine, which looked okay, and then directed the beam underneath to see the right landing gear flopping around, suspended by the hydraulic lines and cables. I reported this and told him to maintain a south heading while I figured out if we had enough fuel for Minneapolis. Being well acquainted with North Dakota, I figured if we didn't, we would be going over Hector Airport at Fargo and could belly it in there. In the meantime we radioed Grand Forks station about the situation and found out the truck driver was shaken, but okay.

Now came the toughest part. "Goody" had to go back and tell the passengers what happened, along with the next plan. (At this time there were no P.A.s on DC-3s for communicating, only face to face.)

Damage to the truck from the collision with the plane.

While he was in back, Minneapolis flight control contacted me on HF radio. I told them our plan and that we had enough fuel to make it to Minneapolis. It was a VFR night without a cloud in the sky. North Central decided to send up another DC-3 with a large spotlight to assess our damage. We agreed to fly over St. Cloud and then follow the Mississippi River down to Minneapolis. Sure enough, chief pilot Gail "Red" Wallis (who also is a marine) and Pete Wall, director of training, were right on course and blinked their landing lights at us over St. Cloud. They looked us over and determined the only damage we had was the right main gear.

The decision was made to belly it in on a foamed Runway 29 Left with the gear retracted. The right gear hanging down would probably separate, and the left gear on DC-3s rotates in the wheel well while retracted. It was now my chance to go meet the passengers. At DC-3 speeds we had a lot of time to brief them on emergency exits, crash procedures, and work with the stewardess.

Minneapolis tower cleared us to land on foamed runway 29L. Goody briefed me that as he flared out I would get the magnetos off, kill electrical power, and turn gas mixture controls off. Just as we were about 100 feet off the ground a crash crew truck crossed the runway in front of us. Oh no, not two trucks in one night! Away we go again, up into the sky for a go-around. (Can you imagine what our eight stalwart passengers were thinking?) We were now getting down to fumes on fuel.

On the next pass we landed. Nice and smooth in the foam, with only a small fire in the right nacelle, which the crash crew extinguished immediately.

Everyone deplaned through the normal entry door. The passengers were met by our PR department. They all elected to take the morning flight to Grand Forks. As crew members we were debriefed by the

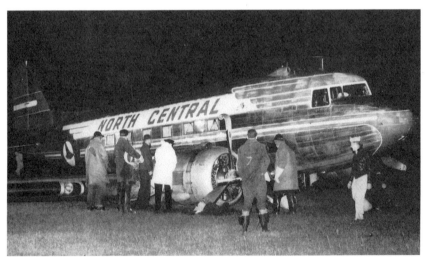

The damaged plane after hitting the truck.

FAA and company officials. We were released to go home and cleared to assume our normal flights the following day.

Goody drove me home to a little apartment we had in Highland Park. The sun was up and the birds were chirping when I tried to sneak in without waking Geri, my wife. She was six months pregnant with our first-born. She heard me and sat up saying, "What are you doing home? You were supposed to be on a three-day trip." I answered, "We hit a truck in Grand Forks and had to come back." She rolled over and immediately went back to sleep. What a worry wart!

The good old days of aviation were considerably different than today. First of all, the passengers were really tough. Every one of them wrote letters to the company for the outstanding job we did. Today passengers would have lawyers suing us, the company, Douglas, the FAA, and everybody else they could name, for trying to kill them. Following is a sample letter that one of the passengers wrote, complimenting us on the incident. The FAA nowadays would ground you until you passed a simulator check. I'll take the good old days!

Who had to pay for the accident? The truck driver, since he drove through signs that read, CAUTION: LOW FLYING AIRCRAFT.

Box 1244
Grand Forks, N. Dak.
June 26, 1957

Mr. Louis E. Farrel
Headquarters Office
North Central Airlines
Minneapolis, Minnesota

Dear Mr. Farrel:

I was one of the passengers on the plane that you helped
take back to Minneapolis last Sunday night.

I want you to know how wonderful I think all the crew
were on that trip. You were all so calm and kept us so well
informed that I really never felt that we were in great danger.

I am very grateful to you for your skillful handling of
the plane.

Sincerely yours,

Dorothy L. Travis

DLT:dt

Letter received from North Central passenger after collision.

NORTH CENTRAL AIRLINES INC.
6201-34TH AVENUE SOUTH
WOLD-CHAMBERLAIN FIELD
MINNEAPOLIS 23, MINNESOTA

H. N. CARR
PRESIDENT

July 1, 1957

Dear Mr. Farrell:

I want to express my sincere appreciation for the excellent way in which you assisted in the emergency landing at Wold-Chamberlain Field on Monday morning, June 24. What might have been a tragic accident was averted through the skill and courage shown by you and the other members of the flight crew.

Sometime soon when you are in the General Office, I hope you will stop by, as I would like to have the opportunity to visit with you.

Sincerely,

H. N. Carr

First Officer L. E. Farrell
North Central Airlines, Inc.
Minneapolis, Minnesota

c.c.
Mr. A. D. Niemeyer

Letter to Farrell after collision from North Central President H. N. Carr.

Paid Buzz Job
By Lyle Bradley

Most pilots get in trouble when they unsafely fly too low. Most aviators love the sense of speed, so the lower the flight the faster it seems. Flying low and fast is fun, but it frequently creates an improved profit for tombstone makers. All aviation groups frown on buzz jobs with a few exceptions at air shows, manufacturing demos, and crop spraying.

In the spring of 1950 I was offered a job to do buzz-type flying daily for good pay. I was in graduate school at Iowa State University at Ames, Iowa. The Hawkeye Spraying Company needed another pilot. I passed the flight test and physical test for the company and decided that graduate school could wait for a few months.

Our company consisted of three Piper aircraft, each outfitted with 90-horsepower engines and a 200-gallon tank behind each cockpit. Personnel were three regular pilots, the boss, who was also a pilot, four flagmen, and two trucks for carrying tools, fuel, personal belongings, records, maps, and extra parts. The flagmen were also the truck drivers and mechanics.

Early April found us in Oklahoma. We moved north as the crops matured, weeds increased, and insects multiplied. Our runways for flying were low traffic country roads or pastures, wherever we could operate (not always safely).

Spraying has limitations. When the wind was over five knots, rain started, or livestock were close by, we stopped. This meant our flying time was pressed into a few morning and evening hours. That's the time for profits. During the daylight hours our time was spent getting people with large acreage to hire us for spraying. At first jobs were plentiful, until a rainless month came and farmers began to wonder if they would get a crop, so our jobs hit a drought as well. At times we barely made expenses.

Each pilot was responsible for mixing the spray being used—mostly pesticides to control weeds or insects. We were careful to follow company instructions, but in the rush to fly the few hours available we had to guess while mixing. One day a car drove up with a United States field man from the Pure Food and Drug Division to check our activity. He spent several hours chatting and watching our operation. He gave us an okay and I did not give him a clue that we were not always that careful while measuring. He showed us literature picturing a chemist eating DDT powder to give everyone a false hope for pesticide safety. (I found out years later that the chemist died of unknown causes in his early forties.)

One morning after spraying a crop close to our road landing spot, we had to stop due to wind. I walked back over the field. I had sprayed parathion, which is a nerve poison, for insects. To my surprise I came across a clutch of baby pheasants, some of which were writhing and convulsing from either the poison or insects that had died. I'm a birder and biologist—this bothered me. My conscience started to tell me that perhaps I was in the wrong business. When I mentioned my observations to others it fell on deaf ears. One pilot, with a chuckle, said, "We might as well poison them as shoot them."

There were few trees to dodge in our area but there were power lines, fence posts, large birds, and a few other obstacles. We did not have a single accident in the group, except for two planes that ended up in the ditch due to cross winds and landing on narrow roads.

One evening, after spraying a field for insects, I noticed my instruments were all doubled (almost like a multi-engine airplane). When I checked a field of cattle, they too were double and blurred. Suddenly I realized that I was being overcome by pesticide fumes from the empty tank. I quickly cut the power and glided the 200 feet into the same field with the cattle. The engine was stopped and I sat there a moment trying to put my thoughts into perspective. When I tried to move my legs to get out of the plane they wouldn't move. Finally I flopped out on the ground and lay there in a helpless prone position with about 50 sets of cattle eyes watching me close by. I felt terrible, mentally and physically. The sun was ready to set and no one knew where I was, except the cattle. I just hoped there were no bulls among them.

I struggled to my feet while hanging onto the support struts of the plane. For a half hour I floundered like a drunk. Finally I could feel nerves functioning in my hands and feet. By closing the tank it prevented any fumes from escaping. I checked the wind, started the plane, and returned to our operating spot. While flying back I made a decision—I'm quitting this business tomorrow.

When I landed the other guys were getting ready to run a search for me. We had a toast for my return. After the toast I shared my plans to quit. There were no tears, no rationale to stay, only silence. Finally the boss indicated that I would have to fly a plane back to Iowa. I had a feeling that they were happy to see me go for several reasons—my questioning the business, a plane needing an overhaul, and profits were down due to the drought.

We operated out of different spots, such as a ranch in Oklahoma, the airport in Goodland, Kansas, the Martin, South Dakota, field, and at an Onida, South Dakota, farm field. One full tank of gas could take me to Ames, Iowa.

Next morning about 0900 I departed and all day fought a strong southern crosswind. When I was about 20 miles west of Ames I had to land deadstick in a farmers pasture because I was out of gas. I barely got out of the plane when a pickup drove up alongside of me and a friendly farmer asked if I had trouble. When I mentioned gas problems, he said, "Jump in, we have tons." I was on the ground for about 15 minutes. I paid for the gas, thanked him for his help, chatted about farming, and was underway.

I was happy to be on my way home. Conversations with my mother had indicated my father was scheduled for an operation at Iowa City Hospital, so I drove directly there. I spent two days at home and then headed back to Minneapolis for the July USMCR drill. I would be back flying my love—the Corsair.

My experience with paid buzz jobs was disappointing, but a good learning experience. I had a few close calls, but overall it was worth the time, travel, and trauma.

Federal Aviation Flight Inspections
By Clyde H. Slyman

The Minneapolis Flight Inspection Field Office crewed DC-3 and Sabreliner NA- 265-80 (twin-engine jet) aircraft with the responsibility of flight checking communication and navigational aids in the National Airspace System. Aircraft accidents involving an airspace system facility, for example ILS, NDB, VOR, TACAN, DME (aviation navigational aids), and so on, required a priority after accident flight check of the involved facility. The accidents frequently occurred during low ceiling, low visibility, and at night. This was hazardous duty.

The involved facilities were flight checked promptly, often under adverse weather conditions. All parameters of the facility were checked to determine in-tolerance or out-of-tolerance parameters. If all facility parameters were within tolerance and the flight check airplane did not crash, the United States government would not be liable in the sure to follow litigation.

At other times, FAA inspections hit closer to home, this time involving our own aircraft. Shortly after the flight-inspected DC-3s were replaced by N265-80 Sabreliners (twin engine jets), my crew was conducting a periodic VOR flight check at Pierre, South Dakota, when the left engine fire warning light came on. The throttle was pulled back to the idle position, but the light remained on. A visual look at the engine did not show any evidence of a fire. We secured and shut the engine down and made a single engine landing at the Pierre Airport. Upon opening the cowling, there was no evidence of fire.

After consulting the FAA maintenance experts at Oklahoma City, we started both engines and flew back to home base in Minneapolis, Minnesota.

The Minneapolis Flight Inspection Line Maintenance checked the fire warning system and discovered that the wiring for the respective engines was not correct. The left engine fire warning light was connected to the right engine and the right engine fire warning light was connected to the left engine. If in fact there had been an engine fire, we would have shut down the good engine, resulting in disaster.

Moral of the story: In an emergency, if you make your situation worse, quickly undo what you did!

An Airworthiness Directive (AD) was issued requiring an inspection of all models of this aircraft. All 12 of the FAA Sabreliner aircraft were grounded until inspected and rewired.

Hunting, Jumping, and Cleanup
By Lyle Bradley

Hunting

In Iowa during 1946 there were bounties on fox and wolves. The last timber wolf was killed in 1910, but a friend collected a $50 bounty on a coyote (brush wolf) because the county auditor didn't know the difference.

I've never approved of bounties. They are a waste of tax money and cause some wildlife number problems. For about a month during January and February of 1946, two of us hunted fox by air. Wayne did the shooting with a 12-gauge shotgun and I flew the plane. We never shot a still fox—we always got it running. Several times I had to almost hit the fox with a wheel of the plane to move them. After retrieving the fox I would open the stomach to determine the food intake. Mice, voles, and a few rabbit parts were the only identifiable foods. A little corn and grass was also mixed with the animal parts. We then turned the fox into the county auditor for bounty.

The five dollars per fox paid for shells and aircraft fuel. After food analysis on the fox we realized we were killing a beneficial mammal, so we stopped hunting them. Those who propose bounties should become better informed before making their erroneous decisions. Aircraft renters and hunters are the only ones who profit.

We had two close calls while chasing fox—we clipped a small tree and flew under some power lines. We enjoyed the aerial hunting but are happy that the practice became illegal about two years after we indulged. I feel guilty today that we harvested twenty-eight red fox and three gray fox under false pretenses.

Jumping Voluntarily

I had worn a parachute for most of my 26-year military career and never had to use it. After talking with a skydiving team, my mind seemed to become wrapped into a parachute, so I found 13 others in our school district interested in skydiving.

We arrived at Stanton Field near Northfield, Minnesota, on a Saturday morning. Our class consisted of our superintendent, nine teachers, three kids of adults, and myself. We started ground school at 0800 and completed the class at noon. At 1300 the first group of three jumpers boarded the plane along with the pilot and an instructor. Each person in our group used a static line (a line attached from the chute to the airplane) to open the chute. Everyone jumped on Saturday except the two oldest adults. A late afternoon storm stopped the activity so we had to return the following day to jump.

Our chutes were the new ones you could steer, so we were not at the complete mercy of the wind, like all aviators were formerly.

The day was enjoyable, informative, interesting, and stimulating. My next jump will be a free fall from 10,000 feet.

I'm happy that I never had to use the "nylon letdown" as a fighter pilot because there are inherent dangers in bailing out of an airplane. At least four of my pilot friends are not here today because of problems associated with bailing out from fighter planes.

River Cleanup

In 1954 I purchased some land including an oxbow lake adjacent to the Rum River in Minnesota. In 1955 Carol joined me in the venture and we raised five children. We loved the water and the wildlife associated with that habitat. The Rum is a beautiful river popular with canoeists, photographers, and a host of other river enthusiasts.

One problem soon became apparent, however. There was much junk and litter in the stream. I canoed, hiked, and drove a car along the river to discover from where the material was originating, but I was unsuccessful. One day I was assigned an engine-time hop in a Corsair, so I took my binoculars and flew the 147-mile length of the Rum River at 2,000 feet. I scanned the banks all the way to its source at Mille Lacs Lake.

My discoveries amazed me. Two cities had their landfills in the flood plain. Three farmers and two livestock dealers had their animal lots in the flood plain. I contacted several people who had exhibited concerns about the river junk. We organized the Quad County Recreational Association and started writing letters to legislators, government agencies, environmental organizations, and many property owners along the river. Within two years the river was rid of the major environmental problems. Today, even with more people living along the river, it is much cleaner.

In 1993 we organized over 400 people in one day to clean every foot of the Rum River in Anoka County. Even Minnesota Governor Perpich joined us for the activity. It is obvious that people want clean water. Using airplanes is a great way for discovering some of these environmental problems.

AUTHOR BACKGROUNDS

Harry Anderson

In 1939 I was turned down for aviation training in Fort Francis, Canada, by the RAF because I was born in Sweden and did not have a birth certificate. My mother obtained a certificate from the pastor of the church in Sweden where I was baptized. I was accepted and entered flight training at the naval air station in Minneapolis, Minnesota. From there I went to Corpus Christi, Texas, where I got my wings.

I was assigned to VMSB-144 as a member of their squadron located at Camp Kearney, north of San Diego. We lived in tents with kerosene heaters, four men to a tent. We flew with VMF-123, VMF-124 and VMTB-143. The squadron VMF-124 was the first F4U squadron in the Marine Corps at the time.

After serving in the South Pacific I went to El Toro, California, to form a new squadron of just graduated second lieutenants. We flew the SB2C and many pilots were killed in training. The plane was taken away from the Marine Corps as unsuitable for our missions.

I requested to train in the Martin JM-1 twin-engine night fighters in San Diego. I was told if you lose an engine on take off, get out prayer beads because you are going to crash. I spent one month flying this plane, which looked like a B-25.

Our group was sent to Vero Beach, Florida, for advanced training, then transferred to Eagle Mountain Lake, Texas, for final training and eventually transferred to China. I had more than enough points to get out of the service by this time, so I took advantage of it. I turned down a regular USMC commission.

Austin J. "Jim" Bailey Jr.

Born 1922.

1941 Northeastern, Boston. Learned to fly in Civilian Pilot Training Program.

1942 Joined the navy.

1943 Graduated Navy Flight School. Pacific War, marine Corsair pilot in VMF-314, earning Distinguished Flying Cross and Air Medals.

1946 Returned to Northeastern University.

1950 Graduated, B.S. Mechanical Engineering. Recalled to active duty, Korea.

1951 In Korea joined Corsair Squadron VMF/A-312, engaged in troop ground support and deep support. Hit by ground fire on deep support near Pyongyang and ditched the plane in the Yellow Sea. In Korea earned Distinguished Flying Cross, Air Medals and Purple Heart.

1952 Joined Honeywell as project engineer and engineering test pilot. Worked in design and development of flight controls, fly-by wire, fire control couplers, side stick, and automatic carrier landing systems.

Test aircraft flown: F3D, F2H-3, F-94, Canadian CF-100, F-100, DC-3, Cessna 310, F-101, Swedish Fighters J-37 and J-35. Involved in simulator study with Lockheed (Kelly Johnson) leading to SR-71. Designated by United States Air Force as flight instructor for the F-101. Performed design review of Mercury capsule cockpit. Development of X-15 Rocket Research aircraft and testing with Neil Armstrong, Al White and Scott Crossfield.

1959-61 CO Minneapolis Marine Reserve Attack Squadron 234.

1967-70 Sweden Honeywell flight test manager and test pilot J-37 Viggen STOL fighter.

Honors: Octave Chanute Flight Award by American Institute of Aeronautics and Astronautics; Fellow in Society of Experimental Test Pilots; Inducted into Minnesota Aviation Hall of Fame, nominated National Aviation Hall of Fame.

Author Backgrounds

Sherman P. Booen

I built and managed radio stations. The Civilian Pilot Training program taught me to fly in October 1940 and I intended to join the Air Corps as a cadet, but was deemed too old at 27.

With a background in radio I signed on for aviation electronics at Dayton, Ohio. I was factory-trained in the use of the electronic autopilot for high altitude (30,000 feet) precision bombing in B-17s and B-24s. From 1942 to 1943 I trained crews in the States and in October 1943 I became a technical representative assigned to Italy and the 15th Air Corps. In 1943 and 1944 I instructed the lead crews bombing Germany with the electronic autopilot connected to the Norden bombsight, along with the use of the autopilot to help bring the big bombers home when the manual controls were disabled.

At end of World War II I returned to radio broadcasting in the Twin Cities.

In 1946 I was commissioned Captain Executive Officer Marine Air Reserve stationed at the Naval Air Station, Radar Squadron 16, and in October 1950 I was assigned to the Armed Forces Radio Network Far East (AFRES). In 1952 returned to my TV job and was named CO of our reserve radar squadron.

Retired as colonel in USMC.

In 1972 I was chairman of the National Conference of the National Marine Reserve held in St. Paul. It was a huge success for the Richard Fleming Chapter of the reserve.

As a civilian, aviation was my life's work. I founded and produced a television program, *World of Aviation*, seen on WCCO-TV for 28 years, and founded and edited *Minnesota Flyer*, a statewide monthly magazine. I was a commercial pilot and was elected to Minnesota Aviation Hall of Fame and Broadcasting Hall of Fame.

In the waning days of my life (age 92) I remain a supporter of all marine functions possible. The Marine Corps has added great value to my life and to my family. Semper Fi!

Lyle Bradley

Flight in birds, insects, and airplanes has fascinated me since my conscious life started in Dubuque, Iowa, in 1924. At nine my Dad and I flew in a Ford Trimotor. At 16 came Pearl Harbor. At 18 I left the University of Dubuque for Naval Aviation tests in Minnesota.

My first training was at Aberdeen, South Dakota, in Civilian Pilot Training. Next was Iowa City, Iowa, for preflight fitness, then on to Minneapolis for E-Base and Stearman biplanes, followed by Pensacola Naval Air Base for BT-13 and SNJ trainers. Wings of Gold were won April 1944. Wildcat fighters (F4Fs) came next, followed by our dream airplane, the F4U Corsair. On the west coast we prepared for combat.

Went to Hawaii for aircraft carrier checkout and then flown to Guam to join VMF-123 on the USS *Bennington* (CV 20). Returned from combat in seven months when the carrier was damaged. After WW II entered Iowa State University in science. In 1950 left graduate school for an aerial crop-spraying job. Our Minnesota reserve recalled me for the Korean War. After a year in Korea with VMF-214 I spent two years as a flight instructor at NAS Pensacola, Florida.

Carried on civilian work while in the Minnesota Reserve Squadron. Became a wildlife warden/biologist in Texas and spent 35 years as a science educator in Anoka, Minnesota. Was a naturalist for state and national parks in summers, and president for eight organizations. During this time married Carol, raised five children, built a house, led over 1,000 field trips, discovered dinosaurs, and traveled to 50 states and 15 countries. Retired as lieutenant colonel with a few awards in 1967.

My years in the USMCR has energized, expanded, and educated me. I've met superb friends, experienced laughs and tears, and spent hundreds of hours flying beautiful airplanes, especially the F4U Corsair.

Thomas (Tom) Brinkman

BS—Aeronautics & Engineering Mechanics, University Minnesota, 1963
MS—Aeronautics & Engineering Mechanics, University Minnesota, 1965
MS—Electrical Engineering, University Vermont, 1977
ASME Southern Minnesota Subsection—President, Vice President, Secretary, 1968-70
ASME Young Engineer of the Year (Minnesota), 1971
President—Scott Hosier W I I Roundtable (Rochester, Minnesota)

I was born five months before the attack on Pearl Harbor, but somehow, almost instinctively I have had an interest in World War II and World War II aviation. I have had the good fortune to make the acquaintance of several South Pacific marine pilots from the original Black Sheep Squadron (VMF 214), and then to develop a friendship with a wonderful group of Minnesota Marine aviators who flew in World War II and in Korea, not to mention interesting postwar careers, and this has been a bright spot in my life.

The pilots in this book "have been there," having flown in combat. I have not. My contribution to this book represents historical research combined with engineering knowledge, having completed aeronautical engineering studies at the University of Minnesota and having completed a rewarding career in engineering, engineering management, and program management. My career spanned 30 years at IBM (Rochester, Minnesota), followed by 10 years at Seagate, Western Digital, and Pemstar (an IBM spin-off). Interestingly, for 20 years of my career I worked on development of read/write heads for computer hard disk drives. This brought me back full circle to aeronautics and engineering mechanics because of the demanding aerodynamic ground effects which allowed heads to fly a few millionths of an inch over the surface of a disk rotating at 7,200 rpm (visualize a Boeing 727 flying several hundred miles an hour at one inch above the runway).

Andrew "Andy" W. Danielson

Born and raised in St. Paul, Minnesota. Attended the University of Minnesota and received a BSL degree in 1954. Received a regular commission in USMC out of the NROTC unit at the University. Attended Basic School at Quantico, Virginia, until January 1955. Started flight training at Pensacola in February of 1955 and received wings June 1, 1956, at Corpus Christi, Texas.

Joined VMF-114 at Cherry Point, North Carolina, and flew the F9F-8 Cougar for one tour. Then went to VMF-531 flying the F4D-1 Skyray. During this period also flew the F2H-2 Banshee, the F3D Skynight and the TV-2, which was the navy version of the air force T-33. Resigned regular commission in October 1958 returning to NAS Minneapolis and joining VMF-213 as a USMCR pilot. Flew the F9F-5 Panther, the AD-5 Skyraider, the T-28 and the R4Q (C-119) Boxcar. With the coming of the R4Q, VMF-213 merged into VMA-234, which then became VMR-234. Squadron moved to NAS Glenview, Illinois, in 1970. Retired in 1992 as a lieutenant colonel after 24 years regular and reserve service.

After returning to Minneapolis in 1958 flew with Northwest Airlines for three years but continued to attend the University of Minnesota Law School and received JD degree in 1961. Practiced law in Minneapolis as partner and trial attorney with a Twin Cities law firm. Was appointed to the District Court Bench in 1971 and resigned in 1976. Was then appointed by President Jimmy Carter to serve as the United States Attorney for Minnesota. Returned to law firm in 1979 and continued as partner and trial attorney. Was reappointed to the District Court Bench in 1988. Retired from bench in 2002. Reside in Minneapolis with wife of 51 years, Vonne. We have three sons and seven grandchildren.

Myron H. Engel

I was born on February 19, 1934, in Wagner, South Dakota. I graduated from Wagner High School in 1952, and then attended South Dakota State University where I joined the Marine Corps PLC program. I was commissioned as a second lieutenant USMCR when I graduated from college in 1956. After graduation I left immediately for Quantico, Virginia. The Marine Corps had a new flight-training program. If you qualified, you were exempt from basic training. I tested for this new program and was assigned to pre-flight training in August of 1956. At the end of flight training I received my wings on August 13, 1957, and then went to MCAS Opa Locka, Florida, for C-119 transition training. In 1958 I was assigned overseas duty at MCAS Iwakuni, Japan, with Squadron VMR-253. In Japan I checked out as an aircraft commander for the C-119.

In 1959, having been released from active duty, I became a pilot for Northwest and North Central Airlines in Minneapolis, Minnesota. I joined the Active Reserve when the marines got C-119s at NAS Minneapolis. I was the second marine reserve pilot to get re-qualified in the C-119.

In 1965, after furloughs from Northwest and North Central, I became a corporate pilot with Honeywell, Inc. in Minneapolis. I retired from the Reserve in 1975 as a lieutenant colonel. On February 28, 1994, I retired from Honeywell. I am married with three children and grandchildren.

Ralph A. "Lefty" Engelking

Commissioned Quantico, Virginia, Marine Base September 3, 1953, Infantry Platoon Leader.

Designated Naval Aviator July 6, 1955.

Assigned Marine Attack Squadron, VMA-332, MAG-31, First Marine Air Wing.

The first designated Special Weapons [Atomic Delivery] Squadron, VMA-332.

Deployed to NAS Iwakuni, Japan, March 1957 to July 1958.

Operated off aircraft carriers USS *Philippine Sea* and USS *Princeton*. Released from active duty July 1958.

Marine Air Reserve NAS Jacksonville, Florida, flying FJ-3 Fury.

Marine Air Reserve NAS Minneapolis, Minnesota, flying AD-5N and R4Q-2 (C-119).

Instructor pilot NAS Pensacola, Florida, March 1962 to March 1965 flying T-28, T-34, and SNB.

Navy Blue Angel support team plane commander, flying R4D-8 and R5D, summer 1964.

Eight and one half years active duty, six years in Marine Reserves, major USMCR.

Retired November 1, 1990, from Northwest Airlines as Captain 747-400.

Author Backgrounds

Louis "Louie" E. Farrell

Born December 5,1931, in Fargo, North Dakota.
Graduated from Bismarck High School, 1949.
College education from Montana State College, Bozeman, Montana.
Enlisted in Naval Cadets 1952. Carrier qualified SNJ-5, F6F Hellcat.
Commissioned as a marine naval aviator second lieutenant, March 1954.
Operational squadron VMA-323, flew F9F-2 & -5 Panther jet, El Toro, CA.
Flew in atomic tests "Operation Teapot," Yucca Flats, 1955.
Korea, 1955, MACS-3. Flew AD-5 Skyraider and SNB Beach Craft.
Atsugi, Japan, 1956, VMF-235. Flew FJ-2 Fury. Exceeded speed of sound.
Pensacola, Florida, November 1956. Instructor Pilot teaching tactics and formation in SNJs and T-28Bs.
Married to Geraldine Alexander (St. Paul girl) in Pensacola, Florida.
April 1957 Hired by North Central Airlines flying DC-3s.
Transferred from active duty directly to reserve MARTD MSP VMF-213.
June 1959 Transferred to VMF-234. The reserves switched aircraft to AD-5Ns. Re-qualified in ADs and T-28B Trojans.
1959 DC-3 captain and checked out in Convair 340/440, North Central Airlines.
January 1962 Reserves received R4Q-2 (C-119) Boxcars. Instructor pilot.
1967 Instructor/check pilot DC-3, Convair 440s, North Central Airlines.
1968 Chief Pilot Minneapolis, North Central Airlines.
1968 Instructor/check pilot CV-580 (Turbo-prop) and DC-9-30s.
1974 Retired from USMCR with rank of lieutenant colonel after 22 years.
December 1979 Instructor/check pilot B727-100-200.
1985 Left chief pilot office for instructor/check pilot in "glass cockpit" B757.
1989 Check out in DC-10 flying the line internationally.
1991 Retired Northwest Airlines, age 60 rule, to enjoy family of six children and fifteen grandchildren.

Harry J. Goodyear

Born in Minneapolis, Minnesota, May 29, 1919. Graduated from Central High, Minneapolis, Minnesota. Employed with First National Bank from 1937 to 1940.

Enlisted as a private in VOM-6R Marine Reserve Squadron at Wold Chamberlain Airport in 1939, called to active duty in 1940. Served in San Diego, California, and at the Naval Air Station, Glenview, Illinois, from 1940 to 1943. Completed naval flight training in 1943. Assigned to Fighter Squadron VMF-122 at El Centro, California. Served in Pacific 1943 to 1945. Attended landing signal school and served aboard aircraft carrier CVE-122 as a signal officer from 1945 to 1947. Returned to Marine Squadron VMF-234 at the Naval Air Station Minneapolis, Minnesota, from 1947 to 1951. Called to Active duty for Korean War and assigned to Naval Air Station Pensacola, Florida, as a flight instructor from 1951 to 1953. Returned to Marine Squadron VMF-234 Naval Air Station Minneapolis, Minnesota, as a squadron pilot from 1954 to 1957. Assigned to VTU Attachment from 1957 to my retirement in 1969 as a lieutenant colonel

Civilian Career
1937 to 1940, Banking at First National Bank, Minneapolis, Minnesota.

1948 to 1951, Mortgage consultant for Hennepin Federal Savings & Loan, as well as Minnesota Savings & Loan Associations, Minneapolis, Minnesota.

1954 to present, Realtor at Goodyear Realty Company and Edina Realty Corporation, Minneapolis, Minnesota.

Author Backgrounds

Richard Hansen

Richard O. Hansen was born in St. Paul, Minnesota, in 1923. Reading magazines called *G8 and his Battle Aces* encouraged him to become a fighter pilot.

Following Pearl Harbor, Dick enlisted in the navy V5 aviation cadet program. He received his wings and commission at Corpus Christi, Texas. After training in TBF Avengers, he went to El Toro, California, where he was checked out in the F4U Corsair. He left the United States on May 29, 1944, and joined VMF-111 at Makin in the Gilbert Islands, and then went to Kwajalein in the Marshall Islands flying similar missions against the Japanese. In January 1945 he was transferred to VMF-224, one of the first squadrons to land at Yontan, one of two captured airfields on Okinawa. There he won the Navy Cross for actions against the Japanese kamikazes.

Following his tour on Okinawa he was sent back to the United States. In August 1945 the atomic bombs were dropped and the Japanese surrendered, changing everything. Dick joined VMF-213 in Minneapolis, a marine air reserve squadron flying F4U Corsairs.

In August 1950, VMF-213 was called to active duty when North Korea invaded South Korea. The squadron was sent to El Toro. The Marine Corps badly needed helicopter pilots, and Dick was one of a number of fighter pilots chosen. By June 12, 1951, he was with VMO-6 in Korea flying mostly Bell helicopters, the kind seen in the MASH TV series, evacuating wounded from combat areas to field hospitals.

Returning to civilian life after his Korean tour, he entered the construction industry. Dick is retired with three children, six grandchildren, and one great grandchild.

Robert A. Kilgore

Born in 1923, I grew up in Minneapolis and attended Washburn High School, where I played hockey and tennis. I went on to the University of Minnesota in 1941, planning to become an aeronautical engineer.

I enlisted in the navy V-5 program to become a pilot. Progressing through the training program I received my Wings of Gold as a second lieutenant in the Marine Corps. Training as a fighter pilot culminated in flying the F4U Corsair. The Corsair was designed for a pilot about 6' 2", not someone like me at 5'6", but with the help of a couple of pillows I managed. Three and a half years later, including a tour of the South Pacific, I returned to the University of Minnesota, only this time in the School of Architecture.

After getting my degree I joined a well-known firm, getting paid the princely sum of $100 a month. Over the years we designed over 50 churches, several banks, libraries, an assortment of other commercial buildings, and a host of private residences. In 1964 I took a course in atomic fallout shelter analysis.

In 1948 I married Fifi, my college sweetheart, and she blessed me with a son and daughter.

In August 1950 our reserve squadron was recalled to active duty for the Korean conflict. I spent the next eighteen months flying helicopters.

Returning to civilian life I kept playing hockey for a number of teams until at age 74 Fifi terminated my hockey career. I still enjoy playing tennis once a week and meeting with my marine buddies once a month after knowing some of them for over 60 years.

Carlyle Lageson

I was born in Albert Lea, Minnesota, in 1918. I attended school in Albert Lea and then St. Olaf College in Northfield, Minnesota. In 1940 traveled for Northrup King of Minneapolis. In December 1940 completed the Civilian Pilot Training (CPT) class. On July 19,1941, I was accepted into the United States Navy to train to be a naval aviator.

After completion of E-Base in Minneapolis, I was transferred to New Orleans for Morse code and celestial navigation, then to Pensacola, Florida, where I was accepted into the United States Marine Corps. Transferred to Opa Locka, Florida, where I received my wings.

In early 1943 I was transferred to Norfolk, Virginia, to complete live carrier landing training, then overseas via San Diego aboard former Admiral Byrd's ship, the Southern Cross, renamed the USS *Wharton*. The skipper of the ship was the same one who took Admiral Byrd to the Antarctic.

The first overseas base was on Espirito Santo where marine fighter and dive-bombing squadrons were formed and trained. I was an instructor for new pilots arriving from the States. In November 1943 I joined VMSB-236 to complete my three combat tours, after which time I returned to the States in November 1944. I then returned to Pensacola as a flight instructor in multi-engine aircraft.

While in Florida, Geraldine Christensen (Jerry) and I were the first couple married in the chapel at NAS Jacksonville on December 21,1942. In December 1945 I completed my active duty and returned to Albert Lea, Minnesota, where I joined my father-in-law as co-owner of the Northern Valley Packing Corporation, which specialized in shipping North Dakota potatoes to eastern markets.

Jerry and I had four children and 41 happy years together. Sadly, Jerry passed away in 1983. I later married a long-time friend and St. Olaf graduate, Jeanne Olson. We live in Albert Lea, Minnesota, and in the winter spend time in Mesa, Arizona. I maintained a marine reserve status until my retirement in 1973.

Goodwin Luck

I was born in St. Paul, Minnesota, on April 16, 1916. I became interested in aviation at an early age, taking my first airplane ride in an Eagle Rock biplane from a small airport near Robbinsdale, Minnesota, at age 12. From then on I was determined to become an aviator.

I attended St. Paul Central High School, then worked my way through four years of college, graduating in 1938 with a degree in aeronautical engineering from the University of Minnesota, with distinction. In August of 1935 my brother, Edward, and I joined the Marine Corps Aviation Reserve Squadron, V06-MR, at NRAB Minneapolis. Edward earned his wings at Pensacola in 1937 and I did likewise in 1939.

At North Island I was assigned to Marine Fighting Squadron Two and qualified for operating off the aircraft carrier *Saratoga*. In November 1940 I was transferred to NRAB Minneapolis mainly as a flight instructor. In early November 1942 I was transferred to San Diego and then assigned to General Mulcahy's ComAirSols staff as an operations officer based on Guadalcanal, Solomon Islands. On June 30, 1943, our ComAirSols staff landed on Rendova Island and became ComAir New Georgia.

After 16 months in the South Pacific I was transferred to Cherry Point, North Carolina. From there I was transferred to the marine unit at Klamath Falls, Oregon, for treatment of malaria. I was later assigned to the marine air wing at El Toro, California, as engineering officer until released from active duty in May of 1945.

The next 35 years I was chief powerplant engineer for Northwest Airlines retiring in 1981.

I was inducted into the Minnesota Aviation Hall of Fame in 2002.

Author Backgrounds

James C. Magnus

Born March 3, 1917, in St. Paul, Minnesota. Graduated from Mechanic Arts High School in 1935. Worked with Great Northern Railroad to 1938, then attended University of Minnesota on a hockey scholarship from 1938 to 1941.

Married Geraldine G. Watzl in Corpus Christi, 1942. After 56 years, we're still enjoying five daughters and many grandchildren. We also had a son, now deceased.

In retirement, we enjoy our golf community of Rio Verde, Arizona, and break for the summer to our cabin in Clear Lake, Minnesota.

My military career started in 1935 as a PFC in my dad's outfit, the Minnesota National Guard 206th Infantry. Airplanes were my future, so I transferred to the 109th National Guard in 1938. Joined U.S. Navy Cadet Program in 1941, where I trained from NAS Minneapolis to NAS Corpus Christi, Texas. Graduated June 1942 as USMCR second lieutenant and OS2U seaplane pilot.

In 1943 went to MCAS El Toro, California, with Instrument Training Squadron 953. In 1944 we transferred to VMR-953 at Kearney, California, and on to Corvallis, Oregon, and then to Ewa, Hawaii.

After World War II worked for Northwest Airlines, then to Hinck Flying Service in Minneapolis, and on to the University of Minnesota as director of aviation.

By 1950 the marines called our Minnesota F4U squadron up for Korean duty, and El Toro MCAS assigned me as a field operation officer.

After Korean tour joined Honeywell as captain and stayed 23 years. Between Honeywell and the Marine Reserves, I enjoyed flying jets from 1957 to 1977.

Having served the military in the National Guard, U.S. Navy, and U.S. Marine Corps, plus private flying at the University of Minnesota Aeronautical Department, corporate flying for Minnesota Business Aircraft Association (president 10 years) and Flightsafety International, I was inducted into the Minnesota Aviation Hall of Fame in 1997. It is an honor to be included with the likes of Charles Lindbergh, Speed Holman, and Watt Bullock, previous Minnesota inductees.

William F. Messerli

Born January 4, 1933, in Versailles, Missouri. Moved to Iowa in 1942 and attended Parsons College in Fairfield, Iowa, from 1951 to 1953. Naval Air Cadet (NAVCAD) August 1953; carrier qualified SNJ-5; designated naval aviator February 1955 and commissioned second lieutenant USMCR at El Toro, California. Joined VMA-323 flying the F9F-5 Panther jet. Spent three weeks in Advanced Survival School at Stead Air Force Base, Nevada. In Korea and Japan from August 1955 to February 1957 with VMA-251 and First Marine Air Wing staff. Logged 500-plus hours flight time in AD-4. MCAS Edenton in North Carolina, February to August 1957. Active Marine Reserves 17 years at NAS Minneapolis and NAS Glenview, Illinois. Retired 1974 as lieutenant colonel with 21 years military service.

B.S. Business Administration 1959 from University of Minnesota. Caterpillar Tractor Company, Sales Promotion 1959 to 1961; 1961 to 1965 William Mitchell College of Law, J.D. 1965. Entered private practice of law in Minneapolis 1965. Messerli & Kramer P.A. currently has 45 lawyers and 125 staff.

I have three children and seven grandchildren.

Ohrn O'Dette

On January 3, 1921, I was born in the old Swedish Hospital in Minneapolis, Minnesota. At ten my mother and father were divorced and Mom decided the best place to raise two boys was in a small town, not the big city. So with my five-year-old brother and me in tow we moved to a small town of five hundred in Braham, Minnesota.

At the height of the depression, 1931, we moved from an upper duplex with all modern facilities to a two-story building with electricity only. Under this condition she started a coffee shop that grew into a full-fledged restaurant.

In 1938 I graduated from high school and spent four years working in a grocery store, telephone company, men's tailor shop, and a movie theater. Then I became a machine operator. In 1942 I was working at the Rock Island Arsenal and the navy was touting a new pilot training program called V5.

I was commisioned in the USMCR and received my wings October 30, 1943. After operational training in PBJs (B-25s), I was selected to go with five other pilots to Pawtuxent River, Maryland, to service test the F7F night fighter. This was the first plane produced specifically as a night fighter, with a twin engine to boot. The highlight of my career!

I returned to the pilot pool at Cherry Point, North Carolina, and then sent to Vero Beach, Florida, for single engine night fighter training. From there I went overseas to join Squadron VMF(N)-541 on Pelelieu. I flew twelve missions and the war was over. No, I wasn't that good!

I spent several months in China at Peking/Peiping/Bejing for the surrender of the Japanese and flew reconnaissance. I returned home for discharge on June 30, 1946.

Jim O'Neil

When Jim was four years old he told his aunt he was going to be a pilot and that he would give her a ride (he did both). He graduated from Bloomington High School and was awarded a football scholarship to St. Thomas College.

In 1942 he applied for the Navy Aviation Program and left for Goodwell, Oklahoma. His first correspondence simply said, "I soloed—Whoopie!" About a year later he was commissioned in the Marine Corps (he switched to the marines as his dad was a World War I marine). In Atlanta they made him an instrument instructor. In September 1944 he joined a Corsair squadron in El Toro, California, and married Wanda, his high school sweetheart. He shipped out to the Pellelau Island in the Pacific where he was attached to a night fighter squadron. When the war ended, he was sent to Peking, China.

Graduated from the University of Minnesota with an aeronautical engineering degree, and got a job with Boeing Aircraft in Seattle in 1949. During this time he remained with the marine reserve squadron in Minneapolis. He was recalled into action for the Korean War and became a forward air controller.

After Korea he joined Honeywell as a test pilot for flight operations until the space program came along. He was the liaison between the astronauts and Honeywell. He was in it at the start of the Mercury (one-man), then the Gemini (two-man) and the Apollo (three-man) programs. He was two years beyond the maximum age limit for the astronaut program, so he joined the commercial end of the Honeywell aviation program. Demonstrated their products at conventions, including the Paris Air Show. He retired from Honeywell at the age of 60 and spent five years consulting.

He was commanding officer of the reserve squadron prior to retirement.

In 1968 Jim became a council member of the city of Bloomington and served for 10 years. Although in excellent health, he died at the age of 69 from complications resulting from eye surgery. He left behind Wanda, his wife of 49 years, two sons, and a daughter.

Herb Pfremmer

Born in Minneapolis, Minnesota, May 31, 1922. Graduated from Roosevelt High School 1940. Enrolled at University of Minnesota in 1941.

Received private pilot license in 1941.

Worked at Fairview Hospital in Minneapolis when Pearl Harbor was attacked and enlisted in the Navy Cadet Training Program. Went to Iowa City for preflight training, Minneapolis for primary flight, and Corpus Christi, where he received his wings. Accepted into the Marine Corps in July 1943 and advanced training in Jacksonville, Florida, in torpedo planes. Served as a Corsair pilot on board the USS *Bennington* 1944 to 1945 in VMF-123.

Returned to Minneapolis. Took a position with Van Dusen Aircraft Supplies as a sales representative, covering four states by Taylorcraft and a 120 Cessna.

In 1951 was distributor for Shell Oil Company and Goodyear tires. Sold these interests and purchased a recreational equipment business, which expanded to include Minnesota's Lookout Mountain Ski Area, with the first chairlift in Minnesota, and the Four Seasons Supper Club. Sold in 1973 and retired.

Married high school sweetheart on October 5, 1943. Family includes four children and many grandchildren.

In May 1975 worked as a public relations representative with a large industrial construction company, retiring again in 1982. Started antique business in Eveleth, Minnesota, named The Unusual Place. Retired again in December 1991.

Active in civic affairs and president of Chamber of Commerce; member of the Mayo Committee and chairman of the Range Delegation for the enactment of the Taconite Amendment in Minnesota. From 1953 until 2005 was lay speaker and interim pastor in various churches of the United Methodist Church.

Hobbies included hunting and fishing, but flying was primary recreation until 1982 when hearing problems precluded the use of radio, at which time for safety reasons he discontinued flying.

C. M. (Tony) Plattner

Born in Walker, Minnesota, on May 29,1930. Attended Hackensack and Walker schools, graduating in 1948, then went to Carleton College in Northfield, Minnesota. Graduated in 1952 with a B.A. in mathematics.

In the middle of the Korean War he became a naval aviation cadet and elected to become a marine pilot upon completion of training. He served at MCAS Cherry Point, North Carolina, K-3, Korea (following the war) and at MCAS El Toro, California, during four years of active duty. He joined the Marine Air Reserves in Minneapolis in 1956 and retired as a colonel in 1984 with 27 years of active and reserve duty.

He worked in California as an engineer for a year in 1957, and then joined the Northern Minnesota Publishing Company, a family-owned newspaper business in Walker, Minnesota. He remained there until taking a job as a reporter for *Aviation Week and Space Technology* magazine in 1962 in their Los Angeles Bureau.

As the magazine's staff pilot he flew and wrote about new aircraft, including such airplanes as the Douglas DC-9 and Boeing 737. He also spent several months in Vietnam reporting on the aviation aspects of that conflict.

Aviation continued to be an important part of his life and he flew commercially in Los Angeles with a group called the Skytypers. This consisted of five SNJ trainer airplanes flying abreast and emitting puffs of smoke to form words and messages.

After leaving *Aviation Week*, he joined The Garrett Corporation, an aerospace firm located in Los Angeles, in 1970, and remained with them through a number of mergers. He retired from the surviving company, Honeywell, in Tucson, Arizona, in 1996. During this time, he served in various public relations, sales, and marketing positions.

He currently lives in Tucson, Arizona.

Author Backgrounds

Clyde H. Slyman

1937 First Flight.

1940 Civilian Pilot Training (CPT), Private Pilot Certificate (Kent State University). October 1942, Naval Aviation Cadet. 1943 CPT Secondary, Prescott, Arizona, flying Waco UPF7. April 1943, Pre-flight School, Fifth Battalion, Delmonte, California. July 1943, Primary Flight Training at NAS Norman, Oklahoma. Flew N2S Stearman, N2T-1 Timm. October 1943, NAS Pensacola, Florida, Whiting Field Celestial Navigation, Morse Code. Flew SNV-Vultee, SNJ, rear seat, instrument training.

February 8, 1944, designated U.S. Naval Aviator, commissioned second lieutenant U.S. Marine Corps. Orders to NAS Jacksonville, Florida, Naval Auxiliary Air Training Facility (Green Cove Springs) for operational training in Corsairs.

May 1944, VMF-924 Corsair, VMF-913 Corsair. January 1945, VRF-1 Naval Air Station, New York. September 1945, VMF-911. Flew F7F Tiger Cat.

1948 to 1950 Attended Kent State University

1950 to 1953 Recalled to active duty, Korean War. 1950 to 1952 VMR-153, Cherry Point, North Carolina. Flew R5C (Curtiss Commando). August 1952, VMO-6 OE, First Marine Air Wing, Korea. January 1953, Headquarters Flight Section, K-3, Korea. Flew R4D-5, R4D-8, SNB. June 1953, Headquarters Flight Section, U.S. Marine Corp Air Station, Cherry Point, North Carolina. Aircraft: R4D-6, R4D-8

1954 to 1958 Attended Kent State University, B.S. and two years graduate school.

December 1958 to April 1984, Federal Aviation Administration (FAA), Flight Inspection Field Office, Minneapolis, Minnesota. Aircraft: Twin Beechcraft, DC-3, Beechcraft Bonanza, Cessna 182, Cessna 206, Sabreliner N-265-80. FAA certificates: Private Pilot; Commercial Privileges, Airplane Single Engine Land; Airline Transport Pilot—Airplane Multi Engine Land, DC-3, N-265

In 1970 retired from U.S.M.C. after almost 30 years reserve/active duty.

Darrell Smith

Darrell N. "DN" Smith was born in Redwood Falls, Minnesota, on April 14, 1922. From early childhood his one big desire was to fly airplanes. Following Pearl Harbor he enlisted in the navy V5 aviation cadet program and in August 1943 he received his wings at Pensacola, Florida. He was commissioned a second lieutenant in the Marine Corps.

He was then assigned to VMF-312, a new fighter squadron being equipped with F4U Corsairs, that arrived at Espiritu Santo in the New Hebrides Islands, south of Guadalcanal, in July 1944. After many frustrating cancellations of assignments, VMF-312 was the first squadron to land at Kadena, a captured Japanese airfield on Okinawa, in April 1945.

Following the Okinawa campaign he returned to the United States on 30-days leave. While there the atomic bomb was dropped and changed everything. He was assigned to a navy Ferry Squadron where he flew N2Ss, SNJs, F4Fs, F6Fs, F4Us, and TBMs to bases throughout the United States,

When released from active duty he returned to Minnesota, and with the help of the GI bill graduated from the University of Minnesota Journalism School in 1949. He also joined the marine reserve fighter squadron in Minneapolis, which was among the first squadrons to be recalled to active duty in July 1950. On the west coast he was put back in VMF-312, which arrived in Korea in early September.

There he flew combat missions from Kimpo in South Korea, then from Wonsan and Yonpo in North Korea, in support of the marine division trapped at the Chosin Reservoir when some 300,000 Chinese entered the conflict. The squadron then went aboard the carrier *Bataan*, where he continued to fly combat missions until he returned to the United States in July 1951 and rejoined the Minneapolis reserve squadron.

Retired from marines as lieutenant colonel in 1982. He is married with four children and four grandchildren. Retired from a career in the printing industry.

Edward Anders Sovik

Ed Sovik was born in 1918 in China to missionary parents. In 1935 he left China to enter St. Olaf College in Northfield, Minnesota. After graduation he studied art in New York and theology in St. Paul.

Sovik volunteered for Marine Corps aviation in August 1941. In January 1942 he was summoned to begin flight training in Minneapolis. Then followed NAS Pensacola, where in November he was given his wings and a commission. Further training followed and then a year at MCAS Cherry Point, North Carolina, where he entered the new night fighter program. He became operations officer of VMF(N)-532, the first single-engine Marine night fighter squadron.

The squadron was shipped to Tarawa in January 1944 and moved with the advancing American actions to Kwajalein, Eniwetok, and Saipan. In October 1944 the squadron was returned to San Diego, ostensibly to retrain in the new F7F Tigercat and then to go back to the Pacific. However, Sovik and other pilots were assigned to Marine Air Group 53, a new night fighter training program at Eagle Mountain Lake, Texas. He was named group operations officer and served until October 1945, when he left active duty.

After graduating from Yale University School of Architecture in 1949, Sovik moved to Northfield to form an architectural firm and teach at St. Olaf. His firm worked throughout the country. Sovik was active in professional affairs, contributed to periodicals, and wrote the book *Architecture for Worship*. For twenty years his firm operated a single-engine airplane, and Sovik's logbook hours doubled. He retired in 1996.

John Wastvedt

Growing up in a small town in Minnesota in the 1930s was a wonderful life. The days were filled with hunting, fishing, swimming, baseball, and of course, model airplane building. I read all the aviation magazines of the time about World War I fighter pilots. I graduated from high school in 1940 and my parents signed me up for Kemper Military School with an infantry ROTC.

When America entered the war on December 7, I was in my second year of college. I immediately contacted the navy recruiting office to volunteer as a naval aviation cadet. By late 1943 I was in a Corsair in the first Marine fighter squadron (VMF-124) during World War II to go aboard carriers. After serving in late 1944 and 1945 aboard the *Essex* in the Far East, I returned to the United States for duty as an instructor in operational training at NAS Jacksonville. I also married my childhood sweetheart, Laurene, and we are still going strong after sixty years.

I finished a degree at the University of Minnesota in aeronautical engineering in 1947, at the same time flying in the ready reserve. Twenty-five years later, including a tour of active duty during the Korean War, I made a career change to real estate syndication that was successful, so I cashed out in 1986. Looking around for something to do I started flying commercial charters and settled in for another career for 20 years. Along the way I retired from the Marine Corps Reserve after 30 years as a colonel.

In 2006 I retired, but not from flying. I have about 10,000 hours. My wife and I own three airplanes: a Mooney 201 for our transportation around the country, a Pitts acrobatic biplane for fun and "whifferdills," and a racing glider for traveling hundreds of miles with no engine. Life is great!

APPENDIX A

All Known Minnesota Marine Air Reserve Members: 1931-1998
(d = deceased)

Adamak, Edward
Adams, Arthur (d)
Albert. Richard
Allen, Ken
Amundsen, Glen L.
Anderson, Harry (d)
Archbold, William (d)
Armstrong, George (d)

Bailey, Austin J.
Banson, Douglas
Barnum, Alymer (d)
Baston, Fred
Bates, J. N.
Battray, R. L.
Bennewitz, Bill
Berg, Richard D.
Bergin, D. T.
Bixby, Walter E.
Booen, Sherman
Bradley, Lyle R.
Bradley, Roy
Brandt, Ray (d)
Bredeson, Neal
Brobeck, W. R.
Broin, Lowell (d)
Bruggemeyer, Roger

Byers, George (d)

Christian, Neil (d)
Christy, James (d)
Cole, Howard
Comstock, Eldon
Conklin, Peter G.
Cornell, Homer (d)
Christmas, D. (d)
Couillard, John
Crocker, Robert (d)
Cunningham, Jilt
Currie, Lloyd

Dahlberg, Robert
Danielson, Andrew
Dickinson, G. N.
Dittrick, Ray
Dodson, R. R.
Doth, Richard
Dudley, William H.
Dugan, Nolan

Engel, Myron
Engelking, Ralph
Enright, John

Farrell, Louis
Fiero, Lewis
Finneseth, Keith
Forsberg, John
Foss, Donald
Frazier, J. E.
Frederickson, J. (d)
Frederickson, N. (d)
Fults, Douglas

Goodyear, Harry
Gordon, C. C.

Hagen, Charles D.
Hallquist, Dennis (d)
Hansen, Richard
Hanson, Howard
Hauby, J. G.
Haywood, Tom (d)
Helfrich, William E.
Hellerude, Arthur (d)
Henderson, Neil
Hoidale, Porter
Holden, William (d)
Honke, Max (d)
Hoops, Duanne
Huber, Jack B. (d)

Irgens, R. M.

Jensen, John D.
Johnson, Chester (d)
Johnson, Helmer
Johnson, Henry "Red"
Johnson, Howard B.
Johnson, Kenneth
Johnson, R. C.
Johnson, Richard
Johnson, Robert G.
Jones, Richard
Jung, Walter (d)

Kegel, Stanley
Kehs, Robert D.
Kelly, Thomas
Kemper, Frank
Kier, Avery (d)
Kilgore, Robert
Kipp, John (d)
Kisport, J. H.
Knight, Edward
Kronkhite, Clifford

Lageson, Carlyle
Lakin, W. L.
Lammerding, R. L.
Lane, Henry
Lars, Roger W.
Laugen, Larry
Lebens, Nicolas (d)
Lee, Robert B.
Lee, Robert E.
Levine, James
Lovett, Thomas
Luck, Ed (d)
Luck, Goodwin

Luers, Charles

Maas, Melvin (d)
Mackin, Gene
Magnus, James
Maher, Marcus (d)
Malcolm, George
Mallberg, Duane
Manussier, J.
Marshall, Fiske (d)
Mathews, G. H.
Mathews, William L.
Maurer, Wesley
McAlpin, John
McCabe, Lyle (d)
McClure, Robert (d)
McCrea, Robert
McGrand, John (d)
McKown, Richard (d)
McNavy, James
McNeely, Austin
Messerli, William
Meyers, Leonard C. (d)
Miller, 0. J. (d)
Miller, R. N.
Mitchell, Norman (d)
Moore, J. R.
Moursch, D. H.

Neff, Barney (d)
Nelson, Donald
Nelson, M. W.
Nentel, J. K.
Niesen, G. L.
Nitz, William (d)
Northfield, Charles (d)
Northwick, C.
Northwick, Ken

Nyman, Melvin
Nyquist, Glen
Nystrom, Thomas
O'Dette, Ohrn
O'Neil, James (d)
Ochock, Louis
Odenbaugh, Thomas (d)
Oliva, Dino
Olson, Arnold (d)
Olson, S. C.
Owens, Sterling

Pack, F. J. (d)
Partridge, J. R.
Pederson, Paul (d)
Peterson, Carl
Peterson, Vernon (d)
Pfremmer, Herbert
Plattner, Clement
Polhamus, Richard
Polhamus, Robert
Pressnell, Larry

Rattway, R. L.
Rawlings, Richard (d)
Redel, Bill
Reid, C. E.
Reinert, J.
Roe, Timothy
Rogers, J. G.
Roisum, Kenneth (d)

Schlapkohl, Charles (d)
Semlyer, Justin
Severson, Martin (d)
Shay, Harold (d)
Sjoberg, Curtis
Slyman, Clyde

Smalley, Laurel (d)
Smith, Darrell N.
Smith, Sam
Sodd, John
Sorenson, Raymond
Sovik, Edward
Sowles, Larry
Springer, G. L.
Stokes, Edward
Stonelake, Joseph (d)
Stub, Jake
Sumner, Bruce
Sumner, Stewart (d)

Sweetser, Warren (d)

Talarico, Angelo
Taylor, Mervin
Teasley, Allen
Thorne, Dale (d)
Torgerson, Russell
Twito, Wayne

Venables, Charles (d)
Ventres, Daniel

Wadden, David

Walbaum, R. W.
Washborn, Arthur
Wastvedt, John
Watzbarger, K. S.
Whiteside, C.
Wojick, Theodore (d)
Woolsey, Blair

Yakel, R. J.
Young, Elwood

Zonne, Edward (d)
Zonne, Emil

Appendix B

A TOAST...
By Lew Fiero
Lt. Col. USMCR

Because their country called, it was freedom they vowed to serve
Young men from farm and city came to boldly test their nerve.
These were fledgling eagles—their pinions not yet dry;
It mattered not, however—their eyes were on the sky.
Into the U.S. Navy, from their oath they did not swervew
Then into Stearman trainers, their energy and interest did verve.
Up into the endless skies—and now it was they knew
What e'er their fate, their call was to the blue!
Open cockpit training done, and finally wings of gold...
The Globe and Anchor they wear binds them to traditions old.
Into a new fraternity—these pilots of new-won skill
Pursue the foe o'er land and sea, their mission is to kill.

These eagles of the Corps are older now, past flying but a dream,
Still bound by the Globe and Anchor, the wings of gold still gleam.
The memories of past conflicts dim, as rapidly pass the years,
And comrades gather to lift a toast as retirement nears.
But now, a solemn glass is raised to those whose last patrol
Sent them into the endless blue to answer that final roll.

APPENDIX C

F4U Corsair Flight Checklists

Standard Checklist: All Flights

1. Fuel quantity aboard.
2. Power plant ground test.
3. Generator output.
4. Radio operation
5. Stick and rudder free.
6. Power plant ground test.
7. Rudder, brake pedal, and seat height adjusted.
7. Shoulder harness: "Locked."
8. Wings: "Spread" and "Locked." NOTE: Check to see that wing fold control is in "Spread" position, that closure doors at wing joints are closed, and mechanical wing hinge pin locking handle is in the "Lock" position.
9. Arresting hook control: "Up."
10. Fuel tank selector: "Reserve."
11. Mixture: "Automatic Rich."
12. Supercharger control: "Neutral."
13. Propeller control: "Max. RPM" ("Down").
14. Cowl flaps: "2/3 Open."
15. Intercooler flap: "Closed."
16. Oil cooler flap: "Open" as required.
17. Alternate air control: "Direct" ("In").
18. Rudder tab: "6 degrees Nose Right."
19. Aileron tab: "6 degrees Right Wing Down."
20. Elevator tab: "1 degree Nose Up."
21. Wing flaps: set as required.
22. Tail wheel: "Locked."
23. Check that safety pins in cabin release handles (painted RED) are properly in place.
24. Manifold pressure limit: 54 inches Hg.
25. Check magnetos and cylinder head and oil temperatures.
26. Open the throttle gradually and smoothly.

Lyle Bradley in simulator.

Diving Checklist

1. Cabin: "Closed."
2. Landing gear control: "Up."
3. Dive brake control: "Off" or "On" as desired.
4. Wing flaps: "Up."
5. Propeller control: 2400 RPM or lower.
6. Mixture: "Automatic Rich."
7. Throttle: "Slightly Open."
8. Supercharger: "Neutral."
9. Fuel tank selector: "Reserve."
10. Cowl flaps: "Closed."
11. Oil cooler flaps: "Closed."
12. Intercooler flaps: "Closed."
13. Maximum RPM Limit: 3600 RPM (not over 30-second duration). All diving shall be done in "Neutral" blower.

Approach /landing Checklist

1. Shoulder harness: "Locked."
2. Tail wheel: "Locked" (for field); "Free" (for carrier).
3. Fuel tank selector: "Reserve."
4. Mixture: "Automatic Rich."
5. Supercharger control: "Neutral."
6. Propeller control: 2300 to 2400 RPM.
7. Cowl flaps: "Closed."
8. Alternate air control: "Direct" ("In").
9. Landing gear: "Down."
10. Wing flaps: Set 30 degrees, or as required, for field landing; 50 degrees for carrier.
11. Arresting hook: "Up" for field; "Down" for carrier.
12. Gun switches: "Off."
Gun charging knobs: "Safe" (push in).

Appendix D

An Aeronautical Engineer's View:
The Vought F4U Corsair and its Contemporaries
(Condensed from the author's book, same title, published May 2006)
By Tom Brinkman

Introduction

The Minnesota Marine aviators who have contributed their WWII, Korean War, and postwar experiences to this book flew an unusually wide variety of aircraft during their lifetimes. During World War II this included Grumman F3F biplane naval fighters, then nearing the end of their frontline service prior to WWII, extending to the ubiquitous Grumman J2F Duck amphibian (scout and rescue), and on into piston engine fighters such as the Grumman F4F Wildcat, F6F Hellcat, and the Vought F4U Corsair. In their post-WWII aviation careers they went on to fly many military and commercial aircraft ranging from the Fairchild C-119 Flying Box Car transport, to jet aircraft such as the North American FJ Fury, Grumman F9F Panther, Douglas F4D Skyray, Lockheed T-33 Trainer, North American F-100 Super Sabre, McDonnell F-101 Voodoo, the Boeing 747 passenger jet, and even helicopters...not to mention many types in between. Most Minnesota Marine pilots in this book, however, flew the remarkable Chance Vought F4U Corsair in the South Pacific, Central Pacific, or Korea. These pilots flew from land bases, large Essex Class carriers (CVs), and smaller escort carriers (CVEs) in daytime aerial combat, night fighter combat, bomber escort, and close ground support. Here is one aeronautical engineer's view of this great warplane.

Design for Air-to-Air Combat

In many ways the Vought F4U Corsair took propeller driven fighter technology and performance to the ultimate level, incorporating a huge amount of innovative design for 1938...driven by the U.S. Navy's charge to design a naval fighter with a huge increase in speed and performance, one which could perform at least as well or better than army land based fighters. Indeed, in aerial combat the Corsair proved fast, superb, and deadly. And as a fighter-bomber, a role it pioneered to a significant extent, it was exceptionally rugged and devastating, carrying the heaviest bomb/rocket load of any single engine WWII fighter bomber of any combatant nation. The F4U's versatility extended to a pioneering and successful night fighter combat record (the F4U-2), a unique approach to photo reconnaissance (the F4U-1P), which allowed a pilot to record results of his own ground strike, and a test bed for advanced engines and advanced weapons.

The basic design and story of the Corsair has been frequently described.... mount the largest available engine on the smallest possible airframe to create a powerful, fast, aerodynamically clean, and as light as possible fighter for naval duty. In fact, the resulting fighter became the world's first 400 mph single engine fighter as well as the fastest shipboard naval fighter both before WWII and throughout WWII, with speeds up to 446 mph. This design produced remarkable performance from the first prototype, but also provided for immense "stretch" in model-to-model improvement and versatility, perhaps more than any other WWII fighter. Due to the Corsair's success, and to the stretch available in its design, Vought was still introducing new Corsair models beyond 1945 for frontline combat service—the F4U-5 (469 mph) in 1946, AU-1 for Korea, and the F4U-7 for the post-Korean era French Navy. It was the last of the great WWII propeller driven fighters, of any nation, to be in production—a span of nearly 13 years from first prototype flight May 29, 1940, to end of production, longer than any U.S. propeller driven fighter.

Corsair design began with the first use of the world's most powerful piston aircraft engine, the Pratt & Whitney R-2800 Double Wasp, 18-cylinder air-cooled radial, rated at a [then] monstrous 2,000 hp (other radials were 1,000-1,200 hp). Radial engines were much more rugged than liquid cooled engines and also did not tend to overheat when idling on carrier decks while waiting in turn to takeoff—the U.S. Navy preferred radial engines before, during, and after WWII, until jet aircraft matured sufficiently for carrier operations. To properly harness this amount of power, Vought added the world's largest fighter propeller (13' 4" diameter; three blades). An inverted gull wing allowed the large propeller adequate ground clearance while also allowing a shorter and hence stronger landing gear. An upward folding wing mechanism was chosen which, as it turned out, allowed more Corsairs to be packed onto a carrier deck than even the successful F6F Hellcat with its more complex wing folding scheme. WWII fighter designers worked at great length to design effective ailerons that would provide good roll rates since this maneuver was key as a starting point before transitioning to several other common fighter maneuvers. Some data shows that the Corsair had the best high speed (above 250 mph) roll rate of any U.S. 2nd generation WWII fighter and essentially as good as any at low speeds.

Design for Ground Attack

The aura of glamour frequently associated with aerial combat in WWII and Korea has always overshadowed the role of the fighter-bomber and of ground attack. However, consider that in the Pacific, twice as many Marine and Navy F4U Corsairs were lost to ground fire as to aerial combat. And the Army Air Force in Europe suffered equivalent or worse losses in ground attack operations. Generally speaking, U.S. WWII fighters were the most rugged and heaviest of all WWII combatants' fighter aircraft. The most rugged American fighters were the Vought F4U Corsair, the Republic P-47 Thunderbolt, and the Grumman "Iron Work's" F6F Hellcat, all with the legendary tough 2,000 hp P&W R-2800 radial engine, good armor, and self-sealing fuel tanks, but also with combat proven durable and tough airframes. The F4U also used a new aluminum spot welding process, both stronger and offering less drag than flush rivets.

The F4U, with its outstanding ruggedness, good range and loiter time, speed, maneuverability, and WWII's heaviest single engine bomb and rocket carrying capability was a perfect partner for ground attack work, and became America's first true fighter bomber. Significantly, Col. Charles Lindbergh, during his Pacific tour as technical representative for Vought Aircraft, visited the Marshalls in September 1944 and showed the Marines, with both local demonstration flights and with actual attacks on Japanese targets, how to takeoff and dive bomb with a 2,000 lb, a 3,000 lb, and a 4,000 lb bomb load. Corsair fighter-bombers could also carry eight-5 inch HVAR rockets (High Velocity Aerial Rockets) under their wings, giving a Corsair the equivalent to the broadside from a U.S. Navy destroyer. As these tactics developed, the F4U was proven to dive bomb controllably and accurately up to an 85-degree dive angle. An extensive dive bombing test in the Marshall Islands in 1944 showed the Corsair to be only 10% less accurate than SBD Dauntless dive bombers, resulting in replacement of the dive bombers by Corsairs in two squadrons. The Corsair was so successful in pioneering the fighter-bomber role and tactics in the Pacific that future naval air direction for fighters and multi-role aircraft was significantly affected. In fact, by war's end the F4U's accomplishments had made specialty dive-bombers and torpedo aircraft unnecessary, although in Korea the Douglas AD Skyraider served as a very effective ground attack/dive bomber, but was not a fighter.

Teething Problems and Design Issues

Based on an aerospace engineering education and a career in development and testing of complex high performance devices, I have found that innovation is always followed by the need for design modifications, and working out "bugs"—and the more innovation, the more bugs. It is part of the history of the Corsair that due to significant issues with the first Corsair's carrier landing characteristics, it failed Navy carrier qualification trials in the fall of 1942. These problems—poor over-the-nose visibility due to the F4U-1's long nose when landing on aircraft carriers, left wing stall/dip caused by high torque at low speed, high bounce on landing caused by stiff landing gear shock absorption, overall cockpit visibility, and aerodynamic ground effects during landing which resulted from the Corsair's large flaps and low inverted gull wing—were all fixed or significantly improved by the next model (F4U-1A), although this required 12 months. As a result of these early problems, the Corsair was given to the U.S. Marine Corps and relegated to land bases. The Marines historically had been given second-rate equipment in a number of areas. But in this case the Marines were given a high performance, war winning caliber aircraft, and history shows that they put the F4U to tremendously good use in the Pacific Theater.

British Commonwealth

The British Royal Navy has had a number of very important firsts in naval aviation. However, during WWII the Fleet Air Arm did not have a truly first rate British developed carrier fighter. As a result, the Fleet Air Arm procured 1,000 F4F Wildcats, over 1,100 F6F Hellcats, and 2,012 F4U Corsairs. The British, not deterred by the rough edges of early Corsair F4U-1 landing characteristics, began modifications almost immediately, including using a curved landing approach to help forward visibility. Corsairs joined the Royal Navy in mid-1943, only four months after U.S. Marine land based Corsairs entered combat, and were operating in multiple squadron strength in early spring 1944, nearly nine months before similar levels of U.S. Navy activity.

Japanese who faced the Royal New Zealand Air Force's 419 Corsairs and their aggressive pilots in the Solomons referred to them as "Whispering Death" due to the New Zealanders' tactic of cutting back engine power to more quietly swoop down onto Japanese troop positions.

Accomplishments in the Pacific

Aerial combat in the South Pacific was extremely intense, fought against Japan's remaining best, hard and harshly trained, combat hardened pilots. The Japanese had a tremendous airpower build up and many of the fiercest air battles of the entire Pacific War were fought here, often with Wildcats and Corsairs badly outnumbered. However, Corsair pilots in the many Marine and one land based Navy squadron (VF-17) knew they had a near quantum leap in power and capability with the F4U, and this greatly helped build a confident, aggressive attitude in combating the dangerous Japanese Zeros and Tonys. Marine Major Gregory (Pappy) Boyington, leader of the successful and famed Black Sheep (VMF-214), while on Espirito Santo stated, "The Corsair was a sweet flying baby if ever I flew one. No longer would we have to fight the Nip's fight, for we could make our own rules." Eight Marine squadrons were credited with 903 aerial kills in the Solomons, and 64% of all Marine WWII aerial victories were in the Solomons against Japan's remaining best frontline pilots. In fact, it was soon recognized that the F4U was the first fighter to dominate the vaunted Zero in the Pacific.

Moving beyond the Solomons and the Central Pacific to the Western Pacific... The U.S. Navy finally approved F4U Corsairs for aircraft carrier duty in April 1944. The first Japanese Kamikaze onslaught occurred in late October 1944 during the retaking of the Philippine Islands. Kamikazes had hit 9 out of the initial 10 Essex-class aircraft carriers within a period of four months (missing the USS Bennington). This compelled the Navy to quickly get the faster, better climbing Corsair onto aircraft carriers. The late war F4U-4 Corsair with its up-rated engine and four bladed propeller was the fastest climbing American fighter of WWII (6.8 min to 20,000 ft; 3,870 ft/min), an important performance feature for urgent kamikaze interception in the Western Pacific. Corsairs finally came aboard USN aircraft carriers in December 1944, and they ran up very large scores. For example, 436 of 637 shoot downs (68%) in the Okinawa campaign during the spring of 1945 were by carrier and land based F4U Corsairs. In addition, Corsairs carried out an incredibly large and effective ground support effort in this bitter, long, and costly battle, earning the title "Sweetheart of Okinawa" from grateful mud Marines, as well as "Whistling Death" from fearful Japanese defenders throughout the Pacific Theater.

Ultimately, the Corsair served on approximately 13 Essex-class fast carriers (CVs) and on approximately six Escort carriers (CVEs) during WWII, as well as on 10 British Royal Navy carriers. Whether flying from land or from aircraft carriers, whether in aerial combat or performing ground attack, the F4U weaved a path of destruction in battle after battle, significantly outclassing Japanese fighters in the Solomons and throughout the Pacific, running up an 11.3:1 victory ratio (2,140 air victories vs 189 air losses), possibly the highest ratio of any WWII U.S. fighter.

How did the Japanese view U.S. 2nd generation fighters?

The F4U-1 Corsair first entered combat in February 1943 in the Solomon Islands. The Japanese sent air intelligence officers to the Solomons in 1943 to determine why Corsairs were shooting down so many Japanese planes. In the end, Japan's Admiral Koga at Rabaul had futilely fed more of his frontline naval forces into defending the Solomons and Rabaul than he had originally intended. There are plentiful post-war Japanese testimonials to "hating the Corsair," and to "hating the Hellcat." But high-ranking Japanese officers, when interrogated at war's end, revealed that they considered the Corsair to be the most formidable fighter in the Pacific. Japanese opinions could vary of course, and another comparative breakdown reported is: F4U—best fighter at any altitude; P-38—best high altitude fighter (turbo-chargers); P-40—best low altitude fighter (New Guinea army arena); F6F—best low altitude fighter (Central Pacific naval arena).

Korea and Early Cold War

The F4U Corsair was indispensable to both the U.S Marines' and U.S. Navy's three year effort in Korea. During the Korean War the F4U was a Jack-of-all-trades, flying 82% of Navy and Marine missions during the urgent first 10 months, and were included in nearly all Navy strike missions throughout the three year conflict. While jets such as Grumman

F9F Panthers and North American F-86 Sabres received more publicity, and the F-86 vs MiG-15 air battles produced more glory, most of the Korean air war was a rough, dangerous, low-level, air-to-ground war. For these heavy duty ground attack operations the Marines and Navy had a WWII retread in the fast, agile, and rugged F4U-4 (446 mph, 4,000 lbs ordnance) and several newcomers—the faster and higher flying F4U-5 (469 mph, 41,400 ft. ceiling, 5,000 lbs ordnance) and the more heavily armored, low altitude AU-1 (438 mph, 5,000 lbs ordnance). Corsair loiter time was excellent at this point—range with drop tanks was 1,950 miles (nearly 9 hours at 215 mph)!

Back in the late 1930s the Corsair was designed to be a dogfighter, and amazingly 12-15 years later it still had some air-to-air "bite." In one instance four of Russia's very fast, very maneuverable Yak 9s, the WWII best of the famous Yak family of fighters, fell to two Corsairs of VMF-312 over Korea. In the night fighter arena Lt. Guy Bordelon, a Navy F4U-5N night fighter pilot, shot down five night time harassment 'Bed check Charlies' and became not only the Navy's only Korean ace, but the only propeller driven, and only non F-86 ace for the Korean War Allies. Captain Jess Folmer of VMF-312 shot down a MiG-15 jet fighter while preparing for a ground attack. During the Korean War, Corsairs were officially credited with 10 air-to-air victories—one MiG-15 jet fighter and 9 piston engine aircraft, mostly late model/high performance Russian types—an admirable record for a remarkable fighter in the age of early jet aircraft. In addition, driven by the frozen winters of Korea, another innovative model Corsair (the F4U-5NL) was introduced—incorporating deicing boots—previously never fitted to a fighter.

Summary

The Corsair design phase took place while biplane fighters were still frontline (but in their twilight), and yet the Corsair proved indomitable in WWII. It also flew in frontline combat roles with early jets in Korea, and later even engaged in combat for France (Indo-China, Suez, North Africa), Honduras until 1977, El Salvador until 1969, and Argentina until 1965, thus sharing active airspace with no less than the U.S. 100 Series jet fighters, the famous "Century Series" jets. In some respects it took longer than desired for the F4U Corsair to reach peak potential, but then so it was also for the P-38 Lightning, P-51 Mustang, and the P-47 Thunderbolt to varying extents.

The F4U Corsair's capabilities were truly remarkable. Fighter comparisons are often made to the P-51 Mustang due to the Mustang's excellent capabilities and accomplishments. In many areas F4U performance matched or exceeded P-51 performance. Probably the best all around U.S. performer in air-to-air and ground attack was the F4U Corsair. Of all U.S. WW II fighters, the Corsair was arguably the finest in air-to-air combat for a balance of power, acceleration, speed, and especially of maneuverability and responsiveness. One of the reasons the F4U had the best harmonized controls was that Vought Aircraft worked extremely hard at a design that provided light stick forces, reasonable rudder forces in most maneuvers, exceptionally effective and smooth ailerons, and massive very effective flaps, all to mate with the rugged powerful 2,000 hp P&W R-2800 radial engine....Vought really "sweated the details." The F4U could transition from one maneuver to the next with little effort, just a little motion on the stick, yet the F4U remained stable, providing the pilot with excellent air-to-air and air-to-ground tracking, as well as excellent controllability while diving. Its aerial handling characteristics are frequently described as a fighter pilot's dream, pilots loved to fly this aerial predator...and it is clear why.

The WWII versions of the Corsair were very fast (417-446 mph depending on model, plus an additional short term boost of 10-20 mph from water injection), exceptionally maneuverable, with a strong airframe, and were a velvet-gloved predator in aerial combat, with possibly the United States' best victory ratio (11.3:1). The Corsair was the bomb/rocket heavyweight lifting champion of WWII for a fighter (4,000 lbs.), devastating in ground attack, pioneered much of "the book" on the fighter-bomber's role, and pioneered American night fighter radar usage. Amazingly, the Corsair performed at these levels with the rugged heavier airframe required to survive repeated aircraft carrier landings. All of this led to the Corsair being manufactured for 11 years (12,571 Corsairs), longer than any other American piston engine fighter in history.

So given all of the foregoing discussion and analysis, what does one conclude as to the 'best of the best'? Well, one of the most telling conclusions comes in a tribute from Major (at the time) Rex Barber, a combat seasoned Army P-38 Lightning ace in the Southwest Pacific. Major Barber flew his P-38 on the difficult, famous, and successful shoot down mission of

Japanese Admiral Isoruko Yamamoto (the "architect of Pearl Harbor") over Bougainville in 1943. He shot down one of two Mitsubishi Betty bombers, very possibly the one carrying Yamamoto. Barber flew a very wide variety of fighters during his career, and his conclusion was very clear-cut..."If the United States had to pick one fighter-bomber to produce in the war, it should have been the Corsair".

GLOSSARY

Acronyms

AA—antiaircraft guns/ordnance
CAVU—ceiling advisability unlimited
CO—commanding officer
CPT—Civilian Pilot Training
FCLP—field carrier landing practice
HVAR—high velocity aerial rocket
IFR—instrument flight rules
LSO—landing signal officer
MCAS—Marine Corps air station
NAS—navy air station
USS—United States ship
VF—Navy fighter squadron
VFR—visual flight rules
VMF—Marine fighter squadron

Aircraft Designations & Ships

BB—battleship
B—bomber
BT—basic trainer
CL—light cruiser
C—transport
CV—aircraft carrier
DD—destroyer
F—fighters
PT—a small, high-speed surface boat
SB—scout bomber
S—submarine

Aircraft: External

aileron tab/ailerons—roll control
arresting hook—for landing on
   carriers
canopy—covering for cockpit
dive brake—slows a fast dive
elevator tab/elevators—climb and dive
   controls
empennage—entire rear part of
   aircraft
engine—power plant of aircraft
flaps—increases lift at slow speeds
fuselage—passages and control wires
   in aircraft
horizontal stabilizer—holder of
   elevators
landing gear—wheels and struts
pilot tube—air tube for airspeed
propeller—radiating blades from hub
radar—radio waves reflected
radio antennae—wire to receive and
   send
rudder—vertical control for direction
   yaw
tail wheel—small wheel on
   empennage
vertical stabilizer—holder of rudder
wing-folding lock—"flag" on wing for
   locking bolts
wing—lift on these to support aircraft

Aircraft: Internal

cockpit—pilot's house
control locks—holds controls to avoid
   damage
control tabs—wing, elevator, and
   rudder adjustment
flaps and dive brakes—slows aircraft
   or increases lift at slow speeds
instruments:
altimeter—feet of altitude
compass—direction of flight
cylinder head—engine temperature
needle-ball—shows balanced flight
oil pressure/temp—gauges for oil
tachometer—RPMs
mixture—controls percentage of fuel
   and air
oxygen—aids functioning of pilot at

night and at altitude
radios—VHF, UHF, etc. for
  communications
RPM—engine revolutions per minute
rudder pedals—floor pedals for rudder
stick or wheel—for controlling aircraft
switch—on and off for engine
  operation
throttle—controls flow of fuel and air
  to engine
wing folding—handle to fold wings
  for storage

Aircraft Manufacturers
B—Boeing
C—Curtiss
D—Douglas
F—Grumman
U—Vought

Aircraft Types: American
Trainer
BT-13—basic monoplane
N2S—Stearman biplane
SNB—multi-engine by Beech
SNJ—advanced trainer by North
  American
T-33—jet trainer used for instruments

Fighter
F4F—Wildcat (Grumman)
F4U—Corsair
F6F—Hellcat (Grumman)
F7F—Tigercat (Grumman)
F9F—Panther (jet)
P-61—Black Widow

Scout Bomber
SB2C—Helldiver (Curtiss)
SBD—Dauntless (Douglas)
TB—Avenger (Grumman)

Multi-engine Bombers
B-17—Flying Fortress
B-24—Liberator
B-25 (PBJ)—Mitchell
B-29—Super Fortress

Transports
C-119—Boxcar, two engines
C-46—Commando, two engines
C-47—Sky Train, two engines
PB4Y—Privateer, four engines
PBM—Mariner (Flying Boat), two
  engines
PBY—Catalina (Flying Boat), two
  engines
R5D (C-54)—Skymaster, four engines

Aircraft Types: Japanese
Betty—twin-engine bomber
Judy—dive-bomber
Kamikaze—aircraft aiming at ships
Nick—twin-engine fighter
Sally—twin-engine bomber
Tony—fighter
Zeke—fighter
Zero—best Japanese fighter

Aviation People
aerologist—weather forcaster
aeronautical engineer—aircraft expert
air officer—controls air operation on
  carrier
cadet—first step in training (before
  wings)
engineering officer—expert in engines
gunner—usually in rear seat
instructor—experienced aviation
  teacher
intelligence officer—briefing officer
landing signal officer (LSO)—helps
  aircraft land on carrier
mechanic—ground tender of engines

Glossary

navigator—copilot or other
ordnance expert—armaments
pilot—controller of aircraft
ship's captain—top decision-maker on ship
squadron commander—decision-maker for a squadron
supply—logistics for operations

Flight Terms

abort—stopping or returning from a flight
airspeed—indicating speed
bombing—internal or external dropping ordnance
catapult—powered aircraft throw on carrier
climb—angle toward altitude
cruise—best level speed for maximum fuel and distance
dive—below level flight
drag—impediment to flight
ground speed—air speed plus or minus wind
landing—completing flight on sea or land
mach—speed related to sound
roll rate—manuever for fighters
shutdown—stop
spin—stalling into out-of-control flight
stall—below flying speed
strafing—using machine guns on low targets
tactics—multiple aircraft maneuvers
tail chase—multiple planes in file
take off—leaving the ground or runway
taxi—from "storage" to take off

Navigation/weather

beam—code of .- and -. overlap to give beam
icing—ice on aircraft parts
link trainer—artificial aircraft on ground
plotting board—pull out by pilot for navigation
radar—radio waves deflected
radio frequencies—VHF (very high frequency) or UHF (ultra high frequency)
wind streaks/chart—streaks, smoke, etc. for wind speed
ZB—on aircraft carriers for homing

Ordnance Types

20-mm cannon—replace machine guns
30-caliber machine gun
50-caliber machine gun
gun camera—phased with guns
napalm—jellied gasoline dropped in tanks
ordnance switches—cockpit controls rockets or bombs
safety briefings—for all

"Radio" Vocabulary

angels—altitude in thousands
bandit—identified enemy aircraft
blanket—clouds in tenths
bogey—unidentified aircraft
cleared—for take off, landing, taxi, and so on
cockeral—IFF switch (to ID friend or foe)
division—four aircraft; made from two sections
flight clearance—VFR or IFR
pancake—landing
section—two aircraft
Tally ho—enemy aircraft spotted
vector—take course heading

Index

Index

O

O'Dette, Ohrn, 3, 6, 242-245, 343
O'Neil, Jim, 3, 301, 344
Oahu, 17, 64, 204
Odenbaugh, Tom, 14, 197-199
Okinawa, 18, 67, 132
Ckinoyerabu, 55
Olathe, Kansas, 83, 151, 246
Opa Locka, Florida, 222
Operation Hand Clasp, 304
Operation Tea Pot, 223
Osaka, 210
OY (observation), 180, 198, 199

P

P-38, 25, 361, 363
P-40, 361
P-47, 358, 363
P-51, 363
PADUKA, 284
Pagan Island, 59-61, 63
Palau, 41, 71, 119, 141
Panther. See F9F
parachute, 40, 62, 110, 129, 134,
    147-149, 266, 280, 289, 323
PBY, 26, 90, 119-121, 203, 366
Pearl Harbor, 13, 17, 33, 67, 203,
    242
Peinovitch, Mike, 142, 143
Peleliu, 18, 71, 119, 141
Pensacola, 57, 74, 83, 116, 136,
    157, 241, 254, 279, 281, 292,
    294, 296
perimeter, 60, 76, 207, 209
pesticide side effects, 318
Peterson, V. A., 26-28, 30, 31

Peterson, Roger Tory, 57, 58
Pete Ross Safety Award, 15
Pfremmer, Herb, 3, 129, 345
Philippines, 18, 41
Piasecki helicopter, 176, 177, 277
Piper Cub, 204
Plattner, Tony, 3, 235, 279, 282, 346
plotting board, 34, 367
Ponape, 90
Pratt & Whitney, 244, 357
preflight, 17, 260, 286, 289, 301
Presley, Frank, 66
PRINCETON, 179, 334
propeller, 28, 221, 222, 229, 235,
    247, 282, 287, 292, 295, 302,
    303, 356, 357, 360, 362, 365
PT boat, 26, 76
Pusan, 20

Q

Quantico, 126, 128, 176, 177, 277
Quonset Point, 114, 126-128

R

R4D, 136, 157, 192, 193, 195
R4Q. See C-119
R5C, 101
Rabaul, 18, 76, 95, 361
Radar Squadron 16, 187
Rawlings, Rich, 224
ready room, 36, 79, 104, 166, 182-
    184, 197, 282
Reagan, Ronald, 30
Red Cross, 214
Rendova, 25-27
Reusser, Ken, 169-172

ORDER FORM

Please copy this page, add the necessary information, and mail it with your check or money order, payable to *Minnesota Marine Air Reserve, LLC*, to:

> Louis Farrell
> Minnesota Marine Air Reserve, LLC
> 2 Bald Eagle Pt.
> White Bear Lake, MN 55110

You can also order at www.MinnesotaMarineWings.com, email LouieFarrell@msn.com, or call (651) 429-7613.

ISBN: 9781930374256

Marine Wings $29.95 each (Hardcover)　　　Qty.　_____

Total: _____

MN residents add 6.5% sales tax ($1.95/book)　　_____

Shipping: $3.50 first book, $1.50 each additional　_____

Total enclosed: _____

Name: _____

Address: _____

City: _____ State: _____ Zip: _____

Phone: (__) _____ Email:_____

You can also order this book online from
DeForest Press at www.DeForestPress.com.
If you'd like to order by phone, call DeForest Press at
763-428-2997, or toll-free at 1-866-509-0604.